Never Again

Also by Herbert S. Parmet and Marie B. Hecht

Aaron Burr: Portrait of an Ambitious Man

Never Again

A President Runs for a Third Term

by HERBERT S. PARMET

and MARIE B. HECHT

THE MACMILLAN COMPANY, New York

COLLIER-MACMILLAN LTD., London

973.917
P241w

Library of Congress Catalog Card Number: 68-23639

FIRST PRINTING

The Macmillan Company, New York
Collier-Macmillan Canada Ltd., Toronto, Ontario

Printed in the United States of America

To Andrew Mark Hecht
To Fanny, Isaac, Joan L.
and Robert D. Parmet

Contents

Introduction

THE PRESIDENTIAL ELECTION in the United States is an American entertainment with serious overtones that takes place every four years. It is a familiar phenomenon to the natives but can be disturbing to those who have not been bred to it. An emigré whose first experience occurred in 1940 said, "It was very frightening to watch you. The name-calling and the vituperation seemed so serious." This comment on our folkway points up an attitude or way of doing things that is not in the least restricted to the election of 1940. However, 1940 was a unique year. The Republicans chose an unorthodox candidate in an unorthodox manner; and never before had a President run for a third term, and never again would it be possible, because of the Twenty-second Amendment that was ratified in 1951.

Yet, to hear the promoters of public interest in the fortunes of a particular party and its candidates, every four years brings a critical test of the ability of the "American way of life" to survive. How many campaigns are inevitably called "the most important in our history"? One can accept the importance of installing the prestigious George Washington in the first place and possibly—but not convincingly—the replacement of Federalists with Thomas Jefferson. Certainly, Jackson's victory in 1828 delineated a definite course, the acceptance of a particular consensus; but even that was launched with uncertain premises. Who knows what may have happened if Douglas or Breckinridge had won in 1860, or if Tilden had been permitted to keep his victory. The ascendancy—accidental, at first—

of Theodore Roosevelt and the subsequent victories of Wilson and FDR all helped to create a particular course or priority of values. In retrospect, Eisenhower's election in 1952 was probably essential and Kennedy's salubrious.

In 1940, with the two-term issue as a weapon, anti-New Dealers, or those who had not been able to adjust to the new responsibilities of American government, argued that the time had come to disarm the "dictator" and to dismantle the machinery. Most vigorous proponents of the Republican party agreed. Nevertheless, their candidate would have to be one who merely wanted to modify the New Deal, which was not an unintelligent way to begin. If the dismantlers and the modifiers together could not exploit the fear of excessive presidential power to begin their rehabilitation in 1940, could they ever win? In short, to argue against a third term was the obvious rationale for those who, if they had it to do over again, would have denied Mr. Roosevelt a first.

The increased growth of centralized government led to accusations that the President had moved Main Street to Pennsylvania Avenue. So the Republican party of 1940—a minority loaded with people out to prevent any new commitments toward "socialism" and convinced that their interests were, after all, more secure on Main Street—got behind a man who wanted to modify and not dismantle.

The election of 1940 was, then, a test of not only whether a sentimental tradition could be maintained but whether the nation's course, which was clearly toward a government that held itself responsible for people as well as for property and toward international responsibility, would become fixed along the lines that had been launched in 1932.

Franklin D. Roosevelt and his opponent, Wendell L. Willkie, did not meet until after the election was over. The loser visited FDR at the White House at Roosevelt's invitation. The President was surprised to find the Republican "a very good fellow" and even talented. Willkie, however, retained many of his doubts about the Chief Executive. Later, FDR sent his ex-opponent as his personal representative on a trip around the world. From that experience came an influential and very popular little book called *One World*. For its author, both the book and the trip were personal triumphs. Then, when the Republican party spurned Willkie in 1944, the President was sympathetic. He said to Frances Perkins: "You know, Willkie would have made a good Democrat. Too bad we lost him."

Both men had not very much longer to live after 1940. Willkie, ten years younger, died in October 1944 of a coronary thrombosis after having been given massive doses of penicillin to cure a streptococcic throat infection. Roosevelt lived only a half year longer. On April 12, 1945, he was killed by a cerebral hemorrhage at Warm Springs, Georgia, just months after his inauguration to a fourth term.

The authors of this book have attempted to provide a comprehensive view of the election of 1940. Not only are the activities and motives of the two candidates examined, but an effort is made to present the "underground" campaign as well. This was an era of ideological struggle that became intensified because of the European war. Some of the repercussions were evident in the United States. There were demagogues like Father Coughlin and anti-war agitation by isolationist groups.

Attention is given to a third stratum of the campaign, the political amateurs, particularly when dealing with Willkie, whose personal appeal provoked even the apolitical into active campaigning. We hope, in this connection, to complicate the oversimplification that his candidacy was engineered and dominated by Wall Street. To do this we have presented fresh material about the Willkie Clubs.

It was our good fortune to have access to the papers of the Associated Willkie Clubs of America, the records of the Eastern Division of the Willkie campaign and the personal papers of Wendell L. Willkie, as well as to the 1940 campaign items in the Franklin D. Roosevelt Library at Hyde Park, New York.

All of these sources have provided rich material, some of which, while ostensibly unrelated to the decisive aspects of the campaign, provides more depth by enabling us to look into the minds of those who were not necessarily opinion-makers but just voters. "For American history generally and many of its specialities," Donald McCoy recently wrote, historians "should wean themselves from an excessive reliance on fashionable, highly literate sources of opinion and information." However persuasive the so-called molders of public opinion may or may not be, it is the great mass of voters that finally decides in a democracy.

Many people were particularly kind and even went out of their way to assist in this work. The courtesy and cooperation of the Great Neck (New York) Library in helping us to obtain material was a valued service. The staff of the Lilly Library at Indiana University worked hard to make accessible the thousands of items from their

Willkie Club collection. Those in charge of the reading room at Hyde Park were also most responsive to our needs. To Edith and Philip Willkie, the widow and the only child of the memorable candidate, we are grateful for permitting themselves to be interviewed on several occasions and for making available their privately held collection of Wendell L. Willkie's papers. Samuel F. Pryor, a man of many and varied activities even during his retirement, graciously gave his time and resources to broaden the authors' knowledge of the intricacies of the campaign. Edward E. Martin went out of his way in Boston to help fill in material concerning his older brother, Joseph W. Martin. John M. Stout, of La Porte, Texas, graciously prepared an excellent memoir of his activities during those exciting days. Others to whom we are grateful for having provided either written or personal interviews are: Harold E. Stassen, John D. M. Hamilton, John Roy Carlson, Morris L. Ernst, Franklin D. Roosevelt, Jr., Mrs. Harold Ickes, Oren Root, Jr., Lem Jones, Lucy and Harry Shackelford, and Representative Hamilton Fish. The authors were fortunate to have had this book edited with thoroughness and understanding by Richard Marek of The Macmillan Company.

Never Again

The Third Term Tradition

THE DECISION of George Washington to refuse a third term as President of the United States started a precedent that persisted stubbornly until 1940. While he was President of the Constitutional Convention he said nothing about his views on presidential tenure. Later on he wrote to Lafayette that he could not see how a President could continue in office, let alone perpetuate himself in it, without the consent of the electorate unless, he said, the country was already "in a state of political depravity." It would be wrong, he stated further, to deprive the republic of a man who could serve his country best in an emergency simply because he was not eligible to run for office again. Although Washington did not accept the Presidency after two terms, there is no evidence that he had changed his mind.

Actually, Washington wanted to retire from public life after his first term. The protestations of his friends that the infant nation needed him to establish stability and prestige finally made him consent to postpone his return to Mount Vernon. But by 1796 George Washington was sixty-five years old, in poor health and in poor spirits. He had served his country for fifteen years and, at his age, could no longer tolerate the increasing quarrelsomeness of the factions within the government. Though these were his genuine motives, the pattern was set.

When the authors of the Constitution considered the question of the Executive office in the Constitutional Convention of 1787, they were obsessed by two conflicting experiences. Because they had lived under a despotic king, they distrusted a strong Executive. Because they had lived under the Articles of Confederation, they were well aware of the impossibility of a system that had no Executive. Therefore the lively and probing debate on various aspects of presidential power and on the methods of election completely overshadowed the length-of-tenure question. A seven-year presidential term with no provision for re-eligibility seemed to have complete acceptance until two weeks before the close of the Convention, when suddenly David Brearley of New Jersey proposed a four-year term without mentioning any limitations to the number of times a President might serve. The proposal passed almost unnoticed.

The most effective contemporary commentary on the Constitution, *The Federalist Papers,* favored the arrangement. Alexander Hamilton, in Paper No. 72, said that he thought it was essential for the Chief Executive to have the feeling that he would be able to finish what he had begun lest he hesitate to undertake a project for the public benefit because, "together with his own reputation," it might possibly be committed to "hands which might be unequal or unfriendly to the task." In addition to the obvious argument that mandated exclusion could deprive the community of an experienced man at a critical time, Hamilton added that, in a national crisis, an ambitious man might be tempted to seize the power he was forbidden. Hamilton asked, "Would it promote the peace of the community, or the stability of the government to have half a dozen men who had credit enough to be raised to the seat of the supreme magistracy, wandering among the people like discontented ghosts, and sighing for a place which they were destined never more to possess?"

Thomas Jefferson, Hamilton's traditional rival, disputed him on this subject as well. As early as 1787 Jefferson expressed doubts about the propriety of more than one term for the American President. Having seen too much of absolute monarchy in Europe, he feared that, under the Constitution, a Chief Executive could be elected from four years to four years until it became a life term. But when the time came, Jefferson accepted a second term because of the bitterness of Federalist opposition. However, he declared firmly that, at its close, he would retire. Therefore, in 1806, when Vermont and then seven other of the seventeen states asked him to serve for a third term, he refused. He said, "That I should lay down my charge at a proper period is as much a duty as to have borne it faithfully." And he added, "That I am sensible of that decline which advancing years bring on; and feeling their physical, I ought not to doubt their mental effect." It seems obvious that Jefferson was motivated by conviction, but it is also possible that the failure of his foreign policy increased his enthusiasm for liberation from the Presidency. Whatever his reasoning, the eschewing of a third term now became a principle, an unwritten law.

Dutifully, subsequent Presidents retired voluntarily after a maximum of eight years in office. James Monroe wrote that the practice now had the force of precedent and usage. Andrew Jackson advocated one term of from four to six years in the first six of his eight annual messages to Congress. But he didn't like it when his enemies took up his idea and proposed twenty or more constitutional amendments limiting presidential tenure that were pointedly directed at him. Because of ill health and advancing age, Jackson retired at the end of two terms and, like Jefferson, left a political heir to carry on for him. With his vast popularity he might well have been assured re-election, but his refusal to run strengthened the tradition immeasurably.

Ulysses S. Grant was the first Chief Executive to make a bid for a triple crown. Several state conventions tried to forestall such a possibility in 1875 by passing resolutions against a third term. Grant, forced to answer, wrote an ambiguous letter to General Harry White, president of the Pennsylvania state convention. In conclusion, he said, "I am not, nor have I ever been, a candidate for renomination. I could not accept a nomination if it were tendered unless it should come under such circumstances as to make it an imperative duty— circumstances not likely to arise." The door was not completely closed, but Rutherford B. Hayes received the Republican nomination in 1876 and won the election.

While the Grants consoled themselves with a trip around the world, the three Grant courtiers—Senators Roscoe Conkling of New York, Don Cameron of Pennsylvania and John A. Logan of Illinois

—planned a crusade to renominate their patron in 1880. In the spring of 1879 a *New York Times* poll showed that five-sixths of the Republican sentiment favored Grant. Everything was prepared when the general made a tactical mistake by returning to the United States eight months too soon. It was too long a period of time to sustain the required level of enthusiasm for the Civil War hero and quite long enough for the opposition to revive the scandals of the Grant Administration and to agitate anti-third-term propaganda.

An Anti-Third Term Convention was called and met in St. Louis in May. As arranged, it passed a resolution opposing Grant's nomination. Nevertheless, handsome, faithful Roscoe Conkling rose to his full height of six feet three inches and delivered a sentimental speech, nominating Grant, to the Republican convention. He quoted the verse:

> When asked what state he hails from,
> Our sole reply shall be,
> He comes from Appomattox
> And its famous apple tree

At the conclusion of the speech applause rocked the house for fifteen minutes. But the Republican nomination went to James A. Garfield. The Conkling faction was partially compensated by the choice of the Senator's New York henchman, Chester A. Arthur, for Vice President.

Grant's defeat can be attributed to outspoken opposition to the third term. Jesse Grant, his son, said that there was more fear of a third term than of his father. The first attempt to alter tradition was a failure.

Except for a Cleveland boom in 1904, which would have meant a third term for Grover Cleveland, which he refused, the subject did not come up again until 1912.

> Washington wouldn't
> Grant couldn't
> Roosevelt shan't

ran a popular jingle that peppered the pages of anti-Roosevelt journals. Technically, "Colonel Teddy" had been elected only once because he had succeeded to the Presidency the first time due to the assassination of William McKinley. But a statement that he had made on November 8, 1904, just after his election, boomeranged later. He said, "On the fourth of March next, I shall have served three and a half years and this . . . constitutes my first term. The wise custom which limits the President to two terms regards the substance and not the form; and under no circumstances will I be a candidate for or accept another nomination." Therefore, William Howard Taft, with Roosevelt's enthusiastic endorsement, succeeded him. He proved to be a disappointment to his sponsor. At the next Republican presidential convention, in 1912, the Taft forces used Roosevelt's words to keep him from the nomination. They said, "We have got to save the country, save the Constitution, save our liberty. We are in danger of monarchy." Consequently, Taft won handily from TR on the first ballot, 561–107. Roosevelt's subsequent candidacy on the "Bull Moose" ticket resulted in disaster for both Republicans. Wilson, the Democrat, won the election.

Theodore Roosevelt's loyal followers tried to interest him in the Presidency in 1915, convinced that only he could handle the intricacies of the European war. The old campaigner, more realistic than his followers, refused because he believed that his preparedness campaign had made too many enemies.

Theodore Roosevelt's defeat was due to the rejection of the man by his party, not to the third-term tradition. Although there had been a National Anti-Third Term League, it had not achieved the power of the one in Grant's time. Many thought that the third-term tradition was now only an academic question.

Woodrow Wilson had written in his doctoral dissertation on government that efficiency in office should be the criterion for presidential tenure, not the calendar. Since presidential power derives from the citizenry of the country, said Wilson, it need not be feared. On June 10, 1918, in Indianapolis, a third-term boom was started for Wilson. *The New York Times* predicted that if World War I was still going on at election time, Wilson would be elected again.

But the summer of 1919 brought a tragic end to the hopes of the Wilson supporters. After tireless weeks of feverish campaigning for his beloved League of Nations, Wilson suffered a complete breakdown. For six months the country was virtually without an Executive, and those closest to the President refused to reveal the true extent of his illness. Wilson was never really well again, and yet some admirers visualized another term. Wilson said nothing about this proposal or about the choice of a successor. In 1924 again there were whispers that the frail war leader had an interest in the White House. But the possibility could not be tested, this time because of Wilson's physical collapse.

Calvin Coolidge would have been a very good subject for the third-term test. Charles D. Hilles, a New York state committeeman, joked, "There is no more danger of Calvin Coolidge becoming a monarchist than there is of his becoming a chatterbox." But Coolidge himself stated, "I do not choose to run for President in nineteen twenty-eight." Without this astonishing declaration made by the President on August 3, 1927, undoubtedly he would have been his grateful party's candidate. He was popular and he had ruled during a period of unprecedented prosperity.

Coolidge, some close to him observed, was deeply wounded when the party failed to draft him and chose Herbert Hoover instead. The excuse offered was that any possibility of such a draft movement was dead before it started because it seemed to have no presidential support. Speculation on Coolidge's motives for withdrawal suggest genuine fatigue, a prescience that saw the coming crash, or miscalculation about his expendability. There is no evidence that he was primarily motivated by a desire to preserve the third-term tradition.

Nevertheless, whatever had been said over the years and whatever the cause of failure, no man had achieved the office of President of the United States more than twice. Historical evidence establishes that Washington did not reject a third term for ideological considerations. And those that followed, even Jefferson, had additional reasons to bulwark their decisions—old age, party politics, illness or political problems. The third-term tradition did, however, achieve a place in the folklore of American democracy. It became an example that was often cited to demonstrate a voluntary safeguard against tyranny. Though in 1940 there was no Constitutional barrier to a President running for a third term, the decision to attempt it would be a major one.

CHAPTER ONE

The Artful Dodger

1

THE LAST WORDS of the presidential oath of office had hardly been uttered in January 1937 before speculation started on who would be the next President. Many Democratic hopefuls, convinced there would be no third term, made plans either to enlist Franklin D. Roosevelt's support or to strengthen their own positions sufficiently to seize the succession. What was a usual phenomenon of American politics now had some novel aspects. FDR wanted to install someone who would continue New Deal policies. But there was none among the possible contenders who did not, in the words of the architect of the New Deal, have some "fatal weakness." And as the second term grew older, the prospect of war in Europe increased greatly. Consequently, even though he was now entering his second full term, many considered Roosevelt his party's and his country's strongest choice.

In 1937 Roosevelt was on the crest of his popularity. Only Maine and Vermont had failed to acknowledge his ascendancy. Already recognized as an outstanding American President, FDR had guided a distraught and despairing country through its worst depression to some degree of restored confidence. His "New Deal," promised casually in his 1932 campaign talks, got off to an energetic start with the enthusiastic response of Congress to the Administration's relief and reform program during the first hundred days in office. Roosevelt was an innovator and a gambler. A chronic optimist, he was willing to try a measure and, if it failed, try an alternative. A group of economists and scholars with fresh insight into the nation's problems were invited to help the Administration. In a brief period of time "the Brain Trust," as they were called, helped to introduce the alphabet agencies, such as the NRA, AAA, PWA, WPA and the SEC. Some of the nation's deepest convictions were disturbed. Roosevelt, as the author of the changes, became his countrymen's hero or villain. While some regarded him as a savior, others, often the wealthy and privileged, dubbed him a traitor to his class. A *New Yorker* cartoon by Peter Arno that greatly amused the President characterized this attitude. A group of elderly, well-dressed ladies and gentlemen were shown calling to friends through the window of an elegant town house, "Come on—we're going to the Trans-Lux and hiss Roosevelt."

Born in 1882, a favored child of an elderly father and a handsome, dynamic mother, Franklin Roosevelt grew up on his family's Hudson River estate at Hyde Park, Dutchess County, New York. He was educated at Groton and Harvard, where he was well liked but was an undistinguished student. He received his law degree from Columbia University and was married to Anna Eleanor Roosevelt, a distant cousin and the niece of President Theodore Roosevelt. FDR's first elective job was as a New York state senator. He fought Tammany Hall's William Sheehan successfully, but he lost most of his friends in the Democratic party. An interest in Woodrow Wilson's "New Freedom" program and admiration for his intellectual capabilities motivated FDR to join the New York Committee for Wilson for President. Later, when Wilson appointed him Assistant Secretary of the Navy under Josephus Daniels, he said that, because he loved the sea, he "would rather have that place than any other in public life." At the Democratic convention in San Francisco in 1920, Roosevelt, only thirty-eight, was nominated to run for Vice President with James M. Cox of Ohio. A hard-fought campaign conducted from coast to coast failed. Warren Harding won the Presidency and FDR returned to a New York law practice.

August 1921 was the turning point of Roosevelt's life. While at his summer house on Campobello Island, New Brunswick, Canada, Roosevelt contracted poliomyelitis. His return to health was painful physically and emotionally. His mother wanted him to retire to Hyde Park and become a country squire, but his wife and his close friend, Louis Howe, believed that his crippled legs need not keep him from a political career—and, in 1928, Roosevelt was elected Governor of New York. Throughout his public life there was a conspiracy of silence about the extent of FDR's physical incapacity. Photographs usually showed him from the neck up or seated in a manner to hide his lower extremities. He was never lampooned about his lameness, nor was his use of a wheelchair publicized. Many people in Europe, even those in high office, did not know he was crippled. There has been much talk by his friends about the psychological effect that polio had on the President. Frances Perkins, his Secretary of Labor, made a particular point of the change from the somewhat supercilious, athletic, impersonal young man with the pince-nez whom she first met in the New York state senate and the Navy Department to the chastened, compassionate, genial, older Roosevelt. She commented that what had been an obnoxious gesture earlier—the shrug of the shoulder and the toss of the head—became incredibly captivating later. How much of this change was maturity and the passage of time can never be determined. Nor can it be known whether his illness turned him politically to the left. However, imprisoned in a wheelchair, Roosevelt had more time to think, to reflect and to understand. He was not bitter, nor did he seem to brood about his health. On the contrary, except for the effects of polio, his strong shoulders and large head gave him the appearance of strength and vigor.

Roosevelt's mind was quick and good at detail. Though he was not an abstract thinker, he could appreciate the brains of others and, with an unerring instinct for quality, absorb and use their best output. He was receptive to originality and initiative. Perhaps it was his illness that made him intuitive and gave him a strong feeling for self-preservation. He was a clever, acute politician—humorous, genial, vastly articulate, with unequaled poise. One of his greatest assets was his spellbinding voice. Senator William Borah of Idaho said that he stayed away from Congress to avoid becoming captivated by his golden voice. "It's dangerous to listen to Roosevelt because he could recite an example in algebra and make it interesting," he said.

FDR's ability to project sympathetic understanding encompassed all kinds of people. Although he spoke like an aristocrat, his words reached the poor. A buoyant confidence in what he said and did transferred itself completely to his public. People thought of him with an affection that somehow they felt was returned.

As for his faults, Roosevelt was often devious because he hated to disappoint his friends. Consequently, after an interview with him, Roosevelt's geniality was interpreted as approval and acclamation. Often this led to future misunderstanding and recriminations by the disappointed seeker of favors. He talked too much, perhaps, because it was his only sport. And like many men who are constantly supplied with a captive audience, he was sometimes repetitive and discursive. His critics found his greatest fault to have been a taste for revenge, particularly against those who threatened his programs. And if he had to choose between reason and the sixth sense, called instinct, he was often guilty of choosing the latter.

An almost feminine, coquettish vacillation both piqued and irritated the electorate throughout FDR's second four years. There were several good reasons, however, for this behavior. The Congressional rebellion against the President's power and possibly against the continuance of the New Deal could best be controlled by a man whose days in office were not numbered. As long as he was a possible candidate he could make policy. On the other hand, if he announced his candidacy he would become more a political figure and less a President, and thus his prestige would suffer. The only answer to the dilemma seemed to be silence. Handicapped by FDR's attitude, as they most assuredly were, the Democratic presidential hopefuls had to proceed as if their chief rival were invisible.

The most logical successor to the Chief was John Nance Garner, his twice elected Vice President. A Texan, with Congressional experience dating from 1902, he was sixty-nine years old but still spry. Nineteen thirty-seven was the critical year for the FDR–Garner relationship. FDR's plan to enlarge the Supreme Court, announced without warning shortly after his second inaugural, enraged the Vice President along with many other office-holding Democrats. The Court had been methodically destroying New Deal legislation by declaring such bills as the NIRA and the AAA unconstitutional as soon as they came up for review. The Roosevelt plan was to add one new justice for each one who had served at least ten years and then failed to resign or retire six months after his seventieth birthday. No more than six new justices could be added. Roosevelt's justification for this proposal was that he believed that the pressing economic and social problems had to be solved "now," not when a Supreme Court, old in spirit as well as body, chose to be agreeable. This may have been, as Secretary of the Interior Harold L. Ickes said, "the most important issue since the Civil War," but it aroused both expected and unexpected opposition. Some of the septuagenarian Senators took it personally, and even some reliable Rooseveltians were appalled at a plan that struck at the sacred concept of Constitutional checks and balances. The institution of the Court, removed from the area of partisan politics, was an oasis in an insecure America that even FDR's great popularity, just dramatically demonstrated by his sweeping electoral victory, could not force his countrymen to abandon. Acting somewhat symbolically, Garner, fearful that the President might expect his support on the issue, packed his bags and retreated to Texas for a long vacation. Garner finally supported the plan only because he was convinced that the Supreme Court would still maintain its independence.

There were other basic differences between the two men over such matters as the unbalanced budget and labor, particularly John L. Lewis, president of the CIO, whom Garner loathed. But it was the idea of breaking the third-term tradition that disturbed Garner the most. However, despite Roosevelt's rift with the Vice President, the Tory wing of the Democratic party was much interested in Garner and did not want to hear his objections to becoming a candidate.

The Gallup poll placed Postmaster James A. Farley at the top of their list of contenders. He was an Al Smith discovery whom FDR adopted after Smith's retirement. An affable, efficient party man, chairman of the Democratic National Committee, he never claimed to have sought office higher than the Vice Presidency. FDR thought that Farley lacked a background in statesmanship. It was his opinion that the Postmaster General should run for Governor of New York in 1938 to replace Herbert Lehman, who wanted to retire— a notion that did not appeal to Farley. Politicians feared that there were other problems connected with Farley's candidacy: his religion, Roman Catholicism; and, more important, the fact that he had never been a New Dealer. Actually, FDR and Farley never had been personal friends, nor had the President ever taken him into his confidence or consulted him on matters of policy. Farley was, simply, FDR's lifeline to the Democratic party structure.

A possible compromise candidate was former Progressive party candidate for Vice President and present Senator from Montana, Burton K. Wheeler. His fight against the Court plan and subsequent break with FDR might endear him to the conservatives, whereas his overall record might make him acceptable to the liberals. It was believed that Wheeler's opposition to the Court plan was in revenge for FDR's rejection of him as a vice-presidential candidate or as a member of the Cabinet. In retaliation for Wheeler's hostility, when the President passed through Montana in October 1937 he ignored the Senator. These episodes lessened Wheeler's chances.

Handsome Paul V. McNutt, once Indiana University Law School's youngest dean and in 1933 Governor of Indiana, was another contender. His political record was both good and bad. His reorganization of the Indiana state government had saved its citizens two million dollars a year, and he had improved the public school system. But there was some question about the legality of the McNutt 2% Clubs, a device to collect money from state employees, and for his use of the National Guard to break up strikes, for which he had been dubbed the "Hoosier Hitler." In 1937, partially as a reward for having endorsed Roosevelt and partially, perhaps, to get rid of him, he was appointed High Commissioner of the Philippines.

An observer said of Jesse Jones's possible candidacy that it was "as loud as the tramp of a timorous kitten." Yet he was most popular with business Democrats. A self-made Texas millionaire, Administrator of the Reconstruction Finance Corporation, he was neither a liberal nor a New Dealer. He was alleged to have opposed the appointment of Hugo Black to the Supreme Court because Black was too liberal.

Although not a well-known national figure in April 1937, Governor George Earle of Pennsylvania was, according to the pollsters, second to Jim Farley in popularity. Earle, from a wealthy Philadelphia family, was a converted New Dealer. He had made a liberal record as Governor, had served as Minister to Austria and would have the support of organized labor and the Pennsylvania political machine behind him.

In addition to the activities of the Democratic aspirants, fear of a third-term effort persisted. The indecisiveness of a poll of Democratic governors taken by the United Press was indicative of uncertainty about a third term. Six governors supported the President for 1940 and three opposed him, stating the third term as their reason. But twenty-nine did not wish to make a commitment. To forestall the possibility of FDR in 1940, four resolutions were introduced in Congress from January to August 1937. All were worded to limit the President's tenure in office. However, the sponsors, among them Senator Edward Burke and Representative Hamilton Fish, failed to bring the resolutions to a vote. Had it been possible, because of the composition of the Congress, one of the bills might have been passed.

Governor Earle introduced serious consideration of the third term with a statement made in June 1937. He said: "There are many leaders of intelligence and honesty in the Democratic party. There are, however, no men in the Democratic party or any other party who reach knee-high in stature, mentally and morally, to Franklin D. Roosevelt. Between the third-term precedent and the welfare of the country, can any patriotic citizen hesitate as to which course he will take?" Proof that the statement was, as Earle commented, made without the President's permission was verified when the press asked FDR to talk about it. He answered, "The weather is very hot." Further questioning by Robert Post of *The New York Times* gained only "Bob Post should put on a dunce cap and stand in the corner." This set the tone for subsequent exchanges on the subject between press and President.

Demonstrably, Roosevelt was sorely tried at this time. He had to manage both rebellious Democrats and threatening dictators. Throughout 1938 the world situation deteriorated. And as the situation worsened, the President became increasingly aware that many New Dealers backed away from any international involvement because they feared it might mean less interest in domestic reform. The New Deal, too, was in grave danger of dissolution. By March 1938 the seven-month-old recession had reduced the Federal Reserve Board index to within ten points of the 1932 low of 69. About ten million were still unemployed, and steel, the nation's weathervane, had lost more than half its business. Roosevelt again asked Congress to grant large sums for PWA, WPA, low-cost housing and NYA, among other agencies. He got his money but only because it was an election year.

One last major reform bill was put through at this time but only after heroic efforts on the part of FDR. The Federal Wages and Hours law was introduced in May 1937 by Senator Hugo Black of Alabama, who later that year became a Supreme Court justice, but it was not passed until June 1938, in a somewhat modified form. Other Southerners fought against it because they wanted to maintain low wages in their part of the country. Senator "Cotton Ed" Smith boasted that a man could live comfortably in South Carolina on fifty cents a day. The bill, when passed, provided that by 1940, with many exemptions, there would be a forty-cents-per-hour minimum wage, a forty-hour week, and children would not be employed in businesses engaged in interstate commerce. FDR was weary but grateful when he finally received the bill for signing.

After the passage of the Wages and Hours law, Congress' opposition to the New Deal was plainly evident. Among the rejected measures were increases in appropriations, a federal theater project and an undistributed profits tax. Several presidential appointments were turned down.

In a desperate effort to save his program, FDR attempted a purge of the Democratic party conservatives. The public was made aware of his decision on June 24 in a fireside chat on party primaries. "After the election of 1936, I was told, and the Congress was told, by an increasing number of politically and worldly wise people, that I should coast along, enjoy an easy Presidency for four years, and not take the Democratic platform too seriously," FDR said. But the President was not content to allow this to happen. He was not convinced that "the people were getting weary of reform through political effort." Quite the contrary, he stated that he was prepared to fight this evidence of defeatism in the Seventy-fifth Congress. He asserted: "Never before have we had so many Copperheads—and you will remember that it was the Copperheads who, in the days of the War between the States, tried their best to make Lincoln and his Congress give up the fight, let the nation remain split in two and return to peace —peace at any price." Roosevelt asserted his responsibility to carry out the liberal principles of the 1936 platform and his right "to speak in these few instances where there may be a clear issue between the candidates for a Democratic nomination involving these principles or involving a clear misuse of my name."

Later, in Barnesville, Georgia, Roosevelt declared that he and their Senator, Walter George, differed on most important public questions. A sharp frontal attack was made by the President on Millard Tydings, the astonishingly popular Maryland Senator who had voted against all significant New Deal legislation. Both efforts failed to shake local enthusiasm for their men. The New Deal's candidate in South Carolina who was to challenge "Cotton Ed" Smith proved to be an embarrassment to his liberal colleagues. Smith's racist campaign was equalled, if not surpassed, by his opponent. The trio of Senators—Tydings, Smith and George—were all successful in the November elections, which was a blow to FDR, but he did achieve the defeat of Representative John J. O'Connor of New York. And it did serve to identify the liberals and the conservatives in the Democratic ranks. Perhaps the "purge" was a mistake, because the President's heart was not really in it. His enemies said that such tactics smacked of the kind of political homicide that characterized the Fascists.

Meanwhile other presidential aspirants appeared, had a brief flurry and then, often, disappeared. Ambassador to Great Britain Joseph P. Kennedy, thought Harold Ickes, was ambitious to be the first Catholic President of the United States. But most Democrats agreed that Jim Farley should have first claim to that title. Also Kennedy was neither a New Dealer nor popular with the State Department because he constantly complained about the "career boys." The Administration left wing resented Kennedy particularly for his alleged role in influencing FDR not to lift the arms embargo against Spain to aid the Loyalist government. And his position on the Jews was contradictory. On the one hand, Kennedy's belief in appeasement made many feel that he was sympathetic to Nazi Germany. Despite this, Kennedy proposed a plan to resettle tens of thousands of Jews, to be rescued from Germany, in the underpopulated areas of North and South America and Africa. *Life* magazine said that such a scheme could propel Kennedy into the White House. It never came off and the Ambassador blamed British red tape. In October, Kennedy advocated that the democracies and the dictatorships agree to a kind of peaceful coexistence, which the State Department thought was going too far. FDR, one week later, in a speech that Kennedy regarded as a slap at him, was most critical of the dictatorships.

The President's natural heir was his very close friend, WPA director Harry Hopkins. At a meeting between the two men Hopkins' candidacy was discussed with what seemed to be great frankness. Roosevelt told Hopkins that he feared that his divorce would be a liability, but, on the other hand, he reasoned, Grover Cleveland had overcome the greater scandal of an illegitimate child. The most serious obstacle to a Hopkins bid for the Democratic nomination was, undoubtedly, the WPA director's health. However, the Mayo Clinic had given Hopkins a two-to-one chance that he was cured of cancer. In spite of drawbacks, FDR said that he thought that Hopkins would do the best job as President of anyone in the running. He was prepared to increase his chances by appointing him Secretary of Commerce as soon as it could be arranged. Hopkins left the meeting convinced that he had Roosevelt's endorsement, and later, in the greatest secrecy, told the story to his best friends. Some manifestations of his support could be detected in certain presidential actions. Press photographs of the President at this time often show Harry Hopkins at his elbow. Mrs. Roosevelt referred to him favorably in her column, "My Day." Arthur Krock recognized his preferential position in October 1938, writing that "If he was No. 1 in June, 1937, he is No. 1-A now." Even Jim Farley placed Hopkins first on FDR's list.

Another active candidate in the President's political family was Secretary of Agriculture Henry Wallace of Iowa. He, like the others, relied on FDR's not running for a third term. Although he was an active New Dealer and to him belonged the credit for the new Agricultural Adjustment Act, he had many debits as far as the professional politicians were concerned. They distrusted almost everything about him—his Republican past, his mysticism and his lack of presence in public.

Paul McNutt unsettled everyone in early February 1938 on his return to Washington to see the President. He had been feted across the country by his supporters and then given a reception in the capital. Farley, having departed for Florida that very same day, was prominently absent from the festivities. Tactfully, while in Washington, McNutt denied that he was a candidate. Enthusiasm for him declined after his return to the Philippines, but he was a comfortable fourth in the Gallup poll in August, replacing Governor Earle. After the November elections McNutt's popularity waned further because the High Commissioner failed to deliver the Indiana vote. Rumors that he had differences with FDR dropped him two slots, to sixth place in the poll.

The fall of 1938 was a very difficult one for the President. In September, Charles A. Lindbergh reported that the German Air Force was the most powerful in the world, stronger than all the other

European air forces combined. The dangerous war crisis, caused by Hitler's demand that Czechoslovakia cede him the Sudetenland, culminated in the acceptance of his demands at the Munich Conference. At first even FDR thought that Chamberlain's "peace in our time" would be a reality. The atrocities against the German Jews caused the United States government to withdraw her Ambassador from Germany, a move that was supported by all except the isolationists and the pacifists.

The November election returns were not as bad as many Democrats had feared. Midterm elections usually reflect a swing to the non-presidential party. FDR's attempt to discipline conservatives in his party had met with partial success. And he retained a Democratic Congress. Republican gains were made in the rural areas of the Midwest and the Northwest. In the cities the Democrats showed up better.

The only liberal or middle-of-the-roader to show substantial gains after the elections was Senator Wheeler, who kept in the good graces of the party regulars by denouncing the party purge. A sudden appearance in fourth place in the Gallup poll was made by Senator Bennett "Champ" Clark of Missouri. A distinguished background in politics along with relatively conservative economic ideas could make him interesting to conservative Democrats. Possibly Vice President Garner preferred him to Jesse Jones.

The election returns satisfied the President. He expected less trouble with the new Congress and realization on the part of certain party members that the ticket for the election of 1940 could not be accomplished without administrative support. "I am sufficiently honest to decline to support any conservative Democrats," he said. Nevertheless, 1938 was a low ebb in FDR's fortunes. Lessening popularity marked the year; a National League to Oppose the Third Term for President was incorporated in New York; in December the Gallup poll still found that seven out of ten voters opposed Roosevelt's running again.

Roosevelt failed to declare his intentions in 1939. Vice President Garner and Jim Farley were now considered the strongest contenders, along with Secretary of State Cordell Hull. The Tennesseean, a former judge who had served in both houses of Congress, was supposedly the President's choice. He was elegant, spare, gray and softspoken, with an unruffled aplomb. His good manners overcame his most obstreperous adversaries. So successful was his record in the State Department that he shuddered to do anything that might mar it. A certain slowness and deliberateness was his greatest shortcoming. Sometimes the President, so frustrated by Hull's reluctance to act, would by-pass him for his Under Secretary, Sumner Welles, the Treasury Department, Harry Hopkins or other shortcuts.

FDR was fully aware that the game of silence that he was playing had many pitfalls; he could never be accused of political naïveté. If, sometimes, he seemed to be two-faced, it was simply his inability to play the hatchet man. He hated to disappoint anyone, although when thoroughly aroused by evidence of disloyalty or betrayal Roosevelt could display his anger. Party division worried the President. On Jackson Day he said, "If we Democrats lay for each other now, we can be sure that 1940 will be the corner where the American people will be laying for us."

Roosevelt's popularity increased in the spring of 1939. In Chicago, "The Third Termers Club," led by Judge John Gutknecht, claimed 50,000 members. The CIO pledged almost unanimous support. Even liberals denied that dictatorship and a third term were synonomous and felt that FDR would save the country from reaction. Henry L. Mencken had his own sour reason for favoring a third term for Roosevelt. "He ought to be made to bury his own dead horse," he said.

Garner had his quota of enthusiastic supporters. In May a "Garner for President" headquarters was established in Dallas, Texas. Big money was backing him because he had become identified with the economy bloc in Congress. Henry Ford announced that "Jack Garner would make a mighty fine President." Roy Muller of the Texas Gulf Sulphur Company agreed with him. Garner's sponsors were not enthusiastic about this support becoming public because they feared that it would lose the Vice President the endorsement of labor. Neither Farley nor FDR took the Garner candidacy seriously, preferring to believe that it was the Garnerites and not the Vice President who wanted the post. However, according to the Gallup poll, Garner was now the favorite, with a 50 percent score.

Increased support for Garner sparked the Roosevelt adherents. News of endorsements for a third term were leaked to the press by such New Deal champions as the Secretaries of Commerce and the Interior and Tom Corcoran and Ben Cohen. Mrs. Roosevelt had mixed feelings about her husband's plans. She asserted that the New Deal was bigger than one man and preferred that he not run again. However, she wanted a liberal to be elected.

In June, Harry Hopkins told the United Press that, in time, he would urge FDR to seek the 1940 nomination. Nevertheless, he was unwilling to give up his own presidential aspirations. In order to become eligible for nomination from Iowa, he purchased a farm there. But shortly afterward he became seriously ill again. It was not a recurrence of cancer but one of a series of mysterious and puzzling illnesses that resulted from the nutritional deficiencies that his earlier operation had caused. A visit to the Mayo Clinic helped him to recover enough to go home to Georgetown, but he was confined to the house for eight months. His presidential hopes were cancelled.

Farley and Garner lunched together in July and had a consoling exchange of grievances. The Vice President announced that he did not want to be President but could not, in any circumstances, acquiesce to a third term. Farley agreed but swore him to secrecy while complaining about the "neglect and kicking about" he had been getting. Later in the month, just before leaving for Europe, Farley paid a visit to Hyde Park.

After dinner with the family, Farley and the President retired to the small study in the north wing. At first the conversation concerned politics and party matters. Whenever the Postmaster General disagreed with FDR he detected a marked frigidity in his manner. Slowly talk turned to a consideration of Democratic presidential candidates. Roosevelt dismissed Garner brusquely with the comment, "He's just impossible." They disagreed about Wallace. FDR favored him. Farley dubbed him a dreamer. When McNutt's name came up the President turned down the thumb of his right hand. Unmentioned were the names of Hull, Jesse Jones, Solicitor General Robert Jackson, Attorney General Frank Murphy, Harry Hopkins and Farley himself. In discussion of the third-term issue FDR said, in an impressive whisper, "Of course, I will not run for a third term." He asked Farley not to repeat this. Then FDR told Farley that he did not want to campaign for a losing ticket. The response was, "Boss, as the party's leader, you'll have to campaign for whatever ticket is selected." Farley asked the President bluntly what kind of candidate he wanted. The answer was that he should be someone sympathetic to the Administration who would continue its policies. Roosevelt did not seem to have anyone specific in mind. Reflecting on the meeting later that night, Farley was rather pleased with himself for his control over his personal bitterness. He also concluded that, until the President finally declared himself publicly, the third-term issue could not be settled. At a press interview the next morning, with a toss of his head and a snappy answer, FDR countered a reporter's suspicion that Farley planned to resign. "He is not," he said. At the Vatican the following month, Farley's reply to Pope Pius XII's question "Will the President run again?" was that it would depend on circumstances and would be breaking an unwritten law that no one had attempted to do in the United States. The Pope laughed quietly and answered, "You know, I am the first Italian Papal Secretary of State to be elected Pope."

In the summer of 1939 Young Democrats at their Pittsburgh convention almost all advocated a third term. Politicians like Mayor Ed Kelly of Chicago and Mayor Frank Hague of Jersey City also supported another four years. The President used a curious divisive technique in which he encouraged rival candidates. It was partly deliberate, partly his inability to tell a candidate to his face that he would not support him. The result was, as calculated, that no significant anti-third-term movement could develop nor could one strong candidate emerge other than Roosevelt.

2

The news of war came over the President's bedside phone at ten minutes to 3 A.M. Friday, September 1, 1939. Ambassador to France William Bullitt's voice carried the tragic information that bombs were falling on Polish cities. Moments later Cordell Hull received the message about the German invasion. Hull said that he guessed it as soon as he recognized Roosevelt's voice on the phone. Secretary of War Harry H. Woodring and Acting Secretary of the Navy Charles Edison as well as Under Secretary of State Sumner Welles also received presidential calls. Response was immediate. The President said that he had an uncanny sense of having experienced the entire situation before. During World War I, when he had been Under Secretary of the Navy, the direct wire to the Navy Department had often brought messages in the night. "It was not strange to me but more like picking up an interrupted routine" was how he described his reaction.

At a solemn Cabinet meeting in the afternoon, FDR picked up the same theme. "History does in fact repeat," he said. The Cabinet was instructed that war problems would be met but the United States would not prepare to fight. As soon as Great Britain and France declared war formally, FDR would address the people by radio. The most pressing difficulty, however, would be the repeal of the arms-embargo section of the Neutrality law, which forbade the sale of munitions to all belligerents, so that the Allies could be provided with the necessary supplies.

In January 1939, in his message to Congress, the President had explained that the blanket arms embargo of the Neutrality law actually favored an aggressor by guaranteeing that his victims could not receive assistance from the United States. Roosevelt and Hull wanted the Neutrality Act repealed but would settle for Executive authority to limit the application of the arms embargo to aggressor states, the President to use his discretion. However, Senator Key Pittman's efforts to guide such a change through Congress had failed in July when the Foreign Relations Committee voted to postpone further discussion of the subject until January 1940. Roosevelt could not wait until then. The situation was entirely too pressing for the democracies.

Ambassador Joseph Kennedy agreed with the President on the intense seriousness of the crisis. A natural pessimist, he regarded the actual outbreak of war as doom for the world as it had been known. Roosevelt thought that part of Kennedy's trouble was his intimacy with the British aristocracy. The President had to calm his quavery-voiced Ambassador when, over the transatlantic phone, he recited the substance of Chamberlain's speech and then repeated over and over, "It's the end of the world. The end of everything."

CHAPTER TWO

"The Stab in the Back"

1

THE WHITE HOUSE mobilized itself into a permanent emergency routine to be followed for the duration. Army and Navy intelligence reported to FDR every day at 2:45 P.M. The State Department sent over hourly dispatches. The President, in the first days, stalled a decision to declare a state of belligerency so he could delay placing the arms embargo of the Neutrality Act in operation. On Sunday night, September 3, he told the American people about the European war. The speech, drafted originally by the State Department, was rewritten skillfully by the President. As was his custom, he had accentuated certain phrases and added new paragraphs. He said that the United States would remain neutral, but "Even a neutral has a right to take account of facts. Even a neutral cannot be asked to close his mind and his conscience." He added, "I have said not once but many times that I have seen war and that I hate war. I say that again and again . . . As long as it remains within my power to prevent it there

will be no blackout of peace in the United States." His voice was
sober, less buoyant than usual, but strangely confident while saying
unpleasant things. His timing was particularly perfect; his diction, as
always, superb.

The next weeks changed life for many Europeans. Gas masks became a correct part of a Londoner's wardrobe. Three million London
children were evacuated from the threatened city for the lovely and,
hopefully, safer English countryside. British ships were being tor-
pedoed unmercifully. Among them was the passenger liner *Athenia,*
which carried fourteen hundred passengers, 292 of them Americans.
The President was anxious to bring Americans back from overseas
and to keep nationals from traveling to Europe so that the difficulties
on the high seas that contributed to American entrance into World
War I would be avoided.

Unable to delay any longer, the United States formally proclaimed
neutrality on September 6. Now, FDR's primary goal was to mitigate
the arms embargo by the use of a device known as "cash and carry."
Although United States shipping would be rigidly restricted, the Allies would be able to pick up their supplies in the United States on
their own ships and, after paying cash for them, take them home.

The trick, however, would be to muster enough Congressional support to pass the new legislation. FDR had already committed himself
to Prime Minister Chamberlain, to whom he had written that "I hope
and believe that we shall repeal the embargo within the next month
and this is definitely part of the Administration policy." It was just as
definitely against the policy of Senators William Borah of Idaho and
Gerald P. Nye of North Dakota, among other isolationist Congressmen. The leaders of the opposition were convinced that the end of the
embargo would be a giant step toward war. Anxious to avoid the
errors of Wilson, FDR tried to make his efforts in the emergency
bipartisan. He invited Governor Alfred Landon, his 1936 opponent
for the Presidency, and Frank Knox, Landon's running mate, to come
to a White House conference on the neutrality legislation.

"I give you my deep and unalterable conviction that by repeal of
the embargo the United States will more probably remain at peace
than if the law remains as it stands today," FDR said to Congress.
Then, candidly, he admitted, "I regret that Congress passed the
Neutrality Act. I regret equally that I signed it." He ended his
speech on an ominous note: "Our acts must be guided by one single

hardheaded thought—keeping America out of war. The facts compel my stating with candor that darker periods may be ahead."

Roosevelt hoped that he had made an impact. The afternoon before, about fifteen Democratic and Republican leaders had been brought into the presidential office to discuss the legislation. In addition, tremendous care had gone into the drafting and the redrafting of the speech. Judge Samuel Rosenman, who more than anyone else had the ability of expressing FDR's thoughts just as he would have himself, had labored over the text the night before with Adolf A. Berle, Secretary of State Cordell Hull and the President. At 11 P.M. FDR went to bed, but Rosenman and Grace Tully, the President's secretary, continued with a new draft until 2:30 A.M. They were up again at 7:00, at which time they went to FDR's bedroom, where they spent the rest of the morning. As he often did, Roosevelt worked sitting up in bed. After completing a draft of a page it would be sent over to Grace Tully to be typed. Several times Secretary Hull was consulted by phone. By 12:30 P.M., very close to the deadline, the last page was approved by FDR. At 2:00 the speech was delivered.

Wearing a blue, double-breasted business suit, the President entered the House of Representatives unsmiling. Even the ovation he received was unacknowledged by the familiar Roosevelt grin and wave of the arm. After the speech FDR, still solemn, left the chamber on the arm of his aide, General Edwin (Pa) Watson. Again the members of Congress and the people in the galleries stood and cheered. The Chief left the building just before a group of men and women, members of the Philadelphia Committee for the Defense of Constitutional Rights, poured into the Capitol carrying small flags and shouting, "No Cash and Carry."

However, these extremists did not represent the majority of the American people. FDR's foreign policy was very popular. The Gallup poll reflected that presidential popularity was 61 percent, almost back to its peak of 62.5 percent when he had been re-elected in 1936.

The "peace bloc" was unconcerned with either the Roosevelt eloquence or the polls. Twenty-four senatorial opponents of repeal said that they were ready to fight it "from hell to breakfast." Henry Ford asserted that the present Neutrality Act was foolproof and its amendment was for the purpose of making money for the munitions makers. America's hero, Charles A. Lindbergh, had somewhat earlier, on September 16, the day before the Soviet Union marched into Poland, urged the United States to shun the war. Commentator Fulton Lewis, Jr., had persuaded Lindbergh to make the address, his first since 1931. The air ace seemed to be following in the footsteps of his father, a Congressman from Minnesota, who was one of the few to vote against America's entry into World War I in 1917. He agreed with Senator Nye, who likened the arms embargo to a traffic light. If it was repealed, the light would turn green, a "go ahead" along the road to war.

Roosevelt must have been pleased, however, by Al Smith's radio address supporting Administration policy. The two men, close friends in the early part of FDR's political career, had been estranged for some time. Smith had been a leader of conservative Democrats who opposed the New Deal. Now, he said, FDR was "so clearly right" that no one with understanding and judgment would oppose him. Delivered with the old Smith verve, the speech made a point of objecting to certain Catholic churches that were making the political issue a religious one. Although Smith's gesture did not result in a real reconciliation, it was a generous move and was warmly received by the man who had dubbed him the "happy warrior."

October was a month of peace rumors. Hitler was firmly established in Poland, but no further offensive was taking place. He let it be known that, if allowed to keep all his war gains, he would be receptive to talk of peace and perhaps FDR could be its angel. France maintained that the German government would have to prove its sincerity by demonstrable acts. Chamberlain and the average Briton were equally sick of uncertainty and Hitler. Peace feelers continued, but, attractive as the idea was to the American President, he listened to his advisers and failed to act.

The President continued to be tense about the fate of the Neutrality bill. He laughed readily, smiled his infectious smile, enjoyed his weekend visits to Hyde Park; but, it was observed, his face was more lined, his eyes more tired and his temper short with newspapermen who pressured him. The Senate had emptied the galleries and the floor itself by its incessant debate. This appeared to be a good sign. But FDR continued to be "almost literally walking on eggs," as he told Lord Tweedsmuir.

All fears were groundless. The desired repeal was passed in the Senate on October 27, by 63–30. The Republican votes had not been needed, but nevertheless the 35 percent Republican support gave passage a satisfying bipartisan slant. In the House, the vote was closer: 243–181.

The British were gratified by the results and the French rejoiced. The German press, however, renewed its hostility to FDR, which it had been soft-pedaling for the last few months.

Now that the United States was to be "the arsenal of freedom," large orders from the Allies were expected. France's were large but England's were almost negligible because Chamberlain was afraid of upsetting British industry. Until May, British orders were slow, a hesitation that cost them dearly later on.

2

The outbreak of war did not change the picture for any of the Democratic contenders. Governor Alfred Landon, however, on the occasion of his visit to the White House, informed the press that he believed firmly that FDR should announce that he would not be a candidate in 1940. All his statement accomplished was that Landon ceased to be considered for a Cabinet post, an idea for a bipartisan Cabinet that Roosevelt had fostered because of the war situation. Mrs. Eleanor Roosevelt stated that she could not see why the war should have any bearing on her husband's candidacy. FDR's mother, on the occasion of her eighty-fifth birthday in September, said, "I don't think my son has the slightest wish for a third term. He is thinking only about the war. He is trying to do all he can for peace." Only the New Dealers saw the war as assurance for a third term. Even the President committed himself only a little. He told Farley that now it looked as if "I could do nothing until the spring, March or April."

Secretary of Agriculture Henry Wallace demonstrated his usual lack of political acumen when, during the most tense moments of the Neutrality legislation debates, he came out for a third term in a statement made in Berkeley, California. Meanwhile FDR was parrying the reporters and laughing over but not answering the jingle that was presented to him:

> He's riding high, and he's riding straight
> He's heading straight for the White House gate.

And the majority of the voters continued to oppose a third term. John L. Lewis was violent on the subject, but the CIO membership wanted FDR to continue the New Deal.

When Ickes brought up the subject of a third term FDR told him that reports from Cornelius Vanderbilt, Jr., from the Midwest revealed that the people were tired of hearing the name Roosevelt. This was reminiscent of one of FDR's favorite stories that had been told to him by "Uncle Teddy." Theodore Roosevelt said, when he was being pressured to run for a third term, that the American people were sick and tired of Roosevelts. "They are sick of looking at my grin and they are sick of hearing what Alice had for breakfast. In fact they want a rest from Roosevelts."

The hopefuls continued to hope, although some realized that their chances were fading. Secretary Hull behaved in a detached manner, assuring reporters that he had no political interests. Burton K. Wheeler admitted that FDR might be in the White House again, war or no war. Farley said sagely that it was natural for all Presidents to consider themselves irreplaceable. But it was the McNutt candidacy that boomed, thanks to noisy and active supporters. By late November 1939, while his managers dreamed of hundreds of delegates pledged on the first ballot, New Dealers began to smell danger. They doubted McNutt's commitment to their views, with good reason, while fearing that FDR favored him.

Wheeler for President clubs were now operating in several states. His appeal was to the isolationists and to those in the agricultural and western states who were opposed to Hull's reciprocal trade agreements. John L. Lewis, now in search of a candidate, showed some interest in him. FDR was furious at the Senator and told a friend that if Wheeler ran he'd vote Republican.

The Garner forces were also seeking to build up state organizations throughout the country to prepare for the primaries in 1940. Sam Rayburn, who had been Garner's manager in the 1932 campaign, was expected to play a major part again.

FDR remained silent both about Garner and about himself. However, he enjoyed twitting the press in his rather heavy-handed style. The Roosevelt humor was never subtle and sometimes offensive to those who did not like to be the butt of jokes. John L. Lewis was one of those.

In November 1939 Roosevelt laid the cornerstone of the Roosevelt library at Hyde Park. After the speech he gave one of his "humorous" performances for the benefit of the press. Picking up a manuscript, the President gazed at it for a few seconds, then looked up suddenly and said, "And may I add, in order that my good friends of the press will have something to write about tomorrow . . ." His meaningful pause was supposed to give the newsmen a chance to hope that his statement would be a revelation about third-term plans. Instead, he finished with "that I hope they will give due interpretation to the expression of my hope that when we open the building to the public it will be a fine day." Gales of expected laughter greeted his words, but it is doubtful whether anyone besides the author enjoyed the joke.

Despite the President's studied disinterest in avowals of third-term endorsement, they continued to be made. Senator William Gibbs McAdoo of California announced that the party wanted Roosevelt again. Unknown to the President, FDR III clubs were started in Georgia, to be followed by similar clubs in other states. Ambassador Joseph Kennedy surprised people when he made the statement that he favored a third term.

Almost every day new supporters were coming out for the President. Arthur Krock commented, "Whatever Mr. Roosevelt may intend, he is obviously enjoying it, however much those may suffer who seriously fear the effect on our liberties of a third term." At the Gridiron Club dinner in December, the Washington correspondents portrayed FDR as the Sphinx. There was constant reference to the anxieties of those whose fate was involved in his delayed decision to run or not to run. Harold Stassen, in his speech that night, called FDR a quarterback who, at one point in the game, "sent Garner and Murphy around the right and Ickes and Wallace around the left and then made a delayed forward pass to Paul McNutt. But halfback Ickes tackled McNutt as he was receiving the pass."

FDR's suggestion that the conventions be held late in July or in mid-August further disturbed the possible candidates. They would surely need at least four months to conduct a campaign. An even more bizarre idea was FDR's insistence that Republican leaders be invited to the Jackson Day dinner, an annual Democratic party event. Roosevelt may have been thinking of bipartisanship, but Representative Joseph W. Martin, a Republican leader, refused the invitation, saying that he'd be out of place at a dinner to raise $100,000 for the

Democratic campaign. Roosevelt's speech at the dinner emphasized the importance of the independent voter. Henry Wallace announced that he hoped that the Democratic nominee in 1940 would be President Roosevelt. James Farley, who had been seated between FDR and Garner, opened his speech with the words, "Fellow candidates."

An interesting development at this time was that the city bosses who had opposed FDR in 1932 now favored him to run again. They held the political power in their own bailiwicks and were ready and able to deliver the vote. Harry Hopkins, early in 1940, gathered together Florida's Senator Claude Pepper, Mayor Ed Kelly of Chicago and Mayor Frank Hague of Jersey City at the Mayflower Hotel in Washington. He called this a historic meeting because the group was to be the nucleus of a movement to force FDR to run again. Now when Henry Wallace and Robert Jackson supported the third term in speeches they were no longer rebuked. FDR just asserted that he hadn't read the speeches.

The foreign press both believed and hoped that FDR would run again. They were fearful that a new American President might not be as sympathetic to their position. In France, Raoul Roussy de Salles wrote in *L'Europe Nouvelle,* "We believe that Roosevelt will accept office for the third time because he considers that he has a mission to accomplish in the world, a mission that does not spring from any mystical source, but from the conviction that events have proven him right, and that he has been on the right path not only as far as it concerns his own country but also the world."

3

Hitler was now anxious to renew the war, believing that his army, air force and armor were indestructible. But his generals opposed him, advising that he wait for the British and the French to make the first move. They sent General Walter von Brauchitsch to convey these views. The general, however, failed miserably to stand up to his leader and had to retreat before Hitler's wrath. The German onslaught was to have begun on November 12, but bad weather intervened.

A few days before, on November 8, 1939, there had been an attempt on Hitler's life in Munich at the Burgerbrau Keller, where

Hitler spoke to commemorate the anniversary of the 1923 Nazi putsch. Shortly after he left the hall a bomb exploded, killing several Nazis and injuring others. Hitler professed gratitude that he had been spared, but Count Ciano, Mussolini's Foreign Minister and son-in-law, was much closer to reality when he reported that everyone was quite skeptical and suspicious that the episode was only a police plot to create anti-British sentiment. This idea seemed to be accurate when Joseph Goebbels, Hitler's Propaganda Minister, reported the arrest of two British agents for the alleged crime. Even the German people regarded the story as rather too perfect and the escape too fortuitous.

The Russians made the next war move. On November 30, at 9:15 A.M., they crossed the border into Finland. The United States was both horrified and angry. Little Finland was a special favorite, perhaps because she always paid her war debts promptly; besides, the Soviet Union was everybody's enemy. Hull offered immediate mediation. FDR begged both sides to refrain from bombing civilians, and, when Russia set up a Communist regime on the Finnish border, the President condemned her in the strongest words used since the war began. A "moral embargo" was promptly invoked, which would shut off completely the sale by the United States to Russia of airplanes, engines, parts and other contraband. The League of Nations dropped the Soviet Union. There was no vote, but not a member attempted to defend the Communist country.

Just before Christmas, a project that FDR had been thinking about since early July was acted upon. Myron Taylor, the retired chairman of United States Steel, was chosen to be the President's personal envoy to the Vatican. Taylor was an Episcopalian. This surprising move was made because FDR believed that the Vatican had many sources of contact with Germany, Italy and Spain. Pope Pius was grateful that the appointment had been made.

Despite the European situation, the Roosevelt Christmas celebration was traditional. The President read Dickens' *Christmas Carol* to his assembled family. His Christmas broadcast was cheerful, dwelling on the fact that Social Security benefits would begin early in the New Year. A turkey dinner with his mother and many of the children and grandchildren ended the festivities. Fifteen stockings were hung at the chimneyplace.

4

Collective security was Roosevelt's primary concern in 1940. To obtain it, he realized, it would be necessary to forfeit part of the New Deal because much of the support for his international program was coming from anti-New Deal conservatives. In his annual State of the Union message, consequently, Congress was asked for increases in armaments and not for any further domestic reforms. The President did say, however, that the process of recovery should be carried on "to preserve our gains." He warned of the danger of a Nazi victory. There was an atmosphere of restraint in the delivery of the speech. It was received in like manner except for one brief light moment. When FDR mentioned "reductions" in the budget, applause started. The President threw back his head and laughed. "But you know you can't have your cake and eat it too," he told them.

Unable to accept the role of bystander while the world traveled toward destruction, Roosevelt felt impelled again to seek a way to peace. He had to try even though he knew such a move was unlikely to succeed. Therefore, he asked Under Secretary of State Sumner Welles, an old and trusted friend, to go as his personal representative to Germany, Italy, England and France. Welles was to offer nothing concrete but just to find out the views of these governments and search for any possibilities for peace. The Soviet Union was not included in the plans because there did not seem to be any hope in that quarter.

Welles saw Mussolini and Hitler and visited the Allies but was unable to accomplish anything. The dictators were hostile and the Allies suspicious.

The Welles mission had been conducted in an atmosphere of mystery. Upon his return to the United States on March 29, the newspapers could only report that he had spent little more than an hour and a half with the President. Complete secrecy about what had been said was maintained. In reality, Welles's reception in Europe had been polite but unenthusiastic. Had there been a glimmer of hope Roosevelt would have exerted his persuasive charm, backed by American power, in a forceful bid for peace. There had been rumors in March, while Welles was abroad, that FDR's therapeutic cruise on the *Tuscaloosa* was really a cover for a rendezvous of representatives of the belligerent nations to talk of peace. This was as fanciful as the President's announcement that his destination was "the cherable islands." Roosevelt returned from his sea voyage browned and rested but without a peace treaty. Regretfully, the nation was told, there was scant hope for peace. The only value of the Welles mission was a bettering of friendly relations with the Allied nations.

The Finnish-Russian peace concluded in mid-March was inevitable but nevertheless a sharp blow to the Allies. FDR's praise of the Finns for their courage and condemnation of Russia for her disregard of Finland's rights mattered not at all. It was a hard peace, much more severe than the terms that had been offered before the war.

Secretary Hull was not surprised when he was informed in the early morning of April 9 that German troops were in Denmark and were landing at Norwegian ports. There had been rumors of such a movement all winter. The Germans had been using Norwegian waters to carry iron ore from Sweden, and to stop this flow of war material to the Nazis the British planned to mine the waters. Thus, between the seventh and the ninth of April, the two enemies were moving toward an inevitable clash. Hitler had taken personal charge of the project. He hoped to make a surprise attack because he was well aware of British superiority on the seas. German troop concentration in the west had been noted, but similar activity along the Baltic had proceeded quietly. Hitler made no public announcement of his next move. Mussolini knew nothing about it.

FDR, at Hyde Park when news of Hitler's latest aggression came, immediately approved Secretary Morgenthau's decision to freeze Danish and Norwegian accounts in the United States to keep them out of the hands of the Nazis. The combat zone was extended to the area of Norway.

5

During the early part of 1940 Roosevelt had not made a decision on the third term. He said different things to different people. To Farley, Hull, Perkins and Dan Tobin he said that not only would he refuse to be a candidate but actually he had made other plans. These might not have been plans so much as alternatives. In January he accepted a position as a contributing editor of *Collier's* magazine at a salary of $75,000. A few days later William Cheyney was shown around the White House and introduced as "my future boss." Miss Margaret LeHand, FDR's personal secretary, reported that although her boss was tired and looking forward to retirement, she wanted him to run again. While discussing with the President who would be the Democratic candidate, he had stated that God would provide. Missy LeHand's retort was that God had better get busy pretty soon.

Garner's candidacy seemed to suffer an eclipse at this time. His office, which had been a favorite retreat for legislators, began to lose its popularity. William Randolph Hearst switched his support from the Vice President to Jesse Jones. By the spring of 1940 Garner's chance of being renominated for the Vice Presidency had also declined.

James A. Farley planned to enter the spring primaries in Massachusetts and in New Hampshire. FDR's "go ahead" on this scheme did not constitute support of Farley but was, simply, part of his pose that he was not, in any circumstances, a candidate. At this time Farley tried to tell "the boss" that he would like to resign as National Chairman. There was no comment made about this feeler. One of the most active Farley men was Joseph Kennedy, Jr., who ran for a delegate's seat at the National Convention.

In February, Chicago was chosen to be the site of the Democratic convention. Farley would not select a date until after the Republicans decided on theirs. FDR approved enthusiastically of the choice of Chicago. Not only was it the birthplace of the New Deal and the President's first nomination but, as he told Harold Ickes, "I am not overlooking the fact that Kelly could pack the galleries for us." And committeemen were not hesitating to say to each other that FDR was the outstanding candidate. Canvassers reported that 90 percent of the leaders either favored or were not opposed to the President.

John L. Lewis, now avowedly anti-FDR, used his considerable power to formulate policy on the 1940 presidential campaign. But rank-and-file members were reluctant to accept his prejudice. "I am one of the millions who want it known that Roosevelt did not let labor down," said one. Another stated, "Mr. Roosevelt took our wives out of boxcars where we were living and he has set our children free and given us dinner buckets."

The International Ladies' Garment Workers Union condemned Lewis for his ungrateful attitude toward the New Deal. The largest independent union in the country, with 250,000 members, it issued a statement delivered by its president, David Dubinsky, that it backed a third term. Formal political activity for the President was started by putting his name in the Wisconsin primary.

Third-term indecision was a strain for all elements in the Democratic party. Even the inner circle was confused. Talk of a draft as a kind of solution was frequent, but its advocates could not answer the question of whether FDR would allow himself to be drafted. Almost everyone now agreed that, if he ran, the President would be re-elected. When, in February, Senator John Bankhead of Alabama became the first New Deal Senator to suggest that FDR state his intentions once and for all, the gentleman in question was fishing off Panama. However, his failure to withdraw his name from the April Illinois primary was interpreted by the Washington analysts to mean that this was the signal to draft him.

Garner was scheduled to be in the same primary as well as those in Georgia and California. FDR said nothing to his Vice President, also ignoring the fact that the Garner campaign "theme song" was to be an attack on the third term. Observers noted that Garner seemed uncomfortable and unhappy at Cabinet meetings. The rumor around Washington was that he might announce his withdrawal in favor of Cordell Hull.

Senator Burton Wheeler, unlike the others, refused to enter any primary in which FDR was a candidate. This was meant as a rebuff to the Vice President. However, the Senator continued to oppose both a third term and the nomination of a conservative and was still available as a candidate.

At this time an episode occurred that wounded the Farley-Roosevelt relationship just about fatally. Ernest K. Lindley, FDR's first biographer and a columnist for the Washington *Post,* published an article on March 4 that claimed to solve the third-term puzzle. The article, which appeared prominently on the first page of the newspaper, stated that FDR, in a discussion with an unnamed southern Congressman—later identified by Farley as Bob Doughton of North Carolina—declared that he would not run again, that he preferred Cordell Hull for President, and for Vice President he wanted either Jackson, McNutt or Wheeler. Farley would not be acceptable to him as a vice-presidential candidate because people might feel that "we were using Cordell Hull as a stalking horse for the Pope."

At a press conference Roosevelt denied knowledge of the article.

This seemed impossible because of its prominent position in the newspaper and the immediate furor that it caused. Two weeks later, on Saturday night, March 16, Farley made a speech at the annual dinner of the Friendly Sons of St. Patrick held at the Mayflower Hotel in Washington. He said, in obvious reference to the Lindley column, "We must never permit the ideals of this republic to sink to a point where every American father and mother, regardless of race, color or creed, cannot look proudly into the cradle of their newborn babe and see a future President of the United States."

At the next press conference after the Farley address FDR stated in answer to a question, perhaps "planted," that not one word of the Lindley story was true. Farley was not satisfied with this belated gesture. He observed that "nothing which ever happened to me politically so wounded me as this article, not so much for itself but because it was generally believed that it had been inspired by the President, and he took no step to offset that impression." Roosevelt behaved with a rather surprising lack of feeling in this episode. It seemed to indicate a deep resentment of Farley and some desire to cause a break with the party chairman.

In March FDR told guests at a Democratic victory dinner, "My great ambition on January 20, 1941, is to turn over this desk and chair in the White House to my successor, whoever he may be, with the assurance that I am at the same time turning over to him as President a nation intact, a nation at peace, a nation prosperous. . . ." This was the crux of the problem. The candidate had to be a liberal and a winner. Although there did not seem to be such a Democrat available other than the President, even he did not want to accept the fact that there was no one to replace him. When Secretary Ickes made the statement that in Illinois everyone believed that only Roosevelt could win on the Democratic ticket, the President snapped impatiently, "Suppose that I became so ill I could not possibly be a candidate? You oughtn't to talk like that. It only means a defeatist attitude is being built up."

The results of the March New Hampshire primary were ambiguous. The FDR slate was victorious but by a slim margin. There was a sizable vote for the delegate pledged to Garner, although the Vice President had not campaigned in the state. This was interpreted by the politicos as a strong indication that anti-third-term feeling was a factor. Nevertheless, the results were sufficiently conclusive to line up the other New England states behind Roosevelt except for Massachusetts. Farley sentiment there was firm. And there was still some doubt whether the American people would elect a President for a third term. Gallup reported only 47 percent favored it.

"Political dog fights," as FDR called them, developed in a number of the states that engaged in spring primaries. In Oregon, which earlier had supported Garner, two factions split over foreign policy. Roosevelt was the victor. North Carolina was instructed for FDR if he should run, otherwise the delegation was free. Florida would give its first support to the President, but if he did not run McNutt would receive the votes. The Governor of Georgia had managed by a ruse to outwit Senators Walter George and Richard Russell, who backed Garner. He ignored a 25,000-name petition to hold a primary.

One of the most delicate situations concerned Texas, because FDR hesitated to get involved in Garner's home state. The President's supporters did not feel this restraint. However, two powerful Texans, Jesse Jones and Alvin Wirtz, Under Secretary of the Department of the Interior, had to overcome the lethargy of the Roosevelt faction which had not overworked itself to line up delegates for the state convention. The best that could be accomplished, after conferences between Wirtz and Myron Blalock, Democratic state chairman, was a compromise whereby the Roosevelt supporters would be yielded about twenty delegates, the rockbound Garnerites about the same number and the remaining third would be ostensibly for Garner but might switch to FDR if, for instance, Garner withdrew. The flaw in the arrangement was that, if the unit rule were invoked, Garner would win.

A dispute arose over the statement to the public to be given out. Jesse Jones and Sam Rayburn both opposed one. But Wirtz and Blalock agreed on a joint telegram, to be taken to FDR first and then to be sent to Blalock and Wirtz by Rayburn and Congressman Lyndon B. Johnson. Rayburn's hesitation was, as Ickes revealed, that "he did not want it to appear that in a Texas political matter a kid Congressman like Johnson was on apparently the same footing as himself, the Majority Leader." But Rayburn finally submitted to the pressure of his peers.

The disputed telegram stated that the state convention would strongly endorse the Roosevelt Administration and that the delegates would vote for Garner as a "favorite son" but would not be part of a "stop Roosevelt" movement. FDR received the two Texans, beaming on them paternally and assuring them that they had "Papa's blessing." According to Ickes, the President treated the two legislators as political equals "with the malicious intent of disturbing Sam Rayburn's state of mind." Probably he succeeded.

Newspaper reaction was that Garner and his team had suffered a distinct setback. The backbone of the Vice President's program, opposition to the New Deal and to a third term, was now broken. From this time on Garner ceased to be a serious threat.

Illinois was decidedly pro-FDR, thanks to such political machines as that of Mayor Kelly's of Chicago. Tammany Hall in New York, however, preferred Garner, as did the Irish-American Democrats in Wisconsin. But after a primary contest there, the New Dealers won twenty-four of the Wisconsin delegation, leaving Garner only three votes. Ohio was the President's simply for the asking.

A number of states lined up against Roosevelt. Maryland, under Millard Tydings, who was unpurged and increasingly popular, and Virginia, in the hands of the Byrd-Glass machine, preferred a conservative. Representative William Bankhead was Alabama's choice, although FDR had some support there. Senator Champ Clark, with the aid of the battered Pendergast machine, fought against New Deal Governor Lloyd Stark for the Missouri delegation. The result was an uninstructed delegation which would probably support Clark if his name was offered.

In June, Congress passed the trade law that extended the President's power to negotiate reciprocal trade agreements until 1943. This had several political angles. Garner's aid to foes of the bill had angered FDR. In Cabinet meetings the estrangement between the President and the Vice President was noticeable. But the passage of the bill was important to FDR's prestige, and it would help Hull, who was the author of the bill, just in case he was a presidential prospect.

FDR had been forced to postpone his regular visit to Warm Springs, Georgia, early in April because of a bad bout with "flu." Dr. Ross McIntire preferred that he not attempt a sudden change in climate. This suited the President, who wanted to watch the trade-treaty contest closely. Later in the month he paid an eight-day visit to Warm Springs, where he seemed to regain his vigor. He drove himself from the "little White House" in his own specially equipped open car, bearing the license plate "FDR," and he smiled in farewell to the cheering crowd of patients. "I'll be back in the fall, if we don't have a war," he cried.

By May 24, *The New York Times* reported, Roosevelt had obtained the necessary majority in the upcoming Democratic convention. Such states as Vermont, Oklahoma, Nebraska, South Carolina and Rhode Island had declared for Roosevelt. Others, such as Montana and Iowa, preferred to support favorite sons on the first ballot but agreed to change their instructions to FDR first and then to Burton Wheeler for Montana and Henry Wallace for Iowa. California was a special case. The two FDR enthusiasts, Governor Culbert Olson and former Senator William G. McAdoo, both wanted FDR slates but represented rival factions within the party. A third faction led by Lieutenant Governor Ellis Patterson, extreme left-wing CIO and Labor's Non-Partisan League spokesman, preferred Senator Wheeler. Another faction, headed by Zach La Mar Cobb, anti-New Deal, anti-liberal and both well endowed and active, favored Garner. A coalition ticket of the pro-third-term groups was arranged by means of FDR's and Ickes' intervention. Ickes commented to McAdoo, "Poor Garner already has one foot in the grave and the other on a banana peel and from this time on it is our duty to speak respectfully of him."

As the states dutifully lined up, the question whether FDR would accept the nomination became a real one. Elliot Roosevelt, from his Fort Worth radio station, broadcast that his father would not be a candidate for a third term unless the people demanded it, but at any rate he would probably withhold the announcement until just before or during the Democratic convention. This of course would keep anti-third-termers from consolidating forces. It also kept soothsayers and pollsters busy. The Gallup poll, in May, reported that Secretary of State Hull would have greater vote-getting ability than FDR because he'd have all of the Democratic vote of 1936 without having to overcome the third-term tradition. Furthermore, he was favored by more than twice as many Republicans as FDR.

Whether or not he would be the candidate, the President was much interested in convention plans. Alben Barkley, temporary chairman in 1932 and 1936, was his choice for permanent chairman. James Byrnes was his preference for temporary chairman, thus giving two Southerners prominent positions.

James Farley had by no means withdrawn from the race. His position in the party gave him power that should have been more meaningful than it was. But it was only in such areas as Boston, which was bitter against FDR, that he found support. Since Roosevelt had sent Myron Taylor to the Vatican, which had greatly enhanced the President's popularity with the Catholics, Farley could no longer count on that segment of the vote. The Postmaster General's attitude combined hurt feelings, because of the President's behavior, and self-righteousness, because he felt that he had been wronged and because he opposed the third term on principle. He undoubtedly agreed with General Hugh Johnson's Jefferson Day dinner speech, in April, in which he said, "It is these veteran Democrats who have borne the heat and the burden of all these close contests. . . . They have carried the fight and the torch and all too often gotten kicks in the pants for their pains." The former NRA chief made special mention in this context "of the loyal, faithful Farleys."

The President retained his hold on the Democratic party by keeping up the third-term mystery. Governor Alfred Landon tried to "smoke him out" by a direct demand that he disavow a third term as the price for Republican cooperation in the national defense program. The Democratic President's answer was that he found himself "too busy with problems of far greater national importance to prepare a political statement."

Because the President's gravest concern was the war, he truly believed that it was unfortunate that the political process had to interrupt the security program. Europe interested herself in the forthcoming elections because it was felt there that the election results would promote either peace or war with the totalitarian nations. They assumed that if anyone other than FDR, even a Democrat, was elected it would be favorable to the dictators. David Dubinsky, speaking at the New York World's Fair, expressed that thought. He wanted FDR to remain in office until "we have absolute assurance that *Mein Kampf* will never be rewritten to include the American continents." And the ILGWU, at their convention, passed a resolution praising FDR which set off a twenty-minute demonstration while representatives from twenty-six states marched through the aisles of Carnegie Hall shouting, "We want Roosevelt."

The German invasion of western Europe increased FDR's popularity dramatically. In August 1939 only 40 percent of the American people favored a third term. By May and June 1940 the figure rose to 57 percent.

6

Perhaps the most ardent opponents of the President's re-election were the spokesmen of those who still felt that separation from the European power struggle was a feasible policy for America. An extreme and most successful example of this attitude was Father E. Coughlin, whose career as a radio priest began in 1926. From his Shrine of the Little Flower in Royal Oak, Michigan, the Canadian-born prelate, whose sonorous voice was overlaid with a slight Irish brogue, warned his listeners of the imminent danger of communism, which he predicted would, unless checked, result in a revolution in the United States by 1933. However, the priest was not a conservative but a critic of the moneyed, whose greed, he said, ignored the teachings of economic justice. His Sunday talks, flavored with colorful phrases, tried to find a solution to domination by the "modern moneychangers," but it had to be a Christian solution.

Father Coughlin became the most popular radio personality of the 1930s. Contributions to pay for radio time poured into his shrine, completely unsolicited. His mail, estimated at 80,000 letters per day, exceeded that of even the President. He was a round-faced, bespectacled, gray-haired, large and chunky man whom his friends found most genial. His voice was often unctuous and his prose sanctimonious, but his listeners admired him all the more for it. At first Coughlin favored the New Deal, calling it "Christ's Deal." But as his influence grew, the radio priest seemed to find the need to become increasingly challenging. In 1934 he struck out on his own with the formation of the National Union of Social Justice, which was more of a political theory than a political party. It was markedly racist and anti-Semitic.

By October 1939 the National Association of Broadcasters wanted to keep Coughlin's weekly hate program off the air. The "Christian Front," a Coughlin-inspired movement, was associated with the German Bund, and the priest followed the Hitler line consistently. After the German-Soviet alliance in the summer of 1939, Coughlin soft-pedaled anti-communism, only to declare, after Hitler marched into Russia, that *der Führer* had saved the world from communism.

More conventional opponents of the Administration's foreign policy were the isolationists, or, as some of them preferred, non-interventionists. They were mainly but not exclusively Republicans. Having been schooled on Washington's advice against permanent treaties and Jefferson's admonishment to avoid "entangling alliances," and further disillusioned by the consequences of United States participation in the First World War, they had been eager recipients of the Nye Committee's findings of 1934. At that time Senator Gerald P. Nye's group investigated the reasons for the United States' entry into war in 1917 and managed to conclude that investors and munitions makers had been the villains, rather than that there had been any such high purpose as making the "world safe for democracy." They were now determined to replace FDR with someone who would not fight unless there was a direct threat to American territory.

The motives of the isolationists differed widely, ranging from those who supported a unilateral foreign policy to those who were actual supporters of the Axis or the Soviet Union. Isolationist Senators such as Wheeler, Borah, Taft and Nye dismissed the war as "just another chapter in the bloody volume of European politics, the usual story of 2,000 years of war over borders and boundaries."

The isolationists could not regard the European war as a moral issue. To them it was the inevitable result of the bungling that was the Treaty of Versailles. The United States, they believed, must understand that intervention in 1917 had brought neither lasting peace nor genuine democracy. Therefore legislation such as the Selective Service bill was bitterly opposed.

Actually, isolationism was more persistent with its Congressional adherents than with their constituents. Many of these lawmakers were older men whose views had solidified in an earlier time. Part of the difficulty was that rural and inland areas of the United States were over-represented in Congress. These legislators' belief that foreign nations were motivated only by rapacious greed and that the two mighty oceans protected the Western Hemisphere blinded them to the plight of Europe. To them, United States entrance into the war would be due to the plotting of self-interested minorities. And there was genuine fear of the horrors of the new type of warfare.

Influential newspapers, such as those of Joseph M. Patterson, Colonel Robert McCormick and William Randolph Hearst, supported the isolationists. Through their reporting many became convinced that Americans must stay at home because Axis superiority would surely overcome Britain and France. Senator Gerald P. Nye declared himself a realist who wanted American action based on an "honest estimate of our national physical strength." Scholars such as Charles Beard and Robert Hutchins of the University of Chicago were extremely articulate supporters of the isolationist point of view. Former President Herbert Hoover was a key figure in the movement. Still bitter over his 1932 defeat, he said that FDR was using international involvements as a cover-up for the inadequacies of the New Deal.

Many young people in the United States were rabidly anti-war. The American Youth Congress, a movement in which Eleanor Roosevelt had been interested, actively opposed American involvement in European affairs. The theme of their conference in the spring of 1940 was "Keep America Out of War" because, they said, "The Yanks are not coming."

On February 10 the President had addressed a gathering of 4,466 AYC members assembled on the White House lawn. From the portico where he stood to be protected from the pouring rain, FDR delivered a "verbal spanking" to the gathered youth. "Do not seek or expect Utopia overnight. Do not seek or expect a panacea—some wonderful new law that will give to everyone who needs it a handout—or a guarantee of permanent remunerative occupation of your own choosing," he said. He added, "One final word of warning: do not as a group pass resolutions on subjects which you have not thought through and on which you cannot possibly have complete knowledge." Roosevelt mocked the "decisive" stand taken by a big local of the American Youth Congress Council against American loans to Finland because, the resolution stated, such an action would force the United States into "the imperialistic war." "That the Soviet Union would, because of this, declare war on the United States is about the silliest thought that I have ever heard advanced in the fifty-eight years of my life," Roosevelt told them. "That we are going to war ourselves with the Soviet Union is an equally silly thought. Therefore while I have not the slightest objection in the world to the passing of futile resolutions by conventions, I do think there is room for improvement in common-sense thinking, and definite room for improvement in the art of not passing resolutions concerning things one does not know everything about," he added.

In a sterner voice the President admonished those young people who called themselves Communists. He told them that though they had the right "openly to advocate certain ideals of theoretical Communism . . . you have no American right, by act or deed of any kind, to subvert the Government and the Constitution." The President's tone sounded overpaternal, patronizing and condescending to a large number of the listeners. This was one of the few occasions when Roosevelt was booed and hissed to his face by an American audience.

Peace rallies, well attended by college students, were conducted all over the country. On April 20 about 10,000 students attended rallies in New York City. The colleges cancelled their classes. At the University of Chicago the campus was lined with 200 white crosses to remind the onlookers of Flanders Field. At Cazenovia Junior College students attended classes on crutches with their heads and arms bandaged to dramatize the horrors of war.

Charles A. Lindbergh, who was one of the most influential isolationists because of his personal popularity, stated in a radio address in May that the country "must stop this hysterical chatter of calamity and invasion." He assured his listeners over CBS that the United States could not be conquered by aerial bombardment. FDR made no comment about the speech, but the isolationists were most enthusiastic. Drew Pearson and Robert Allen, in their "Washington Merry Go Round" column, revealed, at the end of June, that Colonel Lindbergh had been secretly offered the candidacy for President on a third-party peace ticket by the isolationists. But in a speech a few days before, Lindbergh gave no hint of this. Instead he called for a powerful system of national defense and complete abstention from the European war. He denounced the deliberate efforts by an "American minority" to involve this country in war.

In the midst of this sometimes vicious opposition to cooperation with France and Great Britain, a group emerged that had as its objective the defense of the United States through help to these nations. Founded by Clark Eichelberger, director of the League of Nations Association, and William Allen White, in the spring of 1940 the Committee to Defend America by Aiding the Allies was dedicated to the view that neutrality must be replaced by a policy of extending every assistance short of war to Britain and France. The committee was very close to FDR although they were not always in agreement. A distinguished roster of members—political figures, intellectuals, historians, theater personalities and religious leaders—spread the movement across the country. Adlai E. Stevenson was head of the Chicago chapter. Dr. James Conant, Dr. Henry Noble McCracken, Dr. Robert A. Millikan, Paul H. Douglas and William Lyon Phelps were some of the members from the academic community. The vice-chairman of the South California chapter was Douglas Fairbanks, Jr.

Among the committee's objectives was to grant one hundred million dollars to the Allies for the purchase of American surplus commodities for the care of French and English refugees and the repeal of the law barring Americans from volunteering for service in Allied armies. A remarkably effective advertisement written by playwright Robert Sherwood, entitled "Stop Hitler Now," was inserted in major newspapers. FDR endorsed it and called it "a great piece of work." It urged the United States to send planes, guns, munitions and food to the Allies to keep the war from American shores. Sherwood said, "Will the Nazis considerately wait until we are ready to fight them? Anyone who argues that they will wait is either an imbecile or a traitor."

The most significant question, perhaps, was whether or not the committee would be supported by the White House after the next presidential inauguration. William Allen White said: "My relationship to President Roosevelt has been more of a morganatic relationship. I know I had his private support. . . . I never did anything the President didn't ask for, and I always conferred with him on our program." If Roosevelt were not to be the candidate, his party might very well choose someone quite deaf to the needs of the Allies, a man like Wheeler, for example, whose dedication to isolation had become his greatest distinction, or possibly Garner, a rigid anti-New Dealer, or maybe Farley, a symbol of party responsibility. But as FDR himself was quite aware, no one Democrat had emerged with enough appeal or enough experience. And Roosevelt, by keeping his decision to run again or not to run again a mystery, remained in control of the approaching convention.

7

The British had failed to stop the Nazis from overrunning Norway. On May 10, following Hitler's invasion of Holland, Belgium and Luxembourg, Chamberlain resigned. Winston Churchill formed a coalition government. Roosevelt moved instantly to apply the Neutrality Act to the Nazis' newest victims and to prepare for the evacuation of American nationals. The President was concerned that Italy would now "surely go into the war as soon as it seemed a propitious time for her." Secretary Ickes remarked wryly, "To the victor belongs Mussolini."

In four days Dutch resistance was overcome and the Queen and her government fled to London. The Germans then took the Sedan and struck at the supposedly impregnable Maginot line. By the end of May, King Leopold of Belgium, acting alone, ordered his army to stop fighting.

The imminent danger of the fall of France and England motivated FDR to go to the people to tell them frankly what was at stake. The broadcast was scheduled for a Sunday night so that as many Americans as possible would be at home.

On the eve of the speech the small gathering in the President's study was unable to engage in their usual chatter. Even Roosevelt did not enliven his ritual of mixing the cocktails with his customarily optimistic observations. In the speech, the people of the United States were asked to enlarge war plants and to build new ones. At the same time, said Roosevelt, we must not lose any of our great social gains. Any fears that we must abandon our way of life to combat and overcome the aggressors were baseless. "Let us have done with both fears and illusion," he said.

As the war situation deteriorated for the Allies, the President worked from early morning. He would sit up in bed with his sweater or his cloak thrown over his shoulders. By 10 A.M. he was at his desk, where he stayed until six o'clock, with only a lunch break, which he took at a small table in his office. He was on call twenty-four hours a day. Even a plunge in the pool, considered so essential to the President's health, was abandoned. Once or twice a week an afternoon drive provided the only chance for privacy.

The growth of the possibility of Allied failure increased FDR's concern over the disposition of the French and British navies. The French fleet would be vital to France's revival and to the survival of her colonies. Just as important was an assurance that the British would neither surrender her ships nor use them to bargain for a better peace with Hitler. Both nations' Prime Ministers assured the United States that they would not, in any circumstances, surrender their navies. This assurance was necessary to American defense because the combined British, French, German and, perhaps, Italian fleets would be a menace to the American Atlantic fleet. The Pacific fleet could not be spared from its task of keeping Japan from swallowing Asia.

Almost frantic last-minute appeals for the United States to become actively engaged in the war came from French Premier Paul Reynaud. He wanted FDR to get a declaration of war from Congress. At the same time, Churchill demanded that the United States at least declare herself a non-belligerent. But the President was helpless. Only a tiny percentage of the American people favored the United States' entrance into the war.

After the British withdrawal from Dunkirk not the most confirmed ostrich in the United States could hide from the realization of the imminence of a Nazi victory. Sixty-five percent of the American people now answered in the affirmative the question, "If Germany defeats England and France will she attack the United States?"

France now made a direct offer to settle Italy's territorial claims. It was too late. FDR and Sumner Welles wanted to continue to appeal to the Italian leader, but Secretary Hull, who had always been skeptical of the value of the President's personal approach, opposed appealing again to a "bandit."

By June 10 Norway's army had surrendered. Nazi tanks were within thirty-five miles of Paris. French troops had been told, "This is the last quarter-hour. Hold fast." Terrified civilians were fleeing from the French capital, clogging the roads, to escape from the barbarians. Hitler was silent. His armor would speak for him.

Then *Il Duce* declared war on the "plutocratic nations," England and France. Expected as was the move, Premier Reynaud, now at Tours, where the French government had fled, cabled a frantic appeal to Roosevelt to state publicly that the United States would aid the Allies by all means short of an expeditionary force. He promised that France would fight before Paris to the last man. Hull doubted that this would be true, but his greatest concern was still the French fleet. Reynaud must be persuaded to withdraw it to North Africa.

Franklin D. Roosevelt, Jr., was to receive his law degree from the University of Virginia on the evening of June 10. His father, who had agreed to give the commencement address, originally planned a speech that would arouse students, many of whom were opposed to the war, to a realization of the gravity of the world situation. Instead, because of the new development, the President decided to deliver a major foreign-policy address. The telegram that Ambassador Bullitt had sent to FDR included the observation, "What really distinguished, noble and admirable persons the Italians are to stab us in the back at this moment." The phrase "stab in the back," which was originally Premier Reynaud's, stayed with FDR. The original draft of his speech carried the challenging phrase. But it was removed lest it be disturbing to Italian-Americans. As the President rode down south with his wife and his son, he became increasingly enraged at the cynicism of the Italian action. When he delivered the speech he included the challenging phrase. "The stab in the back" had tremendous impact in an address that committed the United States deeply. Roosevelt pledged: "We will extend to the opponents of force the material resources of this nation; and, at the same time, we will harness and speed up the use of these resources in order that we ourselves in the Americas may have the equipment and training equal to the task of any emergency and every defense. . . . Signs and signals call for speed—full speed ahead."

Winston Churchill, listening at midnight with a group of officers in the Admiralty War Room, wrote that when FDR said, "On this tenth day of June, 1940, the hand that held the dagger struck it into the back of its neighbor," there was a deep growl of satisfaction. Before going to bed the Prime Minister, known in his correspondence with FDR as the "Former Naval Person," wrote a letter of gratitude. In the United States, editorials were generally laudatory. So many thousands of wires came into the White House that, for the first time in the Roosevelt Administration, the White House operators required help from a commercial company. Germany expressed irritation and impatience. Italy suppressed the speech.

In June, France surrendered. Premier Reynaud's appeal for "clouds of airplanes" from the United States went unheeded. Britain stood alone. And the United States was committed to her. Franklin

Roosevelt was now confronted with the obligation to make a decision about the next four years. Yet, what might really decide the issue, in addition to the European war, was what the Republicans would do about selecting an opponent. The very reality of the war and the accompanying clamor of the isolationists had made the President all the more reluctant to relinquish his power. That many wanted him to run for a third term was obvious, but the depths of that sentiment in terms of votes was still to be tested.

CHAPTER THREE

"The Darkest Horse in the Stable"

1

SAM PRYOR, the Republican national committeeman from Connecticut, sat in his Greenwich home on the night of January 6, 1938, and as the clock neared 9:30 he tuned his radio to station WJZ, New York. At that moment Pryor and some two million others were awaiting the start of "America's Town Meeting of the Air," a weekly discussion of current issues. About to join George V. Denny, Jr., the program's moderator, was Assistant Attorney General Robert H. Jackson, who was often mentioned as a possible successor to FDR, and Wendell L. Willkie. Willkie was president of the great Commonwealth and Southern utilities holding corporation that controlled eleven electric power distributing companies on both sides of the Mason and Dixon line. But to Sam Pryor, who was an assistant to the president of the American Brake Shoe and Foundry Company and a director of several other corporations, Willkie was more than just another fellow business magnate. He was becoming known as an articulate and independent critic of the New Deal; and nothing pleased Pryor more than a businessman who could answer Roosevelt effectively.

Denny began the program by telling the Town Hall audience that it was not going to be a formal debate. Each man would simply comment on the topic "How Can Government and Business Work Together?" and a question period would follow. "It is not our purpose to widen cleavages but rather to find common ground upon which all classes and all groups of American citizens may work together toward our general welfare," Denny added, and then concluded his introduction by saying that he knew of no subject that was "more interesting or important for this nation."

Jackson spoke first. He recalled the efforts government used to make to help business. Now, he said, the nature of society and the economy have both changed. People expect the government "to furnish steady jobs for all who want to work and to furnish enough goods to make up that standard of living which we have come to regard as American." After all, as Roosevelt had noted in his Commonwealth Club address at San Francisco in 1932, the frontier—that great crucible of individualism—no longer provided the opportunities for those with great personal initiative. We were now living in a highly industrialized society, and whatever industry could not provide must be created by the people through their government. The old dogma that the helpless must help themselves had been repudiated. Directing his remarks to Willkie, Jackson said that the public had become uneasy over the control of a vast system by one great holding company and that people "would feel more comfortable if Mr. Willkie could control only two or three states" instead of six.

Willkie made the most of his turn to speak, not wasting a moment to get at the main point. He noted that it was big business that had enabled such a nationwide radio discussion to take place, that the wonders of free enterprise had made radios available to the average working man. He also ripped into notions that, somehow, men in government wear halos while business executives are evil and that small-business men had interests unlike larger corporations. All thrive under the same conditions. In fact, he said, government restrictions and actions that discourage investments are more harmful to the smaller enterprises, which do not have reserves to cope with hard times. He blandly noted that Jackson had erred by saying that Commonwealth and Southern owned utilities in six states. Eleven states was more accurate. And how could this be considered an evil when the average rates charged by them were lower than that of any utility group in America? Nor was it accurate to attribute this to competition from the Tennessee Valley Authority, because lower rates were also being charged by the Commonwealth and Southern companies that were in the North and far removed from what the government had created to compete with private enterprise.

"I suggest," said Willkie, "that we have now reached the time when we should stop discussing what caused the depression and should direct our attention to how to cure it." Then he said, with greater emphasis: "The real cure consists in convincing the millions of small investors throughout America that the government does not intend to continue its attack on American industry, big or little, for it is these investors upon whom industry depends for its funds." Government and business fail to understand each other, he went on, chiefly "because one thinks and speaks the language of politics and emotionalism," whereas "the other thinks and speaks the language of economics and realism." Then Willkie added: "One thinks economic forces can be controlled by politics, while the other realizes that economic forces are more powerful than either government or business."

He had made his point, clearly and forcefully, and the applause was brisk. Sam Pryor had finally heard an eloquent businessman stand up to the New Deal and argue for private enterprise.

Willkie handled questions from the audience with candor. When a man asked whether he thought big or small business was more likely to hire labor spies, he said that he, for one, was a big-business man who never hired such personnel and that he would repudiate their use by anybody. When someone else asked how, for example, the government should respond to price-fixing by the cement industry, Willkie replied, "I would suggest that Mr. Jackson go to work, if there is anything wrong in the cement industry or in any other industry with reference to monopolistic practices."

The man Sam Pryor and so many other Americans heard that night had succeeded in defying the 1930s stereotype of the "public be damned" type of businessman. Even pro-New Deal listeners agreed that Willkie had outargued Jackson and in so doing had diminished Jackson's stature as a Democratic presidential possibility for 1940.

2

The road that runs northeast from Indianapolis to the little town of
Elwood, through rich Indiana farm country, covers land not nearly so
hilly as that just a few miles to the south. In that prairie region wheat,
corn and hogs were in abundance longer than anyone could care to
remember; and before 1887 Elwood was just another typical town of
the region.

In that year, just before Herman F. Willkie and his family arrived
in Elwood, things began to change. The surrounding fields were found
to contain rich supplies of natural gas. Elwood, with its population of
less than one thousand, became the chief beneficiary. Everything
began to happen at once. Wells were dug throughout the area. Industries, ready to exploit the plentiful fuel, moved in. Glass factories
became particularly important, and the Pittsburgh Plate and Glass
Company built its largest plant in Elwood. A large factory was also
constructed for the American Tin Plate Company. Gas burned from
corner wells and streetlights. In fact, the natural product was considered so available and cheap that it was not, during those early days,
thought necessary to turn off the lights by day: too much trouble. In
five years the population tripled and real estate became a pretty good
investment, as Herman Willkie learned. Blue-collar workers mingled
with the farmers from the surrounding country, the descendants of
the pre-gas age. It was as though the twentieth century had chosen to
preview its technology in a frontier community.

But the cornucopia was not endless. The natural-gas supply had
been exploited too lavishly. The gas began to dry out; lights were
turned off; and by 1893 Elwood and the rest of America were caught
in a new depression. The country was learning that, in the age of
industry, few could avoid the hazards of the economic cycle.

One of those who had lost most of what he had managed to save
was Herman Willkie. Wendell Willkie's father was a liberal Democrat
who considered himself a friend of William Jennings Bryan, the free-
silver advocate from Nebraska. The ills of society and the cause of
the underprivileged were the older Willkie's major concerns. As a
lawyer, which he became after devoting years to public education, he
undertook many labor cases, including one for a fee that was a fraction of the price that had been demanded by the great Clarence

Darrow. At home he showed a warmth and understanding that his children were often unable to get from their mother. Herman avoided imposing rigid rules that would only tempt deception. His most famous son would always remember him as the greatest man he had ever known, and he liked to recall how Herman Willkie would rouse his children early every morning by reciting poetry.

Herman Willkie was born nine years after his father, Joseph William Willcke (as the name was originally spelled), had seen the cause of liberalism crushed in Germany during the 1848 rebellion. In conflict with the authorities after that, Joseph finally fled from the autocratic monarchy and went to America, where his wife and three children joined him in 1861. Herman grew up on a farm ten miles south of Fort Wayne, Indiana. Although his father was a Catholic, Herman adopted his mother's Protestantism and, as a Methodist, attended Fort Wayne College, a secular institution, from which he graduated in 1884. He promptly became superintendent of schools at a place called Milford, where he met and married one of the teachers, Henrietta Trisch, who was also from a German family.

Henrietta was the family's boss. She made the rules and was responsible for what rigidity prevailed. A bright and independent woman, she had been graduated from the Indiana State Normal School at Terre Haute. Few other women of her time and area were known to read two or three books a week. She and her husband were among the founders of the Elwood Public Library and, later, they were elected library trustees. What was particularly unusual for Elwood, or in most of America, was the family's collection of some six to seven thousand books. Perhaps, one might say, an appetite for reading and an abhorrence of injustice were the major elements of the Willkie family legacy.

They had come to Elwood in 1888, when Herman obtained a job as its school superintendent. There was much for him to do. The system was still ungraded and he had to organize a secondary school for the growing community. While leading the high school, he had a reputation as a stern disciplinarian and was called "Hell Fire" Willkie, which was quite unlike his domestic image. In addition, he also read law and was admitted to the bar in 1891. Six years later, despite strong objections from the conservative attorneys of Madison County, Henrietta Trisch Willkie joined her husband's profession and became the first woman member of the bar in Indiana.

When Lewis Wendell was born on February 18, 1892, he was their fourth child. Julia was seven years old, Robert five and Fred only two. The last of Willkie's six children were Edward, born in 1896, and Charlotte, in 1899.

Young Lewis Wendell Willkie started his high-school career without much distinction. Athletics and youthful pranks were more interesting than serious study. Once he created a furor when, with the aid of two friends, he took a human skeleton from a biology classroom and hung the bones from a courtyard tree. He was also the lad who had the bright notion to paint his class numerals on the school walk. That lark brought suspension until he had scrubbed the area clean, a project that took nearly two full days. Still, there was no mistaking him for just another fun-loving high-school student, for he displayed considerable forensic skills and constantly searched for information that his intellect absorbed with profit. It was during his second year that he responded to some good advice. An outstanding and inspiring teacher, Philip (Pat) Bing, gave Willkie a personal lecture about the folly of intellectual laziness. Either that or Pat Bing's dynamic teaching awakened the young man. By the time Willkie was ready to graduate in 1910 with seven other seniors, he had determined to go on to the state university at Bloomington.

While a student at Indiana University he was often seen dressed in a red turtle-neck sweater and disturbing the peace by questioning the Bible, espousing socialism, arguing for the abolition of all inheritances and advocating Jeffersonian democracy. Fighting about leading issues became his varsity sport. Recognizing his early reputation, Willkie later liked to repeat that "Any man who is not something of a Socialist before he is forty has no heart; any man who is still a Socialist after he is forty has no head." As an undergraduate he was a convinced Democrat and a leader of the campus Jackson Club.

Before he could go on to graduate school, however, he had to earn some more money; and in 1913 he went to Coffeyville, Kansas, where he found a job teaching history in the local high school for eighty-five dollars a month. He was a tall, slender and handsome young man, with natural appeal for teen-agers accustomed to traditional teachers. His liveliness and interest in his subject helped to make his classes, and the one in English history in particular, the most spirited Coffeyville had ever seen. His speech was animated and his presentations were witty. He moved around the room with boundless energy and a natural grin. One day a month he declared a holiday from English history and, seated on a corner of his desk, read a short story from O. Henry. One student later recalled her favorite teacher and wrote: "He actually taught us history and made us like it!" Lewis Wendell Willkie was, in addition, present at all pep rallies, where, as the school's leading booster, he won every student's admiration. As leader of the high-school YMCA he lent enough interest so that it became the largest high-school branch in that part of the state.

But he lasted hardly more than one year. The lure of earning more money made him accept a job with his older brother, Fred, as an experimental chemist at the Fajardo Sugar Company in Puerto Rico. Yet he had made a remarkable impression during his brief Coffeyville stay. November 6, 1914, was observed as "Willkie Day" with a special service in the chapel. As he went to the train station, students followed to see him off. When the Coffeyville High School yearbook came out the following May, it carried a full-page tribute to the popular ex-teacher. Included was the statement that "His entrance to our high school was like the ovation of Julius Caesar; he was thrice offered the crown which he thrice refused, and every student was an Anthony." And, as if that were not enough, the yearbook added: "His exalted mind despised small acts and small men. He is a young man of catholic sympathies, but hated with an awful hate, the cowardly, evasive, double-dealing soul, and erased from his list of friends all who possessed such craven spirits. He was four-square before all men."

When he finally returned to Indiana University in the fall of 1915, he compiled a brilliant record at its law school. He won every faculty first prize for scholastic achievement. Already an individualist, he responded to being chosen as the class orator for the commencement program by delivering an address that, appropriately enough for the America of Woodrow Wilson, was called "The New Freedom." In the audience was a majority of the state's supreme-court justices. But that did not stop the youthful orator from delivering a vigorous denunciation of the Indiana law school and the state's constitution. His thesis was that both the state and the school, as well as the nation, were dominated by private economic interests. At the same time he praised President Wilson's domestic reforms and called for their emulation in the state of Indiana. For three days the school's perplexed faculty pondered what to do about their young heretic. His

degree was at stake. Finally, they decided to grant the document and
to bestow his academic honors—but only in the privacy of the administrative office. They hoped they would not soon have another student
like Lewis Wendell Willkie.

As a member of the bar, he practiced for several months in his
home town of Elwood. When the nation went to war in 1917 he
enlisted as a private and then became an officer. It was in the service
that a clerical error referring to him as Wendell Lewis Willkie led him
to adopt the name he preferred. In January 1918, during a leave from
the Army, Willkie married a librarian from the Indiana town of
Rushville who had the coincidental name of Edith Wilk. After a short
overseas tour of duty, as a lieutenant with the 525th Light Infantry
Regiment stationed at Camp De Souge, France, he returned home in
February 1919. Then he took a job with the legal department of the
Firestone Tire and Rubber Company in Akron, Ohio.

3

Harvey Firestone, who made a vain attempt to keep the young
lawyer from leaving the firm by offering to raise his annual salary to
$10,000, said to him: "Young man, I like you, but I don't think you
will ever amount to a great deal." When Willkie asked for an explanation his employer replied, "Because I understand you are a Democrat. No Democrat can ever amount to much." Later, in 1938, when
Firestone was on his deathbed, he sent his son to tell Willkie that his
greatest regret was in having been unable to keep him.

Firestone had been right about Willkie's politics. He was an active
Democrat. He spoke for American membership in the League of
Nations. He worked to abolish the hated anti-labor weapon, court
injunctions, and for the restraint of monopolies. From his father he
had learned the value of civil liberties, and when the state of Indiana
virtually succumbed to the political domination of the Ku Klux Klan
in the early 1920s, Willkie was among their most militant opponents.
He was at the 1924 Democratic convention, the one in which Franklin D. Roosevelt made his comeback after having been crippled with
polio and called Al Smith "the Happy Warrior." Willkie supported
Smith because the Klan was behind William Gibbs McAdoo. He was
also with those who voted to condemn the night-riders.

He rose rapidly through the corporate ranks. When a wealthy utilities tycoon, Bernard C. Cobb, contemplated the formation of a giant utility holding company that would control the stock of many power concerns in the eastern half of the country, he offered Willkie $36,000 a year to work with the company's legal arm, Weadock and Weadock, which meant moving to New York. Willkie joined his new company on October 1, 1929.

In four years Wendell L. Willkie rose to Wall Street prominence by becoming the president of Commonwealth and Southern. Cobb, now retired, had sensed the wisdom of having the corporation run by a man whose politics were compatible with the new national Administration. He advised the board of directors to appoint Willkie. The country boy from Elwood thus secured a job that would eventually pay $75,000 a year.

Appropriately enough, he lived in a luxurious apartment at 1010 Fifth Avenue, but he continued to look like a country boy. His suits were forever rumpled, even though he wore a freshly pressed one every morning. His great shock of dark hair fell over his forehead when he spoke, a characteristic that seemed to emphasize his words. As in Elwood, where his father had usually left the front door unlocked so the children would have no excuse for not returning even in the middle of the night, one could enter his apartment without a key. The interior itself looked as though it had been decorated at random —a mixture of Japanese furniture, Oriental rugs, overstuffed chairs and a fringed lampshade. Over the mantel was a marine picture that was illuminated from above by a bronze light. But perhaps the most unmistakable sign of Willkie's presence was a personal library of some fifteen hundred to twenty-five hundred books, which related to a wide range of subjects, but mainly history, economics and biography. Mornings after a late-night reading bout were a chore for Edith, for her husband's insatiable curiosity inevitably left loose books strewn all over the furniture, as he would consult related works while pursuing the arguments of a particular author, and they all needed to be reshelved. References to his constant reading embellished his conversations. When he wrote a review of David Cecil's *The Young Melbourne* for the New York *Herald Tribune,* he received the kind of fan mail and general praise that would have been appropriate for the biographer himself. Willkie generously donated copies of the book to many public libraries, in Elwood and in other towns. By that year,

1939, he had become a close friend of the *Herald Tribune*'s book-review editor, Irita Van Doren. Years later his widely acclaimed book *One World* was written largely with her editorial assistance.

He had certain habits that seemed peculiar to more conventional people. For example, his belief in his ability to estimate the time correctly within a fifteen-minute period kept him from bothering with a watch. His absent-mindedness also discouraged his carrying a fountain pen, for he was sure to misplace it. He could become so absorbed explaining a point to a companion or excited with ideas that he could not trust himself to concentrate long enough on the mechanics of negotiating an automobile through traffic safely, so he did not own a car, nor did he drive. Food, too, was only something that seemed to get in his way. He ate with enthusiasm, but what went down his throat seemed to matter little. The salad that usually was sent in to his office for lunch at 20 Pine Street, in Manhattan's financial district, was normally consumed at his desk while he went right on telephoning or talking to visitors or doing his paperwork.

The office itself reflected the man as much as did his clothes and his apartment. It was a large corner room with many huge windows, nicely carpeted in green. The leather chairs were light brown. But there, too, was the inevitable pile of books, magazines and newspapers, most of them thrown on top of a big table that stood at one side of the room. Grace Grahn, one of his Commonwealth and Southern secretaries, guessed that there must have been about one hundred books of all types at any given time. The walls were covered with pictures of his father, former Secretary of War Newton D. Baker, former Ambassador to Germany James W. Gerard and several business associates. The whole atmosphere was far from what one might imagine would be the office of the president of one of America's largest corporations.

His politics refused to be consistent with his station. With Mrs. Willkie he was a member of the New York County Democratic organization, which was better known as Tammany Hall. In 1932 he had contributed $150 to defeat Hoover by electing Franklin D. Roosevelt; and receipt #19171 shows that on June 13, 1934, he contributed another hundred dollars to help reduce the debt of the Democratic National Committee. In 1935 both Willkies were elected to the party's county committee, along with James A. Farley and Bernard Baruch. While Mrs. Willkie was perhaps more critical of FDR's New Deal than was her husband, developments had, by that time, begun to fire the opposition of the utilities magnate. He soon regretted having made any contribution to help elect Roosevelt.

Willkie agreed that business had bumbled badly in 1929 and that what had happened was the result of a badly neglected economic and social order. More than most businessmen he realized that the New Deal had saved American capitalism. However, he approved of a role for government only as long as it regulated and protected and did not control and own. The New Deal, therefore, aroused a most articulate enemy when its Tennessee Valley Authority, originally conceived to provide adequate flood control and reforestation, entered the business of supplying electrical power to the area of the Tennessee River, where four of the six Commonwealth and Southern affiliates operated.

In addition to opposing the TVA, he also took on the Public Utility Holding Company Act of 1935, which was a direct attempt to destroy such companies as Commonwealth and Southern. The political involvements of utility magnates such as Samuel Insull had convinced the public that something drastic was necessary to curb and even curtail holding companies. Many, including FDR himself, were convinced that they served no legitimate purpose. What Willkie termed a "death sentence" was the provision that gave the Securities and Exchange Commission, also a New Deal product, power to decide within three years which holding companies controlled "a single integrated system" of power, and only those would be permitted to survive. The Holding Company Act had been a direct result of the numerous abuses by companies with interlocking directorates and "watered stock." Regulations that outlawed long-standing ills were acceptable to Willkie, for Commonwealth and Southern had a clean record; his real fight was against the "death sentence."

Willkie's method demonstrated his Wilsonian faith in the people: He took his fight to them. One of his favorite quips was that "the Tennessee River waters five states and drains the nation." In 1934 the *Literary Digest* carried his picture and noted him as a personality of national interest. By the following year Willkie's speeches began to be published and he had the start of a national reputation. In 1936 he was included in a "March of Time" movie short about the TVA, and appearances on both the National Broadcasting Company and the Columbia Broadcasting System radio networks that year enabled him to attack the TVA and the Holding Company Act as well as some of what he regarded as the excessive assumptions of the New Deal. *Fortune* featured Willkie and Commonwealth and Southern in its May 1937 issue. In August the *Atlantic Monthly* printed his essay on political power, and *Life* gave him space in November. That month the New York *Sun* devoted a special profile to the man who, in the name of Jeffersonian democracy, was crying out for the New Deal really to help end the Great Depression by removing the impediments to business investment. His theme had become clear.

It was also in 1937 that Edward Whiting, a columnist for a New England newspaper, the Worcester *Telegram,* suggested that the articulate critic of New Deal excesses might be desirable as a Republican presidential candidate. Willkie had voted for Alf Landon in 1936 and against FDR, but Whiting did not know that he was still registered as a Democrat. In his adopted state of New York, Willkie was for the mayorality of Fiorello H. La Guardia, the Republican-Fusion candidate in 1937, but the following year, he remained loyal to his own party by favoring another term for Democratic Governor Herbert Lehman against a youthful Republican opponent, District Attorney Thomas E. Dewey. All this time he continued to battle against both the TVA and the Holding Company Act. Willkie's audience also grew wider. Politically, however, he was strictly an amateur and was full of unorthodox positions, as when he referred to the one-man rule of Mayor Frank Hague of Jersey City by saying that "the true liberal must be outraged when the government permits the Mayor of Jersey City to throw union organizers in jail—or eject Socialists from the town—merely because the Mayor of Jersey City is vice-chairman of the Democratic National Committee."

That appearance on the "Town Hall" program in early 1938 was important. A larger audience than ever before heard him speak for freedom for private enterprise, for the basic sources of investment that can stimulate the economy and put people to work. He had not denied that government had a role, nor had he whitewashed capital's shortcomings, but he had declared that virtue is not monopolized by politicians and that, in effect, business and the public had identical interests. Efficiency, he had also said, can be improved with bigness, so that it was ludicrous for the government to act against a corporation just because of its size. Moreover, potential investors quite naturally viewed the impingement by government on one sector of private enterprise as a disease threatening to become more general, thus discouraging capital from further risks. For months after the radio appearance letters urging Willkie to run for the Presidency of the United States filled his mail.

Such ideas were remote. First, Willkie had to defend Commonwealth and Southern's interests. In March of 1938 the Supreme Court, now a "Roosevelt Court," in the wake of the President's political attempt to "pack" the nation's highest judicial body, upheld the Holding Company Act. Commonwealth and Southern thus began years of negotiations with the Securities and Exchange Commission, negotiations which led to the demise of the company eleven years later. Meanwhile, the Tennessee Electric and Power Company, one of Commonwealth and Southern's companies, could not possibly compete against the natural advantages of the government-operated TVA. Only nine days after Willkie's "Town Hall" appearance, he again made news by asking that TVA do the realistic thing and buy out TEPCO altogether. His asking price, based on his accountants' appraisal, was $94 million.

David Lilienthal, the TVA chairman, at first offered $57 million, but Willkie held out for $90 million. Lilienthal went up as far as $67 million and then negotiations stalled. Talks dragged on and Willkie was able to publicize his arguments better by testifying before a Congressional subcommittee. Answering questions from its counsel, Francis Biddle, he said he was not going to surrender TEPCO at a price that would be convenient for the Authority.

The agreement that finally came was sudden. The President had no desire to prolong the squabble. In February 1939, therefore, the deal was resolved at $78.6 million. Congressional authorization was completed in late July. On August 15, in a ceremony at the offices of the First National Bank at 2 Wall Street, three newsreel cameras recorded the actual transfer of the property to the government. When Lilienthal handed Willkie the huge check, the Commonwealth and Southern president looked at it and said, "Thanks, Dave. That's a lot of money for a couple of old Indiana boys to be handling. And for that I'm going to give you a deed for all our Tennessee Electric Power Company properties." One newspaper reporter wrote that the whole affair was a "banner occasion" for Willkie "and he appeared to enjoy every moment of it as it represented what his legion of friends both in and out of the utility industry have described as a 'one-man victory over the competitive inroads of the Federal Government' into the electric power business."

The next day, Arthur Krock of *The New York Times* devoted his column to the question of Wendell Willkie and the coming presidential nominations. It was not Krock's first recognition of the possibility. On Washington's Birthday he had written a report of a conversation in Washington. With the city idle on that day, reported Krock, a group of Republicans were engaging in the favorite American parlor game, picking presidential candidates. A number of names were considered, from the improbable reselection of former President Herbert Hoover through Henry Cabot Lodge, Governor Arthur James of Pennsylvania, Governor John Bricker of Ohio and Governor Leverett Saltonstall of Massachusetts. Their analysis agreed that, while Senator Robert A. Taft of Ohio and Bricker "might eliminate each other by clashing and unsurrendered ambitions," the most likely front-runners were Senator Arthur Vandenberg of Michigan and New York's Tom Dewey.

One Democrat was present, and he asked, "How about that utilities chap, Wendell Willkie?" "He managed to talk himself into a good deal with the TVA," the man pointed out in recognition of the agreement that was to lead to the TEPCO transfer in August. "Take note," the man went on to say about Willkie, "he owns two farms and works them. That's ominous. And, being from Indiana and a lawyer by profession, there isn't any doubt he is a presidential candidate. All Indiana lawyers are."

"If he is a Republican—is he?—you can't wholly count out Willkie," said another man. "But he'll have to go down as the darkest horse in the stable; 1940 will be a little early to bring out a utilities man. But if anyone like that can be put over, I'd watch Willkie. He still has his haircuts country style."

"I don't see how we could expect the Chief to stay out if Willkie gets in the race," said the Democrat. "There's a limit to what flesh and blood can stand."

In March, Raymond Moley's *Newsweek* column pointed out that Willkie would be a high-caliber candidate capable of matching Roosevelt and that he might even succeed behind a "businessman for President" slogan. But Moley was not about to become euphoric. He checked his enthusiasm with the realization that it would be hard to imagine politicians of either party going for a businessman in 1940.

If Willkie was thinking along the lines of Krock and Moley, he was careful to give no outward hint; but, then again, he was plainly being cautious, waiting to see what would be possible. For example, he shied away from some potentially embarrassing publicity that would have linked him to a Nazi propaganda broadcast. An American employed by Reichs-Rundfunk GMBH Berlin, a short-wave station, offered to reward Willkie's compliance with his request that he suggest appropriate songs for a broadcast "dedicated" to the state of Indiana by publicizing the Hoosier's contribution. Willkie promptly declined the honor by pointing out that he had "been in the public press so much that I am quite anxious to take occasions to keep such mentions to the minimum." Then came the following reply from Germany: "I can well understand your reticence in not wishing to have your name mentioned in connection with the broadcast." At about the same time, however, Willkie informed a friend that his only ambition was as a utilities operator and "to get involved in no presidential or other political campaigns." Similarly, Willkie responded with polite notes when others suggested that he support Paul V. McNutt for the Presidency, and he expressed approval but offered no specific commitment for action when Lewis Douglas' name was mentioned. Both men were Democrats attractive to fiscal conservatives. McNutt, administrator of the Federal Security Agency in the Roosevelt Administration, had been Willkie's fraternity brother at Indiana University and had also been Governor of that state. Douglas, whom Willkie described as a potentially "excellent President" when he responded to a booster in February 1940, had resigned as FDR's Director of the Budget in sharp disagreement with the Administration's fiscal policies. "I would do any legitimate thing to see Lew Douglas President of the United States," Willkie wrote to a friend, and left it at that.

That a Republican could win in 1940 had become a real possibility, particularly if Roosevelt held to the two-term tradition. From its near death in 1936, the opposition party had shown viability during the midterm elections of 1938. A coalescense of anti-New Dealers and anti-FDR traditionalists, angered by the Court-packing attempt, frustrated by continuing demands by militant and growing organized labor, and chagrined by the economic plunge that recurred in 1937 and 1938, succeeded in almost doubling Republican membership in the House for the Seventy-sixth Congress, picked up six additional Senate seats and won eight governorships. Such vital states as Pennsylvania, Ohio and Massachusetts were included in the GOP revival. The improved prospects had given the party a long list of eager candidates.

4

There was the District Attorney of New York County, Tom Dewey. He was only thirty-seven in 1939 but had already gained wide public attention throughout the country as the crusading DA, warring against the vicious gangsters who, with the demise of lucrative Prohibition years, had turned to the numbers and protection rackets. Rural Americans were especially pleased to hear how a boy from Owosso, Michigan, had been cleaning up the sordid elements in the big city of New York. So much publicity had been given to his work as a special prosecutor under Mayor Fiorello H. La Guardia that when he ran for District Attorney of New York County in 1937, some polling places in Brooklyn had to put up special signs that said: "Dewey is not running in this county."

His success as a DA made him a formidable gubernatorial candidate against a respected incumbent, Herbert Lehman. A persuasive speaker, Dewey was astonishingly strong in the state's rural areas and carried upstate New York by 619,000 votes. Believing, however, that anti-Semitism accounted for much of this appeal, New York City voters rallied behind Lehman and gave him a 683,000 margin in the city's five boroughs. But Dewey's showing was impressive enough to project the DA as one of the party's best vote-getters. To many, he seemed just the right man to clean up the entrenched corruption of Democratic big-city control that was personified by Frank Hague in Jersey City and Ed Kelly and Pat Nash in Chicago.

There was little doubt about Dewey's ambitions. A small man, carefully dressed and trimly mustached, he often gave the impression of using dubious methods to get his way. By the end of January 1939 he had forced Judge Martin T. Manton to resign from the U.S. Circuit Court of Appeals for having received more than $439,000 from individuals or concerns acting for parties interested in matters handled by Manton's court.

Dewey's reputation soared a few weeks later when James J. Hines, the Tammany Hall leader of Manhattan's Eleventh Assembly District, was found guilty of having been a henchman and paid protector of Arthur (Dutch Schultz) Flegenheimer's policy racket. When anxious reporters pressed Dewey in his 1148 Fifth Avenue apartment about the political implications of the Hines trial, the DA's answer was, "I'm busy being District Attorney." It was dangerous to start a presidential boom too early. But the Gallup poll, which had shown Dewey preferred by 27 percent of all Republicans interviewed before the Hines trial, enough to rate him far ahead of any other name, reported in March that Dewey's candidacy had become the choice of 50 percent.

What was most astonishing about Dewey's bid in 1940 was that he was not a Governor of any state, large or small; he was not a Senator or a member of the House; he was just a big-city district attorney popularly identified with the fight against hoodlums and racketeers. For a major party to choose a man with such limited political prominence, one who was hardly above the Constitutional age requirement for the Presidency, would have meant ranking him with the heroes of some of America's great wars. A significant number of Republicans apparently felt that he had earned that distinction.

Second to the New Yorker in March, according to Gallup, was Senator Arthur Vandenberg. The Michigan Republican had been in Congress since 1928 and was a recognized leader of the party in the legislature. Influenced by Gerald P. Nye's famous investigation of the part played by the munitions industry in bringing about America's entry into World War I, Vandenberg was a solid supporter of isolationism. He had stated that the United States should not be an international policeman and that the best defense against war was a limitation of arms. Until Dewey came close to defeating Lehman in 1938, Vandenberg had been the most widely discussed possibility for 1940. Some, however, thought he might be too controversial. He was for protective tariffs in an age of reciprocity and had a record that was hostile toward labor and pro-business.

Although Hoover, Landon, Lodge and Senator William Borah were also mentioned on Gallup's list that March, Senator Robert A. Taft was the only other serious contender. He was preferred by 13 percent of the Republicans polled. Some observed that both his strength and his weakness came from the fact that he looked like all sixteen million Republicans rolled into one. An isolationist with the firm conviction that America's interest would be best kept by attending to affairs on this side of the ocean, he left many with the impression that what was happening in Europe was not his concern. Yet he differed from other rigid non-interventionists by supporting Administration efforts to repeal the arms embargo. Why should he oppose a

part of the Neutrality law that was so dear to isolationists? His reason
was simple. He could not see that it made much sense to ban munitions while simultaneously continuing to sell materials from which
"munitions can be manufactured, and restriction discriminates
against the little fellow who has no munitions industry of his own."

Robert Taft was a newcomer to the Senate, having been elected in
1938. However, he had been prominent in Ohio politics and had been
placed as a "favorite son" in the 1936 convention. Intelligent, almost
fanatically honest, he was, nevertheless, regarded as cold and color-
less. What support he might develop would come from conservatives,
particularly those in the South.

All three leading candidates were better known than Willkie. The
Hoosier was only an amateur, a Democrat, a utilities magnate, a Wall
Streeter, a man whose fight had emanated from New Deal incursions
into his business interests. But, as Arthur Krock had noted, some
people were thinking of him for the Republican ticket, even if he was
the "darkest horse in the stable." Perhaps they were prompted by
doubts that any of the name candidates could defeat FDR, if "the
Champ" should run again.

5

Sam Pryor was a Dewey man; and, openly at least, he stuck to that
position for some time. But when he heard Willkie on the "Town
Hall" program and then read his articles that the popular magazines
were carrying, he thought he had found the man who could lead
business and America "out of the wilderness." As all professional
politicians in his party, Pryor was ready to subordinate any personal
feelings for or against any particular candidate to the importance of
finding someone with a good chance of winning. This consideration
inevitably made his advocacy of Dewey—or anyone else—tentative.
Pryor had also entertained great hopes for his political ally in Connecticut, Governor Raymond Baldwin, whom he regarded as dynamic
and progressive; but the national committeeman's interest in Dewey
and Baldwin didn't keep him from wanting to take a closer look at
Willkie.

Pryor was also a vestryman of Christ Church in Greenwich. Rich
enough to need no public office for himself but sufficiently ambitious

to be a backstage power, he invited both Willkie and Baldwin to help the church celebrate its two hundredth anniversary on the night of May 2, 1939. Over seven hundred people swarmed into the Greenwich Country Club. It was the largest crowd ever to attend a function held off the church grounds. The senior warden opened the meeting and presented the two speakers, largely for the surveillance of Sam Pryor.

Baldwin recalled Connecticut church history and made some rather uninspiring remarks about the importance of religion to a wholesome society. Willkie, however, used the opportunity to talk about the world. "Hitler and others cannot dim the bright light that made this country the great country that it is which permits us to hold this meeting," he said. Unlike Baldwin, Willkie proceeded to demonstrate that his thinking was preoccupied with larger issues.

Sam Pryor had heard what he wanted. He had no further doubts: Willkie for President, Ray Baldwin for Vice President.

Newspapers became increasingly filled with tidbits about what the Republicans might or should do in 1940. The "boy governor" from Minnesota, Harold Stassen, said the GOP should choose a liberal candidate and platform and accept the social reforms of the New Deal. John D. M. Hamilton, the party's national chairman since 1936 and a man regarded by many as perhaps the best Republicans had ever had, warned the party's Old Guard that any candidate must be appealing to the masses and that a platform should be broad-based. Arthur Vandenberg, whom Krock noted "has the 'right' ancestry, Dutch, and he won't be 60 until March, 1944," won legislative victories in the Senate, and his prospects improved. Frank Gannett, who owned a chain of upstate New York newspapers and was a bitter opponent of New Deal reformers, drew prolonged applause when he told a luncheon meeting of the National Republican Club that the American people should demand FDR's resignation. A few days later a *Newsweek* poll of fifty Washington correspondents predicted that the party would pick a Dewey-Taft ticket and, by a vote of 2-1, guessed that such a combination would defeat the most likely Democratic nominees, Garner and Farley. In early June 1939 a Vandenberg-for-President Club was formed in Detroit by a local real-estate man; but a few days later a Gallup poll showed that, if the elections were held then, the Republicans could defeat Roosevelt by nominating Dewey. A later study of the party's rank and file said that they thought the GOP should select a liberal candidate.

In midsummer of 1939, Taft, opposing foreign loans and intervention in European affairs, said he would be a candidate for the Presidency. But even while he made his announcement, the triumphant record of the DA from New York was still furthering the growth of a Dewey boom. At the same time, Vandenberg's denunciation of a treaty permitting the sale of goods to Japan, refusal to permit Neutrality Act revisions, and his success in Congress had made him another serious entry. This developed despite his statement to Vandenberg Club organizers that he would keep himself "scrupulously detached from the pre-convention campaign." Gallup, in fact, was showing by mid-August that Vandenberg had been gaining rapidly and had moved into second place, although he was still some twenty points behind Dewey.

By the end of November word reached the offices of the Republican National Committee that another man was interested in the nomination: Herbert Clark Hoover was lining up delegates. Colonel R. B. Creager of Texas and Harrison E. Spangler of Iowa, both national committeemen, were already working for the ex-President. And, before the start of the convention on June 24, there would be other entries.

Meanwhile, the Willkie idea was the property of a select circle. On March 3 the New York *Herald Tribune* had printed a letter that was initialed by G. Vernor Rogers, a vice-president of the McClure Syndicate, that suggested the Hoosier's candidacy. At the end of April a New York advertising executive heard Willkie's speech before a Sons of Indiana dinner and exclaimed: "That's the kind of businessman we should have on the Republican ticket for President!" Both *The New York Times* and political columnist David Lawrence followed the appearance of a Willkie *Atlantic Monthly* article on the shortcomings of the economy with laudatory comments. Just as Taft was announcing his own candidacy, *Time* ran Willkie's picture on its cover and noted that he was the country's only businessman being mentioned for the nation's highest office.

6

Willkie made a significant switch during the regular pre-election-day registration period. Edith, whom her husband called "Billie," had suggested that it would be more appropriate for Roosevelt's most articulate critic to join the opposing party. Willkie considered her words and stepped into the booth. When he emerged seconds later he said, "Well, I registered Republican."

"I wonder what the papers will say about this," said Mrs. Willkie.

"Why?" he asked rather naïvely. "What do you mean about the papers?"

"Why, Wendell," she explained, "the way you've been fighting Roosevelt, of course it will come out."

When Sam Pryor went to Willkie's office a day or two later the utilities magnate revealed his new party affiliation. It was also clear to Pryor that if the Republicans wanted Willkie he would be glad to oppose Roosevelt in 1940.

Even though Pryor now had no doubts about the Hoosier's eligibility to be the party's candidate, his own previous commitments in Connecticut, together with Willkie's unique status, kept the national committeeman from issuing an open endorsement. But others, such as Raymond Moley, had no such considerations. The political scientist and ex-New Dealer spent an evening at Yale's Saybrook College talking informally with the students. One boy asked whom the Republicans ought to nominate. Without hesitating, Moley replied that Willkie would be the best man, if the party had the nerve to put anyone forward except political stuffed shirts. Moley also warned about the ominous consequences of four more years of Roosevelt. When he informed Willkie about what he had said at Saybrook, the utilities magnate responded by agreeing to the need to defeat FDR and pledged his own dedication "in whatever capacity it may be best for me to serve." But as to Moley's suggestion that he would be the best candidate, Willkie said he was "flattered" and added: "Some of these days I should like to have a chat with you about the whole question."

General Hugh Johnson was never a very reticent man. He had become a newspaper columnist whose views were sought by opponents of the Administration. On November 21, 1939, he spoke to a large gathering of the Bond Club in New York and told its members that Willkie would make a "very strong candidate" and was an ideal businessman for President of the United States.

At that moment Willkie was in Atlanta. He had gone south to inspect his company's properties. When called to the telephone he heard a newspaper reporter relate General Johnson's words and was asked to comment. "In view of the speed with which the federal government is taking over my business," he replied, "shortly I'll probably have to be looking around for a new job. General Johnson's is the best offer I've had so far."

"Old Ironpants" Johnson was not the first to offer the suggestion, of course; but he had a pungent style, his column appealed to Democrats who were dismayed at what FDR was doing to the party of Jefferson, and thus commanded a wide following. His remark went all over the country, was picked up in numerous news columns and feature stories and, therefore, became the first to incite substantial popular support. During the next few weeks Willkie's mail was filled with those seconding Johnson's remark, but the Hoosier gave no written encouragement.

Willkie knew what he was doing, although his goal was the impossible. However good a candidate he would be, Krock was telling readers, "miracles don't happen any more." After all, the man had no organization, no large financial contributors, no powerful political support. Sam Pryor, ready to defy all this, thought he should announce his candidacy early; and he told that to Willkie.

"Now, Sam, will you just go on down to Florida and have yourself a good vacation, because when we do this it'd better be the right time," Willkie said. "Otherwise, they'll build up enough mud pies to throw at me. You probably wouldn't even want to know me. If they think I'm getting close to Roosevelt, the smears will come out. Let's hold off until the last minute. Why are you so impatient? You want to see me get hurt? You want to see those mud pies fly?"

Sam Pryor went to Florida that December. There he read that Tom Dewey had, as Harold Ickes reported, thrown "his diaper into the ring."

CHAPTER FOUR

"Life Begins in '40"

1

WHEN DEWEY ANNOUNCED his candidacy it was the first of December. Several hundred faithful followers were present as he opened his campaign headquarters at 100 East 42nd Street. His manager, J. Russel Sprague, a Republican leader from Long Island, introduced the official candidate. Other Republicans throughout the state promptly accepted the political realities and lined up with New York's most powerful member of their party. Harold Ickes noted that Dewey's official entry hardly "made a ripple." When Dewey delivered the opening speech of his campaign at St. Paul later that week, Ickes thought it offered "some euphoneous generalities."

Taft of Ohio was also in active pursuit of the nomination. In December he chose Boston for the major address of a New England tour. He championed all of the sacred things—a balanced federal budget, reduction of regulatory measures against business, promotion of private enterprise—but, significantly, he also endorsed one of the

New Deal's major premises, that the government did have a humanitarian function. When Taft was asked whether Ray Baldwin would be acceptable as a running mate, he said he would be "glad to be associated with Governor Baldwin in any way."

But for all this optimism by Taft and Dewey, a published poll of 481 of the 1,728 editors of daily newspapers showed that most thought the Republican candidate would be Vandenberg. The Michigan Senator, whose name had figured prominently for a long time, had stated that his principal activity was to "keep America out of other people's wars." His Congressional reputation had raised his chances, particularly during the fall of 1939. Nevertheless, by spring, the Vandenberg boom had begun to drop from its lofty level of earlier months.

2

Willkie and his friends were keenly aware of the possible goal. They also knew that for a drive to appear spontaneous it would have to be organized with exceptional skill. Being overly aggressive could deprive their man of his potential appeal; so they continued to follow the precaution that had been stressed to Pryor: avoid premature disclosures of intentions. And few of Willkie's activities, little of what he said, were without a purpose. At a dinner of the Congress of American Industry that was held in New York on December 8, he had made some of his usual comments about the dangers to free enterprise when he added: "We shall find, perhaps, that life begins in '40."

Guiding him at this stage, helping to arrange for speaking dates and other fruitful types of exposure, in addition to Pryor, were such people as Russell Davenport, the managing editor of *Fortune;* Charlton McVeagh, a gifted writer and speaker who was close to Davenport; and Harold E. Talbott and Sinclair Weeks, both future members of the Eisenhower Administration. Also helpful were the organizational and administrative talents of Broad Street lawyer Harold J. Gallagher. All were circumspect about their man's real intention. It was an efficient little group that worked diligently behind the scenes to advance Willkie so that he could take advantage of a possibly deadlocked convention.

On the afternoon of January 16, while Willkie was speaking as a member of a panel at the Sales Executive Club, the New York *Sun* carried a story on page sixteen that revealed his new party registration. Moreover, added the reporter, "something like a whispered Willkie-for-President movement" had been under way for several months and noted that his political apostasy might very well be his own recognition of such an opportunity. Meanwhile, at the Sales Executive Club on that day another panelist brought an ovation from the audience by remarking that "the business outlook would be good if we had a presidential candidate like our honored guest, Mr. Willkie."

Three days later, when Willkie read about the death of Senator William E. Borah, a vehement isolationist with the power to block an internationalist, he turned to Russell Davenport and said, "This gives me a chance."

When Willkie spoke at Wooster College in Ohio on January 30 he mentioned having received several thousand letters urging his candidacy. Newsmen then asked him about running. For the first time the Hoosier stated publicly what had been on his mind. "But I'm not running for President," he began. "Of course, it isn't going to happen, but if the nomination were given to me without any strings I would have to accept it. No man in middle life and in good health could do otherwise." Then he added: "But I couldn't go out and seek delegates and make two-sided statements. I value my independence. That's what I've been fighting for all these years."

Arthur Krock's column following the Wooster remark was called "The Care and Feeding of Very Dark Horses." The journalist had found the response to insignificant mentions of Willkie's name as a candidate sufficient proof that he was "a very solid dark horse." A deadlocked convention might even make him a winner. But, wrote Krock, it would be contrary to "American political behaviorism." By stipulating that he would accept the nomination only if it were offered "without strings," Willkie was automatically discouraging the political pros. Only a desperate party would name someone like that. "Mr. Willkie may consider himself a dark horse," Krock pointed out, but the "care and feeding of these political animals is a delicate and gambling business."

But the reaction was not confined to Krock, or Moley or Johnson or, for that matter, to the obvious sources of newspaper support. The

Wooster speech provoked interest in smaller newspapers in different parts of the country. Among them, the *Times* of Bay City, Michigan, suggested that Willkie was precisely the man John L. Lewis had in mind when he had recently threatened to bolt the party if FDR were renominated. And the paper, which noted that Willkie was "quite an everyday person with some startlingly advanced ideas," speculated, without any evidence, that there may have been more than coincidence in the fact that both Lewis and Willkie had made their statements at about the same time. The Springfield (Massachusetts) *Morning Union* praised Willkie's "mental honesty, his straight thinking and direct expression of sound opinion," but was forced to conclude that the "qualities that would enable him to be a good President are the very qualities that seem to make him ineligible. But this will not worry Mr. Willkie, who admits he has no illusions as to the likelihood that he may be nominated." Closer to Willkie's home office, the Wall Street correspondent of the *Christian Science Monitor* compared the "quixotic belief in Mr. Wallace's presidential prospects," which was held by many farmers, with "Wall Street's dream of Wendell Willkie for President."

In mid-February, Willkie followed Raymond Moley's path to Yale and also spent an evening with the students of Saybrook College. In an informal discussion session he developed his ideas coherently and generated enough interest in what he said, particularly in his opposition to bigness in government and business, to compel a number of students to linger on for nearly two hours after the formal end of the meeting. Once again he demonstrated that he could establish rapport with all kinds of groups and that people instinctively felt free to talk with him. But such talents alone can hardly give a man the presidential nomination of a major party.

That Willkie's candidacy had a long way to go before public recognition was apparent when Dr. George Gallup's February report failed to include his name. Dewey, although down 4 percent from January, was still clearly favored by more Republicans than all other candidates combined. He had 56 percent, while Vandenberg and Taft were the only other serious contenders, each with 17 percent.

Most people expected that the first real test would not come until April, when primary elections were scheduled for Wisconsin, Illinois and Nebraska. Dewey's real challenge lay in Wisconsin. The state was part of the isolationist Midwest, and Vandenberg was from neighboring Michigan and better known to its Republicans, many of whom not only sympathized with Vandenberg's isolationist views but also approved of his support of some New Deal social and economic legislation. In short, a Dewey victory there would be an emphatic endorsement. Having lost the last two presidential elections and not caring to forfeit a third, Republicans could then argue that the New Yorker was their most likely winner.

And no man worked harder than Dewey that winter and early spring. His heavily financed campaign, which included a lavishly appointed train, visited a wide area. So much of the District Attorney's time was spent culling votes in the hinterlands that several Democrats back home, evidently eager to save money for the taxpayers, tried to dock Dewey for his absenteeism. The courts rejected their attempt, but the point was made. Dewey continued to press very hard. In Portland, Oregon, on Lincoln's Birthday, he charged that the United States was suffering from an "erosion of capital," which had worn down its productivity to the extent of seven million dollars in the seven years of the New Deal. No wonder, he said, that one third of the people were ill-clothed, ill-housed and ill-fed. Several weeks later, as the featured speaker at the Founders Day rally in the University of Nebraska coliseum, he delivered the major farm speech of his campaign. He attacked the New Deal's farm policy, charging that it had allowed politics—or "policulture," he called it—to triumph over agriculture and outlined his own eight-point program. Even crowds that had gathered for Hoover and Landon in past years were now surpassed by those for the trim, youthful and eloquent New Yorker. Raw weather and alternating periods of rain and snow had failed to reduce the largest turnout in the history of the school's celebration. Nebraska's primary was scheduled for April 9.

Taft, although a declared candidate, contrasted with Dewey by declaring that his presence on Capitol Hill was too important for any extensive campaigning. On the first day of March he appeared before a Lions Club meeting in Wilmington, Delaware, and complained that many New Deal bureaus were dominated by "sympathy for Communist ideals" and that these new extensions of Big Government were aiming more and more at "regulation of business and taxation of success." The Ohio Senator also reminded his audience that, in a recent speech to the American Youth Congress, FDR had acknowledged that he had sympathized with the ideals of communism twenty years earlier when the world had watched the Russians "experiment." Taft, keeping the record straight, did note that Roosevelt had denounced present Soviet conditions. But the President had, he charged, failed to recognize that the ideals of communism were fundamentally at variance with the American system.

The next day Taft turned to foreign policy. He told the National Republican Club that a stay-out-of-war policy should be a Republican pledge. "The Republican party is a peace party," he declared; "the Democratic party may or may not be a peace party." He had little fear of any involvement in Europe's mess before the elections, so there was not much likelihood that foreign policy would become a major issue, unless, of course, the President moved to "involve us in any European quarrels."

Vandenberg, although reportedly slipping, held onto considerable support, even though some of his admirers had no political power. In Philadelphia a model Republican national convention composed of high-school students from three states took their citizenship-training exercise seriously and nominated him as its candidate. To many, Vandenberg did seem the perfect alternative to the young and inexperienced Dewey and to the conservative and rather drab Taft. Granting the desire of most Republicans west of the Appalachians to have as little as possible to do with Hitler's war, Vandenberg was, to them, as safe as anyone else. At least when he warned against sending Americans into battle, one could not say that Vandenberg was wooing each audience with a different tune. Yet even Vandenberg wrote in his diary on February 2 that "probably the best we can hope for from now on is 'insulation' rather than isolation," explaining that an " 'insulationist' is one who wants to preserve all of the isolation which modern circumstances will permit." By March it had become clear that a deadlock among the three candidates could indeed open the field to a dark horse.

3

The Republicans were getting ready. Completing a two-year project to prepare a report for consideration by the Resolutions Committee as the basis of a platform for adoption by the party's national convention, Dr. Glenn Frank submitted a 33,000-word paper that charged the New Deal with ineptitude rather than with radicalism. Two weeks later, the party's national committee decided to accept Philadelphia's offer of two hundred thousand dollars and the free use of its Municipal Auditorium. Thus Philadelphia won over Chicago, which had merely promised to provide a hall and to pay legitimate expenses. But, then again, Chicago was still in the hands of the Kelly–Nash Democratic machine, while Philadelphia was being governed by a firm Republican organization and Mayor Robert Lamberton. To prepare the convention details, a seventy-year-old political veteran from Oregon, Ralph E. Williams, was named chairman of the Committee on Arrangements. Encouraging the GOP with visions of victory, National Chairman John D. M. Hamilton explained that the Democrats were so torn apart and demoralized by factionalism that FDR could be defeated by any one of a half dozen or more men.

Dewey, working overtime to prove he deserved his party's confidence, opened his midwestern campaign with a powerful speech before a large and appreciative crowd in the St. Louis Auditorium. He accused the New Deal of "a fundamental lack of integrity—a cynical disregard of the principles of common honesty," and, turning his pitch to what mid-America wanted to hear, he asked how the people could believe New Deal statements that the nation would be kept out of war. Moving on to Chicago, he made good use of his special train's platform to shake hands and deliver addresses to crowds all along the line, at Alton, Springfield, Lincoln, Bloomington and Joliet. The bad weather made little difference as hands were clasped and the New Deal was mauled. The weather was still miserable, but twenty thousand packed the Chicago Stadium to hear the DA charge the New Deal with intimidation, coercion, extortion and larceny in its administration of relief "for the simple and ugly purpose of corrupting the electorate of the United States." He also accused the politicians in Washington of using WPA funds and relief money to buy votes, which had become a standard Republican charge.

Then Dewey reached Wisconsin, where the primary would be held on April 2. In addition to his other handicaps in competing with Vandenberg for the dairy state, the Senator's delegates vying for Wisconsin's votes were judged by neutral observers as stronger vote-getters than the Dewey slate. At Milwaukee, on the night of March 29, a dismally small crowd turned out, but that disaster was at-

tributed to a lack of advance publicity. Eau Claire's crowd made for
more confidence. One casualty of the great effort was the third finger
on Dewey's right hand, which had become painfully bruised from so
much handshaking. But the campaigner went on to please his Wisconsin audiences by warning that only a strictly isolationist position
could guarantee continued neutrality and then inferred that FDR's
domestic failures were tempting "that man in the White House" to
distract the public by turning its attention to European affairs. By the
time Dewey returned to New York on April Fool's Day he was
suffering from a severe case of laryngitis and could only conclude that
the Wisconsin situation was muddled. He was sure of only one thing:
He had encountered strong sentiment against having the nation join
the war.

Taft's name had not been entered in Wisconsin. And neither
Dewey nor Vandenberg had filed personal nomination papers for the
state's preferential primary. Vandenberg had not even bothered to
campaign there. Perhaps he thought it unnecessary. Clearly, many regarded the Michigan man as a natural favorite to win the state. His
hold on its isolationist German population was considered strong; but
no one could minimize Dewey's efforts. Stopping him was the common need of the Taft and the Vandenberg people.

On the second day of April the results of the Wisconsin primary
vindicated Dewey's hard work. The voters had chosen twenty-four
delegates to the Republican National Convention. And every one of
the twenty-four had pledged to vote for Dewey on the first ballot.
More than two months before any delegates would camp at Philadelphia, the DA was threatening to remove all the suspense from the
show.

After April 9 additional primary votes came in, from Nebraska
and Illinois, and the results showed more of the same. Dewey took
about 55 percent of the Nebraska vote against Vandenberg; it was a
substantial victory but somewhat weaker than his performance in
Wisconsin. In Illinois, where he had run without organized opposition, he was favored by 85 percent of the Republicans. He also did
very well in that state's farm regions, outdrawing by four to three the
FDR vote in the Democratic primary. Such results tempted many to
cross out Vandenberg's name, but there were rumors circulating that
he and Taft would become the ingredients of a "stop Dewey" movement.

Only three days later Dewey moved to enforce his position at home. At an Albany meeting, those backing the DA won control of the party's state committee by electing Edwin F. Jaeckle of Buffalo as state chairman and so took the first step toward ousting the recalcitrant Kenneth F. Simpson as the national committeeman. Simpson's reaction was blunt. No longer did he have any obligation to support Dewey as the state's "favorite son" candidate, he said, and, anyway, the Republican and independent voters of Manhattan did not consider Dewey as the best candidate available.

Even while Dewey was preparing to leave for a second campaign trip to the Pacific Coast, New York County delegates were looking around for someone else to support on the first ballot. Others were also reluctant to support the DA, despite his midwestern successes. Students at a model nominating convention at Bucknell University left Dewey far behind, along with Taft, New York's Mayor La Guardia, Senator Styles Bridges of New Hampshire and Governor James of Pennsylvania and concluded that Vandenberg was their favorite. Iowa Republicans, at the same time, announced that their delegation would support Hanford (Jack) MacNider, a determined isolationist and former Assistant Secretary of War and minister to Canada, as their "favorite son." Publisher Gannett's forces were also trying to attract support. Backed by Representative James Wadsworth and Syracuse Mayor Rolland B. Marvin, as well as by Queens Borough President George U. Harvey, a Coughlinite, he had entered the race with the cry "Throw out the Reds and the Pinks" while, at the same time, preaching non-interference with Hitler. A national Gannett-for-President Committee, with Wadsworth as its chairman, had already been established.

As of that spring, Dewey had done better than anyone could have anticipated. Those betting against him could ask for odds. If America could continue to ignore the European war, it might yet be possible for the Owosso boy—who had shown the big city how to cleanse itself —to sit in the White House.

4

Although here and there one could find news items about Willkie emerging the winner in case of a deadlock, sober people considered the possibility as most remote. Many were puzzled to read in the March 18 issue of the *New Republic* an article by Willkie called

"Fair Trial." In it he complained that the principle of due process of law to safeguard civil liberties had been denied not only to pro-Nazi Fritz Kuhn, head of the German-American Bund, but also to Eugene V. Debs in 1918 and, more recently, to Communist Earl Browder. Wrote Willkie: "Now, you may hate Communism even more than you hate Nazism (and I am surprised at the number of people who do), but if you truly believe in protection of civil liberties, you will wonder whether Browder was sentenced to four years in jail and a $2,000 fine because he made a false statement on a passport application or because he was a Communist party member." That was a strange concern to come from an anti-New Deal capitalist.

That month Willkie also spoke before the Toledo Civic Forum and Rotary Club in Ohio and pointed out that, following the world war, "Businessmen, drunk with power, and a public, drunk with money, broke down the safeguards protecting individual liberties." Then he chastised the irresponsibility of corporations in the Twenties for "playing with corporate structures as with a child's building-blocks, becoming promoters rather than businessmen. And some financiers in Wall Street and elsewhere," he continued, "instead of serving as a link between the savings of the people and the enormous capital needs of industry, became jugglers of finance, concerned primarily neither with the investor nor the investment, but with making money and securing power for themselves." He told of having been present in board rooms and listening to attempts to apply pressure on newspapers and other groups in efforts to eliminate any opposition. Of the regulatory laws that were introduced by the New Deal, he said that many were "sound in principle and most . . . will never be removed from our statute books." His real argument was with what he called the system of "personal government," in which the Chief Executive and not the people appointed the "individuals who write, enforce and judge the rules for the 10,000,000 business enterprises of America." The country was too complex for that: Sufficient allowances could not be made for the multitudinous variations that existed. "Sometimes such a government has been honestly administered, sometimes dishonestly," he said. "But it is not the kind of government to be tolerated by an upright and independent people." The reactions of the Administration to criticism were compared to those of Stalin, Hitler and Mussolini, who "are notorious for their dislike for anyone of a skeptical nature; even the minor voices of opposition disturb them."

He attacked Harold Ickes for calling such opposition "a sin against free enterprise, individual liberty, political democracy and your own self-interest." The present government, Willkie then charged, had the same zeal for maintaining excessive powers that big business once had. "If the government of the United States will sincerely dedicate itself to the purpose of making men free to carry on their economic enterprises, and of making it possible for 'the man with brains to get into the game,' " he concluded, "then this country, with its great trade area, its natural resources and its business genius, will resume an economic progress which will be even greater in the future than it has been in the past."

A few days later *Fortune* devoted major space to the Willkie cause. First there was a two-page editorial by Russell Davenport called "Business and Government," which introduced Wendell Willkie's "We, the People" article. The editorial wondered whether the people were sufficiently sophisticated to accept a man of such progressive, liberal, expansive and truly American principles. Such ideas would eventually prevail, wrote Davenport, but the country should be led by a man who believed in a businesslike approach to solve social problems.

Davenport had been with *Fortune* as its managing editor since 1937. Considered a "maverick intellectual" by his boss, publisher Henry Luce, Davenport had also been concerned about the government's role in business. His first meeting with Willkie had been at one of the monthly sessions of the *Fortune* Round Table, which were problem discussion groups with eminent personalities from various fields. That was in July 1939. Returning home after the meeting, Davenport said to his novelist wife, Marcia: "I've met the man who ought to be the next President of the United States."

"Whose idea is this?" she asked. "His or yours?"

"It's spontaneous," said Davenport. "You see him and you know it."

He invited Willkie to spend a weekend in August with them at the Davenport country home in Connecticut, at the same time making certain to collect some of the other prominent people of the neighborhood. Marcia Davenport found Willkie "a personality to charm a bird from a tree—if he wanted to." Willkie, relaxed but more interested in stimulating discussion than in card games or sports, made persuasive points on the need to transfer the Republican party into a

vehicle of enlightened and responsible opposition, to wean it away
from its hardened isolationism. From that time on Davenport and
Wendell Willkie were close friends. The first fruition of that combination appeared in *Fortune*'s April 1940 edition. Davenport not only
wrote the introductory editorial but also provided his editorial assistance for Willkie's "We, the People" article.

Oren Root, Jr., not quite twenty-nine years old, the grandnephew
of former Secretary of State Elihu Root, a Princeton man, class of
'33, and an associate of the law firm of Davis, Polk, Wardwell, Gardiner and Reed of 15 Broad Street, had never met Willkie. But he
had been impressed when hearing him speak at Princeton in January
1939. Now Root, a member of the Board of Governors of the New
York Young Republican Club, turned past the Davenport editorial to
page 64 and began to read "We, the People."

The article began with some pious Willkie words about political
integrity, with observations about the futility of a politician who tried
to say different things to different kinds of people, because, he wrote,
"The American people are not dumb. They know all about this. They
know that political platforms are written with the idea of being agreeable to as many different groups of people as possible." So he was
about to present a platform that should be approved by "we, the
people." Far from being strictly political, it would borrow from both
parties and be a "foundation upon which we can build—not overnight, but slowly—the economic and moral recovery that we have
been seeking for so long." Then he became more explicit.

He dealt with the growth of governmental power and charged that
"the New Deal has substituted the notion that government is an
asset without which none of us can survive." It represented a throw-
back to the era before our forefathers conceived the laws of human
liberty. The power rightfully belonging to the people had been taken
over by men who *"have acquired a vested interest in depression."*
Nevertheless, the concept of public welfare was upheld as a legitimate
concern of government. At the same level, Willkie wrote, government
"must be responsible not only for the destitute and the unemployed,
but for elementary guarantees of public health, the rehabilitation of
farmers, rebuilding of the soil, preservation of the national forests,
clearance and elimination of city slums, and so forth." He also asserted that any civilized government has had to play a similar role
and that some had gone much further than the New Deal. But we,

wrote Willkie, must be able to accomplish as much without disrupting our economics and "without a philosophy of defeat." Instead of the continuation of a New Deal, he called for a "New World."

Again, he acknowledged the responsibility of business for having caused the depression, but complained that the government's anti-business mentality "has made it impossible any longer to act in a free and enterprising manner." It was an attitude that had hit little businessmen even harder than the large ones, he charged. By doing this, the New Deal had retarded the economy, because a free business had made America great, and shackled investors, lacking confidence, with mutual suspicion inhibiting them, could only hinder productivity. Willkie left no doubt that productivity was the most important basis for a viable foundation; and he declared that the government, instead of being an agent for suppression rather than for free economic growth in a free society, should employ an economic policy *"primarily* for the sake of generating opportunities for private enterprise."

Turning to foreign policy, in the last part of his article, he chose the Russo–Finnish conflict, which had been raging all that winter, to illustrate his points. At that part, his words were welcomed by those Republican businessmen, particularly in the East, who believed that they had an economic as well as a moral interest in Europe. Anticipating his *One World,* he wrote that the modern globe was so small that foreign affairs must influence domestic politics. "It makes a great deal of difference to us—politically, economically and emotionally—what kind of world exists beyond our shores." Then came a condemnation of isolationists for wanting to restrict Finnish aid to non-military purposes, and the U.S.S.R. was lumped together with Germany and Japan as "the aggressive countries today." Freer international trade in a free world was viewed as a way to stimulate our, economy. Willkie acknowledged that Cordell Hull's reciprocal trade agreements had been a major achievement in that direction.

Root's attention was also caught by "Mr. Willkie's Petition." A summary of the long article's main arguments, it was enclosed in a large box on the second page of "We, the People." Modeled after the Declaration of Independence but addressed to Franklin D. Roosevelt instead of to King George III, it consisted of six succinct paragraphs of grievances that summarized Willkie's indictment of the Administration.

In the decade beginning 1930 you have told us that our day is finished, that we can grow no more, and that the future cannot be the equal of the past. But we, the people, do not believe this, and we say to you: give up this vested interest that you have in depression, open your eyes to the future, help us to build a New World.

. . . you have separated "business" and "industry" from the ordinary lives of the people and have applied against them a philosophy of hate and mistrust, but we, the people, say: business and industry are part of our daily lives; in hurting them you hurt us. Therefore abandon this attitude of hate and set our enterprises free.

. . . you have undertaken vast new obligations, which we support. But because you have not applied to these obligations the ordinary standards of business judgment, you have lost our money by the billions and we, the people, say: give us a businesslike administration that will act as the steward of our prosperity; that will ensure the social progress that is now threatened; and that will manage our affairs at least as intelligently as we manage our own enterprises.

. . . under the banners of reform, you have usurped our sovereign power by curtailing the Bill of Rights, by short-circuiting the states, and by placing in the hands of a few men in executive commission all the powers requisite to tyranny . . . we do not want monopolistic government, any more than we want monopolistic industry. Give us back the powers that our forefathers declared to be ours; liberate us to govern ourselves by *law.*

Because you have concealed from us the amount of our real taxes, and because you have hidden from us the real nature of our expenditures, you have specifically usurped our power over the public monies, and we, the people, say: give us as much information concerning our government as we expect to get concerning our own enterprises, so that we may control the vast sums that it has become necessary to spend.

You—the politicians of both parties—have muddled our foreign affairs with politics; with vague threats and furtive approvals; with wild fears and inconsistent acts; and we, the people, say: give us a foreign policy that we can trust and upon which we can build toward the future. We are against aggressors; we are for foreign trade; and we recognize that our own standard of living can be improved only by raising the standard of the other countries of the world.

Such words were enormously appealing to those Americans who still believed that even the complexities of the federal government in the middle of the twentieth century could be handled most efficiently by men with business skills. The tone was, nevertheless, progressive, although somewhat naïve; its appeal was to those who felt, as did Root, that in Willkie the country would have a President who not only appreciated the equation of liberty with freedom of enterprise but who also understood that America's security and economy could not be separated from what was happening in Europe.

Perhaps, wondered Root, there was a way to find out how many others wanted this man in the White House, even though little over two months remained before the convention. After all, Willkie's own willingness to run had become quite clear. On the night of April 4, after George V. Denny had introduced him as a potential presidential candidate, he had addressed a "Town Hall" meeting on "Liberalism" and had said he was not a candidate "in the slightest sense of the word" and added that he had not the "slightest delusion about being nominated." However, he was quick to say, "In order to preserve my intellectual well-being, when the question has been put to me as to whether I would accept the nomination, I have said yes. No man in my position of life would decline it."

Only the latter part of the statement was really candid. Those familiar with political jargon could surmise that the speaker was a willing candidate. Willkie's friends, on the other hand, were glad to hear that his campaign was losing some of its subtlety.

Root finally found a device. He wanted a mature and well-informed test group. To accomplish this, he drew up what he called a "declaration," which really embodied Willkie's own "petition," and spent $150 to have a few thousand printed by the Pandick Press of New York City. Then, hoping others interested in duplicating the declarations would turn to that press and do so at their own expense, he spent the night of April 9 with some friends mailing the petitions to members of the Yale class of 1924 and the Princeton class of 1925. One copy went directly to Willkie. Root explained that he had not informed him in advance because he desired to avoid any inferences that the move was anything but a voluntary and spontaneous effort. His main concern, he stressed, was for the Republican party to respond to the critical issues facing the nation by choosing a candidate who was ready to forsake isolationism by providing responsible leadership. This, Root pointed out, Willkie was in the best position to do; and he hoped that the association of his own name with that of a prominent American statesman of the past would help to contribute to Willkie's cause.

On April 9, the same day that German troops started to roll over

Scandinavia, Willkie was a guest on "Information Please," a popular weekly radio program that pitted a panel of well-informed writers and editors against questions and problems submitted by listeners. The master of ceremonies was Clifton Fadiman. Other personalities who appeared that night were Christopher Morley, John Kiernan and Franklin P. Adams. Willkie had had some reservations about making such an appearance because friends had argued that it would be undignified. But Kiernan and Adams finally persuaded him to join them.

Fadiman introduced the guest as a "real, honest-to-goodness tycoon." Then millions of listeners heard Willkie handle himself with humor and knowledge as he answered technical questions about the Constitution and literature. He showed familiarity with both *Nicholas Nickleby* and the life of Matthew Arnold. When Fadiman observed that he must have had plenty of time to read, Willkie replied: "I wish I did." The president of Commonwealth and Southern was far from the stereotype of the "devil" businessman of the Thirties. More than any other single appearance up to that date, his performance on the program gave him a wide popular following.

How the program may have influenced Oren Root's one-man crusade will, of course, never be known; but the first response to the declarations was a request from Russell Davenport that he and Root meet under the clock of the Biltmore Hotel. Davenport put things plainly to the young man: Willkie wanted Root's activity stopped for at least the next few weeks. His personal campaign threatened to upset the efforts being made by the Willkie people to avoid premature exposure. Moreover, Root was making a nuisance of himself, Willkie felt, by having girls on Fifth Avenue solicit signatures from pedestrians. One unsuspecting young lady requested Edith Willkie's but was turned down. Root, handsome and enthusiastic, managed, however, to convince Davenport that his method was worth trying and that, if successful, it would begin a drive that could acquire sufficient momentum to prepare the way for Willkie's candidacy. So convincing was the young lawyer that he was invited to have breakfast at the University Club with Willkie himself. Willkie also listened and was gratified, but he told Root that he intended to remain aloof from the petitions. It was too early for a campaign to enroll delegate support.

Four days after Root's declarations had gone out, *Herald Tribune* readers scanning the public notices at the bottom of page two saw the following appeal:

Wendell Willkie for President! Help Oren Root, Jr. organize the people's demand for Willkie. Send Root a contribution to 15 Broad Street, New York.

Then things became more hectic at Davis, Polk, Wardwell, Gardiner and Reed, where Root worked. Letters flooded in; petitions and money covered Root's desk. The telephone rang constantly. Root, it soon became plain, could no longer inflict this new campaign on his firm. Finally, he took a leave of absence and, with some of the contributions received, rented a "hole in the wall" at 660 Madison Avenue. He had wanted to find out about the pro-Willkie sentiment. He had his answer.

Four days after his original letters were sent, Root had to print twenty thousand more declarations. Contributions came in at the rate of two hundred dollars a day. Willkie-for-President clubs began to proliferate. By the opening of the party's national convention in June, the Pandick Press alone had printed more than 277,000 petitions, each with space for fifteen signatures; and twenty other presses had also turned them out.

Feeling that Root's people were getting too much publicity, Charlton MacVeagh and Davenport set up a rival headquarters at the Murray Hill Hotel. Their group called itself the "Voluntary Mailing Committee for Distributing Willkie's Speeches." "What happens at the Republican convention in Philadelphia next month," explained its secretary, K. B. Emmons, "is only secondary to our main purpose, which is to let the country at large know about Mr. Willkie's ideas and his personality." For them simply to have become part of Root's forces would have required Willkie to abandon his plan to avoid any premature pursuit of delegate support. Willkie's own explanation of his goals had been similar to Emmons'.

Willkie's public appearances in April certainly had that goal in mind. At the annual District of Columbia correspondents' Gridiron Club dinner, he was present with a number of top politicians and journalists. Even Harold Ickes was able to enjoy Willkie's good-humored talk, possibly because Willkie jokingly referred to the Secretary as his candidate; he had already said that several people were capable of doing at least as good a job as FDR. When, in the course of a debate with Willkie on the third-term issue, Ickes recited some doggerel poetry, the Republican quipped: "Mr. Ickes will have to write better poetry than that if he wants my vote." No doubt Willkie had impressed the correspondents. His qualifications for the Presidency were the main topics of gossip that night.

More important was Willkie's speech in New York on the twenty-fifth. Speaking at the Hotel Waldorf-Astoria, before the annual dinner of the Bureau of Advertising of the American Newspaper Publishers Association, he delivered a basic and clear-cut statement of his views. He appealed for a Jeffersonian concept of liberalism and urged its adherents to preserve that concept by defeating the New Deal.

Those publishers who agreed with him, and there were many, found their Republican candidate at the Waldorf. Particularly active in Willkie's behalf, thereafter, in addition to Ogden Reid of the *Herald Tribune,* were Roy Howard of the Scripps-Howard chain and John and Gardner Cowles, publishers of the Minneapolis *Star* and the Minneapolis *Tribune,* as well as the Des Moines *Register* and *Look* magazine. The Cowles brothers later arranged for Willkie to speak in Minnesota. An appealing candidate had been discovered by some people who could help to promote him.

5

By the first of May, Oren Root had announced that 200,000 had signed his declarations. Root, however, knew better than to rely on signatures alone. Shrewdly, he made use of all possible contacts, taking particular care to reply to letters that seemed to have come from individuals who, for one reason or another, might organize a local Willkie-for-President club. Those who replied early to Root's original distribution of declarations were prized enlistees in the drive.

One was an energetic businessman named Donald J. Smith of Montclair, New Jersey. Smith had been born in Indiana, and, moreover, as everybody who knew him was quick to learn, he was also one of Willkie's fraternity brothers at the Beta Theta Pi house. Now he was a Wall Streeter, the president of the Fundamental Group Corporation, a sales organization for the national distribution of shares of three investment trusts. As early as February 1938, Smith claimed, he had asked Willkie to run for the Presidency. According to Smith, Willkie had then replied: "Donald, no red-blooded American who thought he could run the government would dare turn down the nomination on any ticket." Willkie's increased opposition to FDR moved him closer to Smith's traditional Republicanism.

Smith's efforts, begun during the winter, illustrate the early grass-roots methods followed by the Willkie vanguard. On Smith's business trips to wide areas of the country he boosted Willkie at luncheons and at fraternity gatherings. Smith succeeded in interesting Kenneth L. Cooper, a securities salesman, in organizing clubs in Oregon. In California, Smith enlisted another old fraternity brother, and one who had served in the Army with Willkie, Allan B. Maxwell, a Hollywood life-insurance broker. Maxwell, in turn, brought together a group that organized a Willkie club in Los Angeles on May 16 and also printed ten thousand additional declarations, all for forwarding to Root's office. Smith, meanwhile, sent several hundred personal letters to friends and acquaintances, enclosing reprints of the "We, the People" article, offering, at the same time, to make additional reprints available free of charge in small quantities or larger amounts at cost. Requests for thousands of copies followed. Others were able to see the article when the *Reader's Digest* offered an abridged version. That spring, Smith, in addition to inspiring a Willkie movement in New Jersey, was also instrumental in starting clubs in San Antonio, Atlanta, St. Louis and San Francisco.

In Smith's own state of New Jersey, a viable movement had already begun by mid-May. On May 11 the Bergen *Record* noted that businessmen and bankers of Bergen County were particularly active supporters. In Hackensack there was a "New Jersey Committee for Wendell Willkie." A mass meeting was held on the evening of Monday, May 20, the night before Jersey voters would cast primary ballots to select delegates to the conventions. For the Republicans, only Dewey's name was listed. But within the week or ten days prior to holding the elections, Willkie clubs had already appeared in a large number of New Jersey towns, and others were being born every day. George Dwight, a Manhattan insurance broker and president of the Rumson Republican Club, as well as a Willkie club founder in his town, declared that their immediate aim was to give Willkie a large write-in vote to challenge the presence of Dewey as the only Republican on the ballot. "Dewey is not as popular with businessmen and farmers as many appear to believe," said Dwight. "If our plans go right, Willkie will poll a large-sized write-in vote." Others also joined in the drive. A prominent New Brunswick attorney announced that "anyone interested" in Willkie could pick up petitions from his office in the National Bank Building.

In Baltimore, Kirk Landon not only organized the Maryland chapter of the Willkie-for-President Committee but was also instrumental in establishing additional clubs in Charlotte, Greensboro and Winston-Salem, all in North Carolina.

Pennsylvania was organized by William H. Harman, the vice president in charge of sales for the Baldwin Locomotive Works of Philadelphia. Harman, having received on Thursday, May 9, the suggestion that he enlist in the cause, then moved with incredible speed. The next day he rushed to New York to consult with Root, and after agreeing to undertake the effort in Pennsylvania, Harman went to work on Saturday to round up an organization and secure a headquarters. On Monday, offices were rented on the seventh floor of the Land Title Building in Philadelphia. Forty letters were sent out inviting Philadelphians to serve on the committee. By Wednesday, May 15, the office was officially opened for business. Harman had already written to friends throughout Pennsylvania to find people who could open additional Willkie clubs. Furthermore, he asked Root to suggest key contacts in other areas.

Others showed similar enthusiasm. A New York exporter who lived in Camden, Maine, read the newspaper story about the young lawyer's activity and requested an opportunity to collect signatures. He wrote that "After I return to Maine I would be very happy indeed to undertake there the continuance of this work, at my own expense." Within the next two weeks he sent two hundred declarations to others as far south as Texas and as far west as Chicago. Even before his return to Maine he had written to three friends in that state to pave the way for a Willkie drive up there. When he reached his home town on May 2 he took personal charge of the incipient movement. By the middle of the month, Maine had a Knox County Willkie-for-President club.

Throughout New England others were forming similar drives. Phillips Ketchum, a prominent Boston attorney, joined with his wife to circulate declarations in Massachusetts. On May 16 he opened two offices in the city. Ketchum enquired about Willkie's labor record, and Root wrote back: "I don't know much about Mr. Willkie's labor record and think, as you suggest, that he probably has not got one. He did tell me that there has never been a strike in any company with which he has been connected." In Hartford, Connecticut, another group, composed mainly of insurance men, lawyers and representatives of other businesses, formed the nucleus of a boom in that state. By the middle of May committees were working for Willkie in 129 Connecticut towns, and the headquarters in the capital city had received more than one thousand signatures from Hartford alone.

Such early activity was greatest in the Northeast, but this emphasis should not overlook the enthusiasm that was being shown throughout the country. For example, a woman in Shepherdstown, West Virginia, a little town just across the Potomac from Antietam, resourcefully obtained the use of a window in an unoccupied store on the community's main street. There, in a space about twice the size of a daily newspaper, she posted on the window the headlines about Willkie and then embellished the display with favorable cartoons. She kept her postings up to date daily, thereby adding to the attraction. Local citizens of Independence, Kansas, met on May 15 to organize for the first time in Alf Landon's state. Petitions began to appear in Elwood, Willkie's home town. The Elwood Industrial Bureau distributed them to the local drugstore, the offices of the Elwood *Call-Leader,* the town's municipal building and other places of business for the convenience of those wishing to add their signatures. One of Root's Princeton classmates headed a group in Missouri that began mailing out the declarations with instructions that each recipient of a blank petition was to get fourteen other signatures. Substantial interest was also shown in the South, where conservative Democrats opposed to the New Deal began to participate in the Willkie movement. Within three weeks after Root had first sent out the declarations, Pandick Press received orders for seventy thousand additional copies, others were being printed in Massachusetts and Iowa, and from forty-two states had come unsolicited contributions of fourteen hundred dollars.

Some people, like Tom Dewey, attributed Willkie's following to the "station-wagon crowd." Others called them the "country-club set" and saw the drive as a conspiracy by advertising and other business interests. Strictly defined, however, a "conspiracy" would have involved an organized movement, whereas the only real organization,

as skillful as that one was, came from the small group of amateurs
and pros like Davenport, Pryor, Gallagher, Root, MacVeagh and
others. But a glance at the composition of the various Willkie clubs,
in all parts of the country, leaves no doubt about what kind of people
responded to the overtures that were being extended. A typical club
was led by a community's bankers, financiers, lawyers, real-estate
people, insurance interests and owners of a multitude of small businesses. Added to their ranks were many who, in the era of Theodore
Roosevelt or Woodrow Wilson, would have been called "progres-
sives," for they were the doctors, newspaper publishers and other
crusaders against what they regarded as limitations on personal freedom. Only this time their scorn was directed toward big government
rather than big business. They felt that FDR had to be replaced
before a third term would enable him to accumulate still more power
and defy additional traditions. They were joined by many white-collar
workers and schoolteachers, people traditionally hostile to bigness of
any kind. Those in small towns responded with the most enthusiasm.
To them, Willkie was a man concerned with maintaining their vision
of democracy not only at home but abroad. They were, to a large
degree, members of the "country-club set." They were the affluent,
the college-educated, and came from families that were prominent in
the world of business or the professions who regarded America as a
business society that should remain that way. They were, for the most
part, conservative but not reactionary. For them, Democrats were a
collection of alien minorities, corrupt city bosses and dangerously
militant labor.

Perhaps it was not so coincidental, but 1940 was also the year when
a special survey made by Dr. Gallup showed that, after a decade-long
loss of confidence, Americans were beginning to have more respect
for businessmen.

The fact that Willkie was the president of a great utility holding
corporation that had offices in New York's financial center made it
easy for people to attribute his momentum to support from big business. But there was no real reason why vested interests should have
been more attracted to him than to the other Republican candidates.
As far as commercial interests were concerned, the records of Taft,
Dewey and Vandenberg were satisfactory. Not only were they tested
politicians with conservative domestic views, but they had never been
Democrats nor had they ever spoken so eloquently about the abuses

of business and about the need for reforms. Furthermore, business-men usually find it more expedient to press their cause through politi-cians rather than through one of their own, who might possibly have to try too hard to convince voters of impartiality.

On May 21, just as the Willkie drive was gaining major attention, a midwestern industrialist with vast international connections conveyed his fears to James V. Forrestal, then a banker with the New York firm of Dillon, Read & Company. "The greatest menace to the utility industry," wrote the industrialist, "lies in the current campaign of Wendell L. Willkie for the Republican presidential nomination." He accused Willkie of seeking publicity in a manner that was sure to force politicians to act to stifle utilities and wrote that the continua-tion of such a campaign would eventually lead to government owner-ship of all power companies. "His indiscreet speeches are not only made solely in the interests of his political ambitions," the industrial-ist wrote in a confidential letter to Forrestal, "but they completely overlook the fundamental fact that the utilities must sell their prod-ucts to Democrats and Republicans, conservatives and radicals alike." Eight days later he informed Forrestal that Willkie's aggres-sive campaign must be due to bad advice. "In these times, the head of a utility holding company ought to be as unobtrusive as possible."

Whether or not businessmen thought Willkie would aid their inter-ests, Willkie had great popular appeal. He came along with a fresh apolitical image at a time when the public was weary of politicians, when so much had been written and said about corrupt big-city bosses like Frank Hague and Ed Kelly and Pat Nash, and when politicians were turning the world over with multiplying alphabet agencies in Washington and with territorial conquests, violations of basic freedoms and pusillanimous deals in Europe. There was little doubt that Wendell Willkie, for one, was presenting his views in an honest and open manner, that he believed all he said and, moreover, that a lot of his points were long overdue. He was particularly attrac-tive to those Americans disillusioned by both Munich and the efficacy of the New Deal.

Willkie's appeal had a more subtle basis. The frustrations of fight-ing out of a decade of depression only to be endangered by the renewal of world war had convinced Americans to look on as mere observers; but extending aid to England without becoming one of the belligerent nations could satisfy a moral dilemma, and a candidate like Willkie attracted followers simply because he was not a politician. Those disturbed by the New Deal were precisely the same people who could best identify with Willkie as a fighter for liberty and property. Joining him was to participate in a modern crusade against corrupt politicians, who were the leaders of city machines, and such other evils as "big government" and a Chief Executive with an "alien" desire for power, particularly if he were to disregard American tradition by running for a third term. Within less than a decade people had sought solutions by turning to Franklin D. Roosevelt, Huey Long, Dr. Frances Townsend and Father Charles Coughlin. The newest crusade was now forming behind Wendell Willkie, who was inspiring different Americans to combat thèir frustrations by taking political action.

There was, for example, the wife of a roadhouse proprietor in Montana who had relieved the boredom of her husband's business by engaging, for the first time in her life, in political activity. She had become the executive secretary of the local Willkie club. That meant her name appeared on the club's letterhead to the right of a photograph of her hero. "I had little thought," she wrote to him, "that my name would appear in official capacity right beside your photo." But she was distressed because her husband had complained that her partisan activity was embarrassing him with some customers and he was insisting that his wife give it all up. "I believe in the cause," she lamented in a pathetic letter to Willkie, "and find that to give up now" would be "taking away what little joy I have found in a long time."

And, during those weeks in May, enough was happening to convince hundreds and thousands that what they were doing was not an ordinary diversion from dull rural existence and was, in fact, more valuable than any routine civic responsibility, more important than any selfish pride in being associated with a worthy and patriotic cause. Hundreds of newspaper editorials noted the growing phenomenon of the Willkie crusade. "Here is a first-class effort at direct democracy," said the Bridgeport (Connecticut) *Telegram*. "Nobody can be fooled. Nobody can make a trade, or indulge in the 'fixing' so dear to the politicians. The people, for a miracle, are being given a chance to say what they think." In Montana, the Billings *Morning Gazette* scoffed at columnist Raymond Clapper's statement that Willkie should maintain his independence by not becoming a candidate with the rebuttal that "This yearning for perfection is getting a bit thick." Also, in that same region, the Laramie (Wyoming) *Republican & Boomerang* welcomed a possible Willkie candidacy by declaring: "He expresses most forcefully the viewpoint of the small businessman who has earned every dollar he has. We need a President with that viewpoint!" An important Democratic paper, the Philadelphia *Record,* recognized the prominence of Willkie's drive by saying that "If Willkie is as liberal as he says; if his foreign policy is what he declares it to be; if he likes as much of the New Deal as he says he likes—then Willkie should be out fighting *for* re-election of President Roosevelt as the surest way to his objectives." Then it concluded: "Willkie is simply a smoke-screened Hoover." It took a newspaper from Willkie's home county, the Anderson *Herald,* to really summarize what was happening: "Throughout the nation there is a spontaneous movement growing stronger every day, every hour, every minute. And Willkie isn't doing anything about it, because he can't. He couldn't stop it if he would. This is the people talking and you can't shut them up. So, if there is a deadlock in the convention, it is an even bet that the man on the inside of the track running like greased lightning will be none other than Wendell Willkie of Elwood, Madison County, Indiana and the nation." On May 13 a liberal periodical, *The Nation,* commented: "The Wendell Willkie talk has lost its virgin archness and become hopefully serious."

When the Gallup poll's latest findings were issued on May 8, Willkie's name appeared for the first time. He commanded the preference of 3 percent of Republican voters. Not much of a dent, particularly since Dewey's post-primary surge had sent his figure up to 67 from a March rating of 53. But it was good enough to place fourth, behind Vandenberg and Taft. A difficult climb remained and there was little time left. But Willkie was getting more attention than ever and accepting every speaking engagement he could handle.

6

It was on May 11 that Willkie made his first speech before a group of Republican regulars. The primary victories for Dewey and the support for Taft and Vandenberg had lent credence to the notion that the Midwest was isolationist. Certainly, that section of the country, the heartland of America, with its lingering Anglophobia stemming from the fight for "free silver" during the last decade of the nineteenth century and the concurrent distrust of everything Wall Street embraced, was the most anti-war region. Influential throughout a large portion of the area was Colonel Robert McCormick and his Chicago *Tribune,* which had opposed American participation in collective-security arrangements since the days of Wilson's fight for the League of Nations. In November 1939 midwestern representatives had been the only Congressmen from any region to cast a majority of their votes in favor of keeping the arms embargo. Even the catastrophes of mid-May 1940 moved the Midwest less than any other part of the country. Its large German-American population could hardly become enthusiastic about going to war to help England defeat the homeland. And this was the area that Willkie entered right after Hitler had invaded Holland and Belgium.

His trip had had its beginnings on the night of April 25, when he addressed the newspaper publishers in New York. After that Waldorf speech, the Cowles brothers offered to help arrange for appearances in Iowa and Minnesota, where their newspapers were located. They also pointed out that the members of the Republican state committee were planning to meet in St. Paul on May 11 to commemorate the anniversary of Minnesota's admission to the Union. That would give Willkie an opportunity to face his first audience of party regulars. "You have nothing to lose," they pointed out, "and you might catch on in a big way."

Willkie agreed. The Midwest had to be won. In fact, he scheduled two other major speeches for the week of the Cowles-arranged appearance that was slated for St. Paul and managed to do some politicking before going on to the Minnesota city. To reporters he said that his mission was to sell his belief that the United States must give substantial aid to those fighting against Hitler and pointed to the latest news from the Lowlands to support his stand. The newspapermen did not need much perception to know that they were looking at a genuine candidate, one who eagerly posed for press photographers, especially when Willkie said that, while he would not make a direct campaign for delegates, he would be happy if somehow all this activity should lead to his nomination.

At St. Paul his speech was only a partial success. All the ingredients for publicity were there. The Cowles brothers had purchased air time over a national CBS hookup and had, in addition, secured the services of Governor Harold Stassen, the designated keynoter for the coming convention, to introduce the visitor. Their coup could best be appreciated by Willkie when he suspected that the "boy governor" was somewhat uneasy about being linked with a Wall Street magnate. For the radio audience, Willkie read from his script and, as he did, realized how lifeless his presentation sounded. He again condemned the New Deal's excesses, again calling for aid to the democracies, praised the attempt to legislate a ceiling on campaign contributions that Congress was considering as an extension of the Hatch Act of 1939, and supported reciprocal tariffs. But the speech, as Willkie well knew, was a dud. A prepared script always inhibited his naturally flamboyant style. As soon as the prepared portion had ended and his thirty minutes of air time had expired, he backed away from the microphones and said, "Now I'm off the air and I don't have to use so damn much fine language. What I have been trying to say is, we sure got to get rid of that bunch, and I'll tell you how to do it." Then the real Willkie spoke. "Everytime Mr. Roosevelt damns Hitler and says we ought to help the democracies in every way we can short of war," he said, with all the fervor of a revivalist, "we ought to say: 'Mr. Roosevelt, we double-damn Hitler and we are all for helping the Allies, but what about the sixty billion dollars you've spent and the ten million persons that are still unemployed?'"

The audience loved it. After his forty-five-minute extemporaneous talk, many jumped up and shouted "More! More!"

The Cowles brothers, who had wanted to hear Willkie perform before a group of professional Republicans in the Midwest, were happy. Glowing reports were carried by the press within the next two days about how Wendell Willkie was now right up front as a candidate with the other three leading contenders. One report even said that the Minnesota delegation was considering a plan to split their first-ballot votes four ways. Willkie supporters claimed that the candidate had already obtained voluntary pledges of delegate votes on early ballots from at least eight states. When he spoke at Indianapolis and Des Moines during the following week, his audiences were equally responsive. Becoming increasingly confident, Willkie said to John Cowles: "I want to lick the Champ."

7

During the first half of May, events continued to move quickly. Davenport announced that he was leaving his job at *Fortune* to give full time to the crusade. Oren Root expanded his one-man committee by adding twenty-five others to circulate the petitions and guide the setting up of clubs. Tom Dewey, still cultivating the West, warned Kansans against "social slavery," and then returned to New York with the message that the country was "absolutely determined to keep out of war." Norman Thomas, the Socialist party candidate, preached relentlessly against foreign commitments. In Great Britain, the diplomacy of expediency had collapsed as Winston Churchill replaced Neville Chamberlain as Prime Minister. Publisher Henry Luce, who was in Europe, wired one of his editors on May 12:

The remarks of Roosevelt and the Pope sound wonderful here. I am practically prepared to become a Catholic and a third termer unless the opposition offers some small degree of competition. Unless the others move awful fast, it looks like Davenport's man is the only Republican who can get this home-coming vote. . . .

Regardless of all else, the United States is indulging in complete and criminal folly unless it proceeds at once to build every single military airplane it can possibly make in the next six months. Never mind who uses them, never mind who pays, but for God's sake, make them. . . .

If *Life* and *Time* fail to sell this idea now, it probably won't matter much what these estimable publications say in years to come. The Germans have one weapon greater than all their army and that is the blindness and stultification of those in every country who are too fat to fight.

"Davenport's man" was doing very nicely. Oren Root, addressing a meeting so large that it had to gather in a church across the street from his "hole in the wall" headquarters, said that clubs had formed all over the country. And Davenport revealed that he had drafted Robert L. Johnson, president of a magazine syndicate and one of the founders of *Time,* as an assistant.

In Philadelphia, on May 16, the Committee on Arrangements for the Republican convention was in an all-day session at the Bellevue-Stratford Hotel. The committee's task was to provide for most of the details, even for distributing tickets to the public for seats in the galleries. Seventy-year-old Ralph E. Williams, its chairman, had been presiding all day. As the time neared five-thirty, a proposal was passed to keep the session going until seven to complete the pre-convention details. Williams stood as he spoke. His hands clenched the back of a chair. Suddenly, he fell to the floor. Dr. Louis Chodoff was summoned. The doctor, finding that Williams had suffered from a stroke, had him taken to Jefferson Hospital, where he died. The next day the party's national chairman, John D. M. Hamilton, announced that the Committee on Arrangements would be headed by Samuel F. Pryor, Jr., of Greenwich, Connecticut.

CHAPTER FIVE

Closing the Gap

1

THE DAY SAM PRYOR was appointed to head the Committee on Arrangements, Dr. George Gallup's American Institute of Public Opinion reported that polls would have to be more attentive to the "Willkie boom" that had "started almost overnight." A rating of 3 percent just two weeks earlier had advanced to 5. Even though it still left him considerably behind the three leading contenders, the important momentum had shifted to Willkie. He had, in short, become the "dark horse" most people were talking about. The real importance of the contest, however, would be determined by whether the nominee had a realistic chance of winning the election. The mid-term victories of 1938 had been one good omen for Republicans, but what Gallup reported in May 1940 seemed to buoy their hopes even more. The survey said that while the Democrats were getting stronger in ten states, the GOP had gained in the thirty-eight others. And, furthermore, those Democratic gains were in states already lost to Republicans, such as in the South and in border areas.

It was, however, becoming just as clear that Roosevelt's greatest asset was the deteriorating international situation. An opposing candidate could either endorse the Administration view and hope to convince the people that he would provide better leadership or develop an alternate course to sharpen the issue. Willkie, in his St. Paul speech as well as in Des Moines, had continued to stress his support for FDR's attempts to prepare the country for a possible war. At times, as in Brooklyn on June 18, Willkie's emphasis on the need to stay out of war reflected public opinion with accuracy but seemed to reconcile his views with the Republican isolationists. His statement that "No man has the right to use the great powers of the Presidency to lead the people, indirectly, into war" lent itself to terse and sometimes sensational headlines, such as "MUST AVOID WAR, WILLKIE DECLARES." But for those following his words with care, Willkie's theme was clear: Encouragement of private investments and less harassment by the government would contribute to the kind of productivity that would ensure peace through stronger defenses. In Des Moines he told a Shrine Auditorium audience that "Airplanes as well as all other equipment are produced only by skilled men in adequately financed industries." It was a direct response to the President's request of May 16 for the production of fifty thousand airplanes, a position Willkie called "theoretically correct." Referring to the prewar difficulties of Leon Blum's Popular Front government in France, the Hoosier emphasized the need for a strong, unfettered economy. Merely issuing a "wishful declaration" for more planes was inadequate, he said. In one stroke he appealed to both the New Deal's opponents and to the growing numbers who agreed with the President's view of the international situation.

Even isolationist complacency was jarred by Hitler's rapid blitz of the Lowlands. In Kansas, while Taft was telling a Topeka audience that the country should concentrate on domestic issues to prevent the New Deal from using the international crisis to extend its powers at home, Republican leaders were almost united in noting the rising concern about the European war. Sympathy for the Allies was mounting daily. Writing from Chicago, a *New York Times* correspondent noted that audience reactions to Willkie's speeches seemed to indicate that the so-called "isolation belt" of the Midwest had changed its traditional viewpoint since the German invasion. The Cincinnati *Times-Star* said that the Ohio delegation would almost certainly be influenced by the latest developments. For the first time, Gallup reported that most Americans believed that the United States would eventually enter the war, but that did not mean they were ready to do so voluntarily.

That the fighting could not be ignored had become clear. The difference between Willkie's position and that held by moderate isolationists was over whether the United States should extend direct aid to Europe's falling democracies, which carried the risk of actual involvement, or merely to concentrate on building defenses at home. Thus, on May 17, Dewey said in New York that a national defense board should be established and that the "defense requirements of the nation should be completely removed from politics." His point was in basic accord with the President's request for a preparedness program of more than one billion dollars, which still looked like a lot of money in 1940. But instead of calling for increased aid to the Allies, Dewey was careful to say only that existing orders should be filled. The next day Taft told a St. Louis rally that the nation should "stop playing with the idea that we may enter the war and devote ourselves to a genuine program of defense." At Warrensburg, Missouri, Alf Landon also endorsed the President's call and even termed the address "splendid."

In contrast was the minority who refused to believe that the Nazis were the real villains. Representative Hamilton Fish of New York, who was in line to become chairman of the House Committee on Foreign Affairs in a Republican-controlled lower chamber, warned that Roosevelt had become Churchill's willing accomplice in leading his nation to war against Germany to make the world safe for international communism. He denied being an isolationist, saying he was actually a non-interventionist who wanted negotiated settlements of disputes rather than American involvement in foreign wars. In August 1939 Fish had conferred with German Foreign Minister Joachim Von Ribbentrop at the latter's hilltop villa near Salzburg, and then, as one of the twenty-eight delegates to the Interparliamentary Union Congress that met at Oslo, Norway, the next day, he appealed for a thirty-day moratorium resolution for the peaceful settlement of the Danzig issue, which Ribbentrop had told Fish would provoke Germany to fight. But the vast majority of the delegates spurned Fish's appeal, and the Congressman was left with the belief that FDR had sabotaged the proposed moratorium. Every effort made by the President to prepare for a possible war or to help England was regarded by the man from New York's Dutchess County, FDR's home district, as another move to involve the United States in an unnecessary and unwise war with Nazi Germany. Irish-Americans, despite their loathing of Hitler, retained their antipathy to getting into a war on the side of England, and many people of German extraction found it hard to believe that the war was all Hitler's fault. Thousands belonging to the German-American Conference of Greater New York held a great festival, on the day Lindbergh spoke, to celebrate Hitler's victories. At a park in North Bergen, New Jersey, they sang, danced, drank beer, took target practice at a shooting gallery and admired a plaque of *der Führer* that was illuminated by two large candles.

But in a different place in New Jersey another German-American, Wendell Willkie, told a crowd the next day of the importance of coordinating national resources to strengthen defenses. Five hundred attended the luncheon meeting at the Raritan Valley Farms, near Somerville, which was sponsored by former Senator Joseph S. Frelinghuysen. Willkie spoke extemporaneously and the crowd was enthusiastic. One day later, on May 21, New Jersey Republicans voted in their primary elections.

Dewey was the only regular candidate on the ballot. The write-in-vote movement for Willkie was less than one week old. The result, then, was a tremendous psychological boost as well as a credit to the efforts of those working under people like Donald J. Smith. While Dewey received a not unexpected 256,659 votes, another 18,792 Republicans bothered to write in Willkie's name.

By the third week of May, Dr. Gallup could only confirm the obvious: The Willkie boom, already a political phenomenon, was spreading. Some people, such as newspaper columnist Dorothy Thompson, even suggested the possibility of presenting a bipartisan front by urging the two major parties to offer a joint ticket in November: FDR for President and Wendell Willkie for Vice President. That, they reasoned, would be perfect proof of America's regard for the European democracies.

FDR was not too busy to note Miss Thompson's suggestion. To his friend, New York attorney Morris L. Ernst, he wrote on May 18: "Do try to get this silly business of Wendell Willkie out of her head."

2

Hoosiers seem to have the loyalty and state pride often associated with Texans. Indiana had not contributed a President since Benjamin Harrison, and so Willkie's home state began to awaken to the new possibility. In Elwood a big torchlight parade was planned for the evening of May 20. Posters advertised both the town's good fortune and its most famous native son. Arthur E. Harrel, the leader of the local Willkie-for-President club, expressed the common sentiment when he said, "We confidently expect this to be the beginning of a triumphant parade to Washington." Over a prearranged wire that night, after his return from the day at Raritan Farms, Willkie used a telephone in his Fifth Avenue apartment to address the Elwood rally. Novice that he was, Willkie readily understood that it was much better for a presidential candidate to be identified with the little Indiana town than with Wall Street. Actually, by this time, Willkie's private property consisted of five large working farms that he had bought on the advice of accountants as the soundest protection for his investments against the fluctuations of the economy, and all were located in the area of his wife's town of Rushville. But except for a few who complained that Willkie had deserted them, Elwood did not care. They were glad to help him perpetuate his identity as a Hoosier.

Some of Willkie's old Beta Theta Pi fraternity brothers, having given up on Paul McNutt, were eager to mobilize support. Harry M. Shackelford, who had roomed in the fraternity house with Willkie and was now advertising manager of the Johns-Manville Corporation, was one of the former Democrats who felt that the New Deal was out of tune with Jeffersonian principles. In early May, "Shack" phoned Willkie and asked if his old friends could support him. The offer was promptly accepted. Then, at a Wall Street luncheon, plans were made to give him national exposure that would reinforce his identity with mid-America. And it had to be done with the limited financing that his friends could provide.

One thing they did not want was a plush affair at the Waldorf-Astoria. Instead, they turned to the Manhattan Center, a hall that was frequently used for labor rallies. For the night of May 21 they planned a Hoosier box supper. Little cardboard red schoolhouses, each filled with an apple, a piece of chicken, a dill pickle and potato salad, were available at the hall for one dollar. Using his advertising connections, "Shack" sold the Columbia Broadcasting System's public-affairs department the idea of broadcasting a Willkie speech from Manhattan Center free as a newsworthy event rather than as a costly political commercial. CBS then offered thirty minutes of free time on a 132-station national hookup.

Willkie, however, was reluctant to speak for that long. All he knew, he explained, could be delivered in fifteen minutes. The candidate, a devotee of the printed word, did not seem to understand the potential power of the electronic media. So, to ensure against disaster, a prominent baritone named Edward Nell was obtained to stand in the wings ready to sing if Willkie failed to use his allotted time or faltered along the way. In addition, to aid the effort to dilute Willkie's Wall Street image, Dr. William Howe, who had taught English to the candidate at Indiana University, was persuaded that it was his patriotic duty to help prepare the speech and to introduce Willkie in an unpresumptuous, folksy manner, with his arm around the candidate's shoulder.

Four thousand admirers, mostly natives of his home state, filled the Center. So many thronged into the huge ballroom that Lucy Shackelford, Harry's wife, had to delay the fire department from barring the doors to additional visitors so that at least a major portion of the speech could be completed without any disturbances. Professor Howe followed his instructions perfectly, put his arm around Willkie and recalled Indiana school days. Then the candidate spoke about the consequences of a German victory. Rather than exhausting his message before the half hour had ended, Willkie ran out of time. Nell never got a chance to sing. The entire affair, with its national exposure, had cost the old fraternity brothers only three hundred dollars.

A dispatch from Indianapolis that same day suggested the possibility that Indiana might adopt Willkie at the last minute as its "favorite son," particularly if there seemed to be no obvious convention winner by the time its delegates got to Philadelphia. Also that day *Look* magazine came out with a Willkie article that urged FDR to run again as a means of providing a clear-cut test on the issue of the New Deal and its philosophy of government intervention.

Other Hoosiers, however, those more traditionally Republican, remained unconvinced. Willkie's political conversion had been too recent. Former Senator James E. Watson, when approached by Willkie, refused to extend his support and said, "No, Wendell, you're not my type of Republican."

"I admit I used to be a Democrat," said Willkie.

"Yes, Wendell," Watson explained. "If a whore truly repented and wanted to join my church, I'd welcome her. I would greet her personally and lead her up the aisle to a front pew, but I'd be damned if I'd ask her to lead the choir the first night."

3

As the titular leader of the party, Alfred M. Landon's opposition could be a formidable obstacle for Willkie. As one of the more liberal and international-minded Republicans, Landon could be a very valuable addition to the Willkie drive. Landon's own position during the past year had been one of coolness toward all the leading candidates. He had even contemplated supporting Joe Martin as a move to prevent any one man from cornering a majority of the delegates and thus committing the party even before the convention. He had had this in mind when he secured the minority leader, Mr. Martin, as the chief speaker at the 1940 Kansas Day celebration. By the end of March, Landon's calculations showed enough delegates behind his thinking to keep the convention from being blocked and taken over by conservative and isolationist Republicans. Of late, however, he had begun to accept the idea that, despite his faults, it would be best to go along with the man who had won such impressive primary victories, Tom Dewey, as the most reasonable candidate; but he continued to hope for someone better and withheld a direct endorsement for the DA. At the same time, Landon regarded Willkie as inexperienced and too close to eastern business interests, whose support for the utilities magnate was perhaps too ardent for comfort.

After Landon's meeting with FDR on May 22 he joined Herbert Hoover in New York. Then, telling reporters he might also see Willkie, he went to Greenwich on the afternoon of May 24 to spend the night at Arthur Calvert Smith's home. Smith, a neighbor of Sam Pryor, had worked for Landon during the 1936 campaign as a speechwriter and was also a good friend of the Kansan. Pryor had asked Smith to arrange a Landon-Willkie meeting for the morning of May 25.

Willkie had just returned from more midwestern appearances. At Kansas City he had warned that a strong military posture was impossible without a viable industrial base and cautioned that the Republicans would become "America's first fifth column" if they endorsed coalition rule and dropped opposition to the New Deal, a point of view which drew a great volley of cheers from the members of the National Republican Club. Then he went on to Greenwich for the meeting with Landon.

It was their first get-together. Pryor's hope had been at least to "neutralize" Landon so that the party's titular leader would not be one of Willkie's active opponents. Just two weeks earlier Landon had scoffed at the grass-roots agitation for Willkie as "simply absurd" and had objected to nominating an amateur and refugee from the other party. But, as Landon listened to Willkie, he was not untouched by the man's ability to charm and persuade. After all, Landon's own campaign had accepted many basic New Deal premises. Landon did not forget about Dewey that day; he was yet to be convinced that Willkie was a serious contender. But he left Greenwich realizing that it was not outlandish to think of the Hoosier as an alternative. Sam Pryor had done his job.

Three days later the Greenwich *Time* said that it was possible that Connecticut's sixteen delegates to the convention would all vote for Willkie on the first ballot—"if," the paper cautioned, "the 'dark horse' shows the necessary strength."

4

The fortunes of the leading Republican aspirants were clearly tied to the public's willingness to recognize the need for a firm stand on the war situation, and only Willkie took the initiative. Vandenberg's isolationism had become less appealing and, at the start of the critical convention month of June, he appeared to be going nowhere. Dewey's people, keenly aware of their candidate's vulnerability to charges of inexperience in foreign affairs as the international situation worsened, tried to keep their man from slipping from the peak he had reached in early spring. Their headquarters claimed that a poll by Emil Hurja, formerly a statistician for the Democratic National

Committee, showed that the DA's national percentage was at 66.3, ranging from 52.9 along the interventionist Eastern Seaboard to 79.6 in the Rocky Mountain states. Dewey clubs were also claimed for twenty-two states. At the same time, Taft was the clear favorite of the Old Guard regulars, and his strategy was to stand as the man around whom the anti-interventionists could rally.

Some party leaders did appraise the Senator from Ohio of the changing public attitude toward Europe. In St. Louis, Republicans from eight states warned of spreading sentiment throughout the Midwest for aid to the Allies. Landon also cautioned him to soft-peddle isolationism. Taft, however, expressed his own convictions and stressed the need to maintain strict United States neutrality; and, on a swing through Tennessee, Georgia and Alabama, he charged the Administration with having failed to prepare the country for an attack. When FDR was asked whom the Republicans were most likely to nominate, he replied that it would be Taft. Even he was underestimating the increased willingness of the American people to do something about Hitler's rampage.

But west of the Mississippi, Willkie, too, was more cautious. In St. Louis, he told Missouri's convention delegation that although he wanted to be President, "I don't intend to compromise any of my views." Nevertheless, his major speech from that city on the night of June 6 only quoted Churchill's "blood, sweat and tears" but failed to call for direct American aid. He spoke, instead, the language of those businessmen who wanted an unshackled economy to improve the nation's preparedness. At Lincoln, Nebraska, the next day, a Chamber of Commerce audience heard him proclaim proudly at the outset his business affiliation. "I'm in business and proud of it," he said. "Nobody can make me soft-pedal any fact in my business career. After all, business is our way of life, our achievement, our glory." He observed that Hitler's conquest of Europe had confronted the nation with a serious challenge. Yet, instead of calling for a military response, he advised "competence and efficiency" and left no doubt that such goals could be obtained only by giving business a freer hand.

5

By mid-June, little over one week before the convention, the Gallup poll placed Willkie in second place with 17 percent. Dewey, although still ahead, was off sharply. "This is one of the most remarkable phenomena that I have ever seen in American politics," wrote Harold Ickes. Raymond Clapper's newspaper column noted that "The lack of enthusiasm over the regular candidates—Dewey, Taft and Vandenberg—is astounding." "His sudden transmutation," observed Arthur Krock, "from the dark horse without rider or backer if not an actual convention possibility with a number of good jockeys garbed in his colors and considerable delegate backing, has made Mr. Willkie first-rate news." An item on the editorial page of Mr. Krock's paper considered with amusement the fallacy of continuing to refer to Willkie as a "dark horse." Dark horses, it pointed out, are supposed to come from nowhere and take the convention by surprise. Willkie is being taken too seriously to have a legitimate claim to the category, said the article, and, besides, the Republican party had many others who better fitted that description. Administration leaders, at the same time, were paying Willkie the compliment of fearing his nomination.

On June 12 the Willkie drive was able to announce another boost. Present with the utility man in the national capital that day at a meeting of the Washington Press Club was Representative Charles Halleck of Indiana. Halleck, too, had graduated from Indiana University and, also like Willkie, had been a member of Beta Theta Pi. His support would not only indicate some Congressional strength for Willkie but would be significant as an important "favorite son" endorsement from his home state and go a long way toward minimizing the Wall Street label. Halleck, however, was at the early stage of his own career and, understandably, feared that such a move would jeopardize his standing with the party regulars. But National Chairman John D. M. Hamilton, although necessarily neutral in public, had already decided that Willkie would be the party's best candidate; and so Hamilton had worked behind the scenes with New York investment banker Frank Altschul to convince Halleck to take an important step. As Willkie walked to the head table, from which he would address the newspapermen, Halleck stopped him and said:

"Wendell, there's a story out about you running and my nominating you. I just want you to know as you walk in there that if you're ready to go I'm ready to go."

Then, while delivering his off-the-record speech, Willkie paused and said: "Now, this is on the record. I'm going to be a candidate for President and I shall be put in nomination by my fellow Hoosier, Charles Halleck of Indiana." He also revealed that Representative Bruce Barton of New York would deliver one of his seconding speeches.

The Barton support was significant. Barton was from the "Silk Stocking District" of Manhattan, Kenneth Simpson's county. Simpson, already committed to Frank Gannett on the first ballot, was on the same day being replaced as a national committeeman by Dewey's campaign manager, J. Russel Sprague. A vigorous drive by Dewey to purge Simpson, which had already succeeded in electing Edwin F. Jaeckle as the New York state chairman of the party, was concluded at a meeting at Albany's Hotel Ten Eyck. The fifty-five to thirty-seven vote against Simpson gave Dewey control of his state's delegation but, at the same time, created deep bitterness among those New Yorkers loyal to Simpson. The Simpson ouster also antagonized upstaters such as Syracuse Mayor Rolland B. Marvin, who was supposed to go to the convention ready to support Gannett. Dewey had hoped that the Gannett delegates would be released to him after one or two ballots. In addition to Barton, Walter Mack, Jr., president of the Pepsi-Cola Company, was another Manhattan delegate for Willkie. Therefore, as Dewey tried to tighten his grip on the state's delegation, the forces behind Gannett and Simpson were preparing to counterattack at Philadelphia. Dewey's ambition had become self-destructive.

In Illinois, too, an effort was made to stop Dewey. The state's delegation was for the DA because he had, after all, won the primary there when he had run unopposed. But their support was unenthusiastic and they refused to be bound to him after the first ballot. Dewey's cousin and manager in the state, Leonard Reid, was forced to admit on June 13 that the New Yorker was being hurt by the worsening European crisis. The anti-Dewey drive was being led by both the Taft and the Willkie forces.

New England was, perhaps, the weakest area for both Dewey and Taft. State after state had rejected their overtures and, instead, planned to name "favorite son" candidates. Connecticut was ready to support Governor Baldwin. Massachusetts was expected to be split between Senator Leverett Saltonstall and Joe Martin, the party's minority leader. Both New Hampshire and Maine leaned toward Senator Styles Bridges. The Republican state convention in Rhode Island remained loyal to its young governor, William Vanderbilt, after beating back a Dewey movement; and Vermont planned to send its delegates to the convention without any precise instructions. Willkie, seeing the fertile area of "favorite sons" and unpledged delegates, left on June 13 for a quick tour of the region.

Early on the morning of the fourteenth he was met at Boston's Old South Station by Willkie volunteers and leading Massachusetts Republicans. As large crowds of commuters stopped to watch, they took him to breakfast at the Statler Hotel. Outside his hotel suite the corridor was filled all day by volunteers, party leaders and delegates. At a private luncheon the ex-dark horse talked to thirty-one of Massachusetts' thirty-four delegates and all the alternates, plus two delegates from Maine. He urged them to consider which man had the best chance of winning in November. At a press conference later that day he was asked whether he would accept the vice-presidential designation, and he responded emphatically "No—absolutely not." Then he said, "I'm not just running for public office. I'm in this presidential contest because a lot of people want a successful businessman in the White House. They like my views on government and want to see me nominated."

That night he spoke to more than eight thousand Massachusetts Republicans. An unofficial poll of the state's delegation, taken after the session, showed that at least twenty-two planned to vote for him on the second ballot, after they had discharged their obligations to either Martin or Senator Saltonstall.

In Pryor's private plane Willkie then flew to Hartford. Heavy rain fell as he spoke to three hundred admirers from the steps of the state capitol. Then he called on Governor Baldwin, and at a luncheon given at the Bond Hotel he met all sixteen Connecticut delegates. He also declared: "If elected President I would like to have both Governor Baldwin and Sam Pryor with me in Washington." By the time Willkie left the state, he was sure of getting all its votes by at least the second ballot.

He ended his New England tour with a speech at a rally in Providence, Rhode Island, where he received the support of Governor Vanderbilt. At least six of the eight Rhode Island votes seemed ready to go for him on the first ballot. After having been a guest of honor at the Governor's estate in Newport, he returned to New York with assurances of being supported by most New England delegates.

6

"He is a new species in politics," wrote William Allen White in an article about Willkie that appeared in the June 17 issue of the *New Republic*. He bothers regular Republicans, said the prime mover of the Committee to Defend America by Aiding the Allies, because he refuses to use their language and "apparently scorns their inner-temple ritual and delights to make a record which knocks galleywest their cat-footed strategy for this campaign." White referred to the tons of pro-Willkie literature that he noted was coming from "Wall Street," thereby accepting the popular oversimplification of the Willkie drive, and decided that "The Willkie creed apparently is that to business belongs the spoils." But, on examining the candidate personally, the Kansan had to admit that he had become one of his admirers. "He calls wah, war, and fahmehs, farmers, and flourishes his flat 'a' with a wallop. He grins easily, but I never heard him give a belly laugh. He chuckles. But don't be fooled by that coy dimple. Don't let that adolescent smile deceive you, for it rhymes with guile and he has got plenty of it. He makes quick and final decisions and does a big day's work in a six-hour day."

The Republican party was startled on June 20 as its leaders were already beginning to gather in Philadelphia. Two prominent members of the GOP, Henry L. Stimson and Frank Knox, had accepted places in FDR's Cabinet. Stimson had been Hoover's Secretary of State and now, at the age of seventy-three, was to head the War Department. Knox, a Chicago newspaper publisher and Landon's running mate in 1936, became Secretary of the Navy. For some time the President had been considering such bipartisan appointments to strengthen the nation's defense efforts. Now, particularly to promote legislation to start the conscription of men under a selective service system, he had made his move. Both men were confirmed internationalists as well as Republicans, but their acceptance of the President's appointment was viewed by many as an act of party treachery. "Having entered the Cabinet," declared John Hamilton, "these men are no longer qualified to speak as Republicans for the Republican organization." He maintained that they could not be loyal to both their party and to the President. Wendell Willkie, at Bay City, Michigan, when the news came, reacted with the simple statement that "Each conscientious individual has to determine such things according to the dictates of his own conscience."

Republican platform writers were thrown into confusion by the new development. The issue, as they saw it, was to what degree they should label the Democrats as warmongers by heralding themselves as the "Peace party." The first reaction to the news about Stimson and Knox led them to consider a strong isolationist position; but it was Alf Landon, who headed the Resolutions Committee's subcommittee on defense and foreign affairs that was assigned to write the foreign-policy plank in the platform, who declared that nothing had happened to affect the party's policy writers.

As the delegates were arriving at Philadelphia, Dr. Gallup issued his latest pre-convention findings. They showed that Willkie was secure in second place with 29 percent and that Dewey, although off five points in little over a week, still led comfortably with 47 percent. Taft and Vandenberg had fallen far back, each with just 8, but former President Hoover had advanced to within two points of the senators. Since March, added Gallup, Willkie's popularity had shown five successive increases, and then he concluded that such "shifts and changes in opinion are a clear indication that GOP sentiment on candidates is far from crystallized. It is significant, too, that, as the war in Europe developed, the number of Republicans who are undecided has grown. Today's undecided vote of 34 percent," he pointed out, "compares with only 26 percent a month ago."

Throughout the nation, supporters flooded the delegates with pro-Willkie petitions and telegrams. Oren Root announced that about four and a half million Americans had already signed such petitions. There was more and more talk of a Dewey and Taft coalition to stop the onrushing Hoosier. While Willkie could claim only about less than one fourth of Dewey's first-ballot strength, there was little doubt about his reserve power, which meant that the failure of anyone else to win on an early ballot could mean a rush to Willkie by released delegates committed to "favorite sons" and by those lukewarm toward Dewey, Taft or Vandenberg.

The Willkie volunteers had conducted an amazingly effective mail campaign. Harold Gallagher, for one, had compiled lists that showed the names and addresses of all delegates and alternates. Some entries included useful background information about each person—which candidates they seemed to favor, their wealth and prominence, etc.—such as the note after the name of a Nebraska man that read, "Banker and stockman. Reputed wealthy. No war record." Information from Indiana reported that, while the national committeeman was for Willkie, he had not contributed to the state's fund, so that he was not so influential as he might be. The Willkie volunteers also sent promotional material to influential persons in various areas. Al Cahlan, publisher of the Las Vegas *Review Journal,* was advised to support Willkie because the others had no chance of winning. "It seems almost a certainty that Willkie is not only going to be nominated, but stands one hell of a chance of being elected," he was told in mid-June. Also, extensive contacts were made with key people in virtually every state. A letter from a friend in Portland, Oregon, advised Gallagher that Senator Charles McNary could play an important role. "No one knows Oregon politics any better, if as well, than does Senator McNary," he was told, "and as you no doubt know, he has his finger upon the political pulse probably as well as anyone in the country. If he is prepared at the proper time to pass the word, I would say that there would be little question that you would get the bulk if not all of the votes of the Oregon delegation." The efforts of Gallagher, the members of the Volunteer Mailing Committee and the national coordination of the Willkie clubs by Oren Root resulted in a carefully planned and detailed approach to the problem of selling Willkie and stimulating and fanning that much of the enthusiasm that was spontaneous. Little was left to chance.

Moreover, Willkie was making himself known and getting vast exposure throughout the country, particularly through several press interviews and a rigorous schedule of speechmaking. In June alone, during the three weeks before his arrival in Philadelphia, he spoke at the following places:

June 6	St. Louis
June 7	Lincoln, Nebraska

June 10   Hamilton, New York
June 12   Washington, D.C.
June 14   Boston
June 15   Providence
June 18   Brooklyn
June 20   Bay City, Michigan

The nation's press also responded. On June 19 he won the support of the Scripps-Howard newspaper chain. Seeing him as the only Republican candidate with a chance to win, their editorials said the nation will listen to him as well as to Roosevelt. On June 20 New York's *PM* proclaimed that the nation's papers were climbing aboard the Willkie bandwagon.

One exception was the New York *Daily News,* which concluded a vehement denunciation of the Willkie boom by saying: "If the Republican leaders think they can elect as President a charming and attractive man who develops, however, from a very smart corporation lawyer to a big shot in the electric power holding company game, who lives at 1010 Fifth Ave., N.Y.C., and who offices at 20 Pine St., N.Y.C., then all we can say is they don't know the Mississippi Valley."

7

Willkie arrived in Philadelphia by train at 2:15 on the afternoon of Saturday, June 22, two days before the convention's scheduled opening. The large crowd that met him at the station included newsmen and Halleck and Davenport.

"Do you have more than the seventy votes on the first ballot as you claimed in Washington?" asked a reporter.

"I'm not one of those fellows who juggle figures," said Willkie. "You'll have to go to the mathematicians for that. All I say is that I've expressed my views on national problems around the country. I've met delegates and I'll meet some more in town."

The Willkie party, after posing for photographers, went by automobile to Broad Street, where he stopped at the Land Title Building to visit the headquarters of Harman's Willkie club.

By the time he emerged from the building, word of his presence had brought crowds into Broad Street. Wearing a straw hat that was slightly tilted to one side, Willkie grinned and waved to the crowd. The reception was exciting and the candidate could do no wrong. People cheered from the windows of the office buildings, even as he passed the sedate and aristocratic Union League Club.

"Will you answer questions?" shouted a man in the crowd.

When Willkie said he would try, the man asked: "Are you a liberal?"

Willkie said that that depended on a definition of the term.

Walter Tooze, chairman of the Oregon delegation and a Taft supporter, wanted to know how he stood on the reciprocal tariff.

"I am for it in principle," Willkie quickly answered. "I believe that after the war the wider and broader the trade area the better."

Tooze, whose state was for more tariff protection, turned away muttering unhappily. Willkie, hearing his reaction, walked through the crowd and placed his hand on the delegate's shoulder.

The surprised delegate looked at Willkie and said, "I want yes or no on the reciprocal tariff."

"Yes, I am for the principle of the reciprocal tariff," Willkie explained. "As a matter of fact, I believe the reciprocal tariff was initiated by President McKinley and carried on by President Taft."

Tooze said that Willkie was mistaken, but some people in the crowd supported the candidate's version of tariff history. Provisions for reciprocity had been included in the high and protectionist McKinley Tariff of 1890. When this was pointed out, Tooze seemed overwhelmed. "I am against you on the tariff, but I like you" was all he could say.

That afternoon Willkie met with a large group of supporters. Then he conferred with Senator David Reed of Pennsylvania. The meeting was important because of the stories that many Keystone State delegates were under pressure to vote for Willkie rather than give their first-ballot support to Governor James, their "favorite son." Only one delegate of the state's seventy-two was ready to commit himself by saying he would vote for Willkie from the start. But, later, the delegation decided to hold a caucus on Monday, one hour before the start of the convention.

Dewey and Taft had also arrived that day, and both were interviewed by the press. Dewey's conference was in the Crystal Room of the Walton Hotel, his headquarters. The place was decorated with

American flags and pictures of the DA and his two sons. Taft, who had driven from Washington in his own car, received the journalists in his headquarters on the mezzanine floor of the Benjamin Franklin Hotel. Both men were emphatic about denying the existence of any deal to stop Willkie; and, like the Hoosier, they were unwilling to accept second place on a ticket with anybody else. While Dewey said his first-ballot strength would net him "upwards of four hundred votes," Taft refused to state any figure. He would only venture to say that his victory would come on the "last ballot." Taft also refused to comment on any of the issues, holding that he would prefer to await the platform as presented by the Resolutions Committee. Dewey, however, advocated aiding the Allies while keeping out of the war. Nevertheless, a few moments later, when he was asked whether he favored selling American warships to aid their cause, Dewey said, "No. We haven't half enough warships as it is." He would agree to sell only the surplus ammunition that may be left from the last war. Both men did agree that the nominations of Stimson and Knox should be confirmed; and Dewey denied that Hamilton or anyone else had actually "read them out" of the party, which was true.

"Do you want to say anything about the Willkie boom?" Dewey was asked.

"I am still lost in admiration for the technical skill with which the job has been done," he replied, skillfully minimizing notions that the surge had resulted from a spontaneous popular uprising.

8

Willkie aide Harold Talbott had an idea. Why not demonstrate Willkie's popularity in a way that would reach every delegate? Oren Root listened to his plan and agreed to send out letters urging what was by then called the Associated Willkie Clubs of America to send their members to Philadelphia so the delegates might be impressed by their numbers. Root also dispatched messages requesting the clubs to bombard the delegates with telegrams and letters. Harold Gallagher used his good American Bar Association connections to phone local members to get out more pro-Willkie telegrams, and Talbott himself solicited similar support from businessmen throughout the country, hoping their employees would be convinced to do the same. Henning

Webb Prentis, Jr., the president of the National Association of Manufacturers, sent letters to political leaders advising them that a Willkie–Dewey ticket would have the best chance of winning. In New Jersey alone, three hundred thousand had signed the petitions. A straw poll conducted by the Los Angeles *Times* reported that Willkie got more votes than all other candidates combined. And William L. White, the son of the Kansas editor, reported the sudden mushrooming craze for Willkie among Republican intellectuals and said they were for him "only because they believe he is on the level. They think he is smart without being clever. . . . he is politically inexperienced enough to say exactly what they are thinking."

Already on Willkie's side, but forced by his position to maintain an official attitude of neutrality, was the party's national chairman, John D. M. Hamilton. Hamilton's first awareness of Willkie's potential strength had come after the Nebraska primary, when he learned that several members of that delegation who had been elected to support Dewey were privately prepared to switch their votes to Willkie on subsequent ballots. When Sam Pryor roomed with Hamilton one night in a Washington hotel, he woke up early the next morning and saw that the national chairman was writing. Pryor asked what he was doing. "Well, you won't believe it, Sam," explained Hamilton, "but I'm writing a nominating speech for Wendell Willkie. I just think that this man is the only man who can beat Roosevelt. I'd like to leave the platform and go down and take my seat as the member of the delegation from Indiana and make the nominating speech."

Several weeks before the convention began, at the New York home of Mr. and Mrs. Ogden Reid, publishers of the New York *Herald Tribune,* both Willkie and Taft were invited to dine. Also present were J. P. Morgan & Company director Thomas W. Lamont, British Ambassador Lord Lothian and Dorothy Thompson. The two candidates were asked how they felt about aiding England. Willkie repeated what he had said so many times before about how America could not stand by idly, while Taft was noncommittal. Their reactions confirmed Willkie's support from the Reids and Lamont.

For all his political inexperience, Willkie realized that his amateur status was a source of popular appeal. He claimed to have spent only about four thousand dollars on his effort to be nominated, and that was mostly for travel expenses for himself, Mrs. Willkie and Fred

Rahter, his secretary; and when reporters at Philadelphia asked for an explanation of his position, he replied:

I have no campaign manager, no campaign fund, no campaign head-quarters. All the headquarters I have are under my hat. I have no ghost writers. I've entered into no deals or understanding with any political leaders or anybody else. If I accidentally am nominated and elected President of the United States, I shall go in completely free of any obligations of any kind.

He was, of course, being coy. He had made it all sound so simple and accidental. One may become President of the United States by accident, but nobody is nominated that way. Yet, while it was clearly good strategy for him to maintain an overt air of haphazardness about it all, to those at Philadelphia his statement contained a good deal that was accurate. Even the hotel accommodations, which were limited because of his late start as a candidate, seemed meager and amateurish when compared to the others. Willkie's did appear to be in his hat. Dewey had seventy-eight rooms in the Hotel Walton. Taft's people had rented one hundred and two rooms in the Benjamin Franklin. Vandenberg had forty-eight rooms, mainly in the Adelphia Hotel. Even Frank Gannett commanded the Harvard Club plus Benjamin Franklin rooms. The party's national committee occupied the entire fifth floor of the Bellevue-Stratford. And the Willkie entourage had only a two-room suite on the sixteenth floor of the Benjamin Franklin, although, with Pryor's help, a two-room suite was obtained at the Warwick for the personal use of Mr. and Mrs. Willkie. There was, in addition, Willkie Club headquarters in the Land Title Building and a store between the Bellevue-Stratford and the Ben Franklin. The inadequacy had not been planned—but it was perfect.

It was nearing midnight that Saturday when Willkie and his wife were leaving their headquarters to return to the Warwick when they met *New York Times* writers Arthur Krock and Turner Catledge. The two men readily accepted Willkie's suggestion that they accompany him to his suite. There they asked Willkie whether he had decided on who would serve as his floor manager. Both Krock and Catledge were then astounded to hear Willkie say that he knew nothing about such a function and had never given any consideration to making such an assignment.

Krock then patiently explained the need to have people serve as liaison with the delegates on and off the floor. Their main function was to win over the future votes of delegates who had fulfilled their previous commitments on earlier ballots and now chose to go elsewhere—largely, of course, because their man could not win. To attract such wavering delegates, Willkie should depend on men of recognized influence within the party. Such floor leaders would work together as a squad under the general direction of the floor manager.

Willkie seemed vague about what Krock was saying. His reply was simply that Charlie Halleck had, after all, been chosen to nominate him and that Bruce Barton of New York would make a seconding speech. But, the two newsmen pointed out, Halleck's responsibilities as a member of the Resolutions Committee that had to draft a platform would keep him from attending to all the requirements of being a floor manager. Furthermore, the task of winning delegates could hardly be left to one man.

After that late-hour session the bewildered Krock decided that Willkie had merely tried to exploit his image as a political novice. Surely one of his many friends and advisers must have corrected such ignorance. Catledge, however, disagreed with his colleague and believed that Willkie's response had been genuine. The subsequent testimony of those closest to the candidate, as well as the events of the next few days, also suggests that Willkie was not feigning naïveté.

Harry Shackelford went to see Halleck at the Congressman's headquarters in a back room of the Hotel Walton. Appalled at the accommodations for the Representative and fraternity brother who was slated to nominate Willkie, "Shack" arranged for space in the hotel's only other available place, a salesroom on the mezzanine floor. At least it was larger. But it was so poorly furnished that when Governor Baldwin of Connecticut came in there weren't enough seats. So the three men—Representative Halleck, Governor Baldwin and "Shack"—held their first convention "conference" in the bathroom. And there, using the toilet as a chair, Governor Baldwin said he was ready to give Willkie all sixteen votes from Connecticut on the first ballot. The assumption was that, in return, Baldwin would be nominated for the Vice Presidency.

Baldwin's position was also made known when, at Sam Pryor's

suggestion, John Hamilton gathered a group of Willkie's supporters at his Bellevue-Stratford suite and met with them throughout the night. Most of the Willkie corps was present, including some new enlistees. Baldwin repeated that his state would become the first to go over to Willkie in its entirety from the start. Mayor Marvin of Syracuse, previously one of the New Yorkers for Gannett, drew a bead on Dewey by declaring his "sincere belief that Wendell L. Willkie is best equipped to be the Republican standard bearer in these critical times" and said he would also vote for him at the outset. Two other upstate New Yorkers also went along with the Mayor. Since some members of New York's big delegation were leaning toward Hoover, Dewey's state was already melting away from the DA. Willkie was also able to finish that night with assurances of some support from every state except Mississippi, South Carolina and Louisiana. And John Hamilton advised the group that Governor Stassen would be ideal as the Willkie floor leader.

But the party's 1936 presidential candidate, Alf Landon, continued to resist the Willkie appeal. The Kansan's direct influence was over his eighteen-vote delegation and it was not certain that he could control the entire number; yet his position did make him an important figure, for the same reasons that had prompted Sam Pryor to set up the Greenwich meeting in May. When Willkie tried, however, to see Landon that Sunday night in Philadelphia, he was able to succeed only with the aid of Arthur Krock. When the two men finally got together, only hours before the convention was scheduled to open, Willkie was quizzed about some of the blitzkrieg tactics being used by his supporters, including the stories about enthusaists with unlimited funds buying delegates and financing a fraudulent campaign of letters and telegrams. Willkie was able to convince Landon about his personal honesty and high purpose but was unable to leave with the former nominee's assurance of support.

When Senator Vandenberg arrived that Sunday, he claimed he would win on the sixth ballot. He also denied reports that he would join with Willkie in return for a Cabinet post or the vice-presidential nomination—rumors that were not entirely without substance. Willkie had approached the Senator at the Carlton Hotel in Washington for his support, but Vandenberg had rejected the overture with the statement that both he and Willkie would be the principals in the final showdown at the convention.

Further breaks for Willkie took place the next day, Monday, June 24. The Baltimore *Sun* reported that the head of the Maryland delegation had said that Dewey could not get his state's unanimous loyalty after the first ballot despite his unopposed primary victory there. An informal poll of the Marylanders showed that most of the delegation had decided to abandon Dewey for Willkie. At the Pennsylvania caucus fourteen members from the western part of the state announced they would switch from Governor Arthur James to Willkie on an early ballot. Governor Ralph Carr of Colorado also revealed his agreement to second Willkie's nomination and to serve as one of his floor managers. The news item immediately inspired speculation about the disposition of his state's twelve votes that had been counted for Dewey.

On that day as well, the Republican party's twenty-second presidential nominating convention began.

CHAPTER SIX

"We Want Willkie!"

1

NOBODY READ THE NEWSPAPERS that Monday morning with more anxiety than Tom Dewey. "FRANCE YIELDS FLEET UNDER ARMISTICE, GIVES UP WEST COAST, HALF OF COUNTRY; BRITAIN AND PETAIN REGIME IN OPEN BREAK," announced *The New York Times*'s banner headlines. Already conscious of the fact that Dewey had reached his high point in public-opinion polls in April, before the most recent tragic events in western Europe, J. Russel Sprague and his organization had the task of trying to prevent the latest developments from destroying their man's chances.

For Sam Pryor, as chairman of the Committee on Arrangements, an overt neutrality was necessary. He was wise enough, however, to realize that exploiting the gravity of the international situation would undermine the Dewey cause and help Willkie. Pryor's idea was to convey the feeling of a cathedral when the delegates entered Conven-

tion Hall, to realize that the whole world was watching how the
United States would react, to understand that they would be choosing
a man who might very well have to lead a nation at war. So carnival-
like accouterments, such as the sale of hot dogs and souvenirs, were
banned from the hall. Even selling food was limited to the restaurant
and cafeteria and removed from the hands of vendors. Unlike any
other convention, this one would be seen as well as heard by a larger
audience than the limited thousands lucky enough to get into Philadelphia's Municipal Auditorium. The National Broadcasting Company assumed the full cost of relaying video pictures to the some fifty
thousand people with sets. A special coaxial cable was supplied by
the Bell Telephone Laboratories to feed the images into the New
York City area. The Republicans could be seen in action on depart-
ment-store sets and by visitors to the RCA exhibit at the World's
Fair. Accordingly, Pryor's committee designed the convention's
schedule to correlate with radio and TV time.

The auditorium itself was a large double-decked indoor stadium
that could seat about seventeen thousand. The rostrum was placed at
the open end of what looked like a huge horseshoe. Before it was a
thousand-pound bronze eagle worth six hundred dollars and decorated with silver stars and evergreens. It stood on a red, white and
blue pedestal. In the front rows sat the delegates, with the closest
seats being allocated to states with the best record for Republican
loyalty, such as Maine and Vermont. The 1936 Republican catastro-
phe had made that determination easy. Each state delegation was
marked by a standard in the shape of a little elephant that carried a
small American flag in its trunk.

As columnist David Lawrence pointed out, the mood of the delegates was to "get Roosevelt," to label the Democrats as the "war
party" and to link the cause of patriotism with non-interventionism.
But even on that issue the range among the Republicans was as great
as among Democrats, with those behind Willkie hoping for an Administration favoring aid for the Allies. The desire to end the New
Deal was their common goal.

Even before National Chairman John D. M. Hamilton rapped the
gavel to open the first session, news came of a last-minute stop-Willkie attempt being directed by a group of forty Representatives and
Senators from the Northwest. Some participants at a meeting had
warned that a utility magnate at the head of the ticket, especially one

associated with Wall Street, would be swamped in their states and, of possibly greater local concern, would simultaneously destroy the chances of other Republican office-seekers. They then issued a statement, with eight signatures, requesting the delegates "to nominate a candidate for President whose personal views will present an opportunity for a clear-cut vote on foreign and domestic issues in harmony with the Republican record in Congress." Willkie was not mentioned by name, but it was obvious the statement was aimed at him.

An open supporter of their position was Senator Charles McNary of Oregon. He had served in Congress longer than anyone else from the Northwest and was popular with farmers, as he had been one of the principal authors of the twice-vetoed McNary–Haugen Farm Plan in the 1920s. He was even highly regarded by labor, which praised him as a "progressive" for having supported many New Deal social and economic reforms. But where Willkie had favored reciprocal trade agreements, McNary represented his region's desire for greater tariff protection. Where Willkie was ready to awaken American responsibilities in international matters, McNary was an isolationist. More significant, however, was their difference on the public-power issue, for McNary had been a leading promoter of the Colorado River power development program and had fathered the Bonneville Dam project, consistent with the Northwest's demand to have the government harness and operate such natural resources. While praising the report of the dissenting Congressmen, McNary claimed that Willkie's drive would collapse as abruptly as it had arisen.

McNary was far from alone in doubting that the Willkie boom could last much longer. Most newspaper columnists were also perplexed, even though Wall Street betting commissioners Baldwin & Company placed even odds on a Willkie victory. The key was the inability of anyone really to control the convention, so it was obviously going to be open and unbossed.

In such a situation no delegate could escape being besieged by those seeking switches to another candidate, and raids on delegations were reported all the time. Tension was high and rumors were plentiful. Senator Vandenberg, resigning himself to the realities of the situation, commented that "Everybody's mad at everybody else around here except me." He, like Willkie, was banking on a deadlock. "The only smoke-filled room this year will be in Chicago, and the smoke will come from one long cigarette holder" was his tart observation.

A Willkie madness was inundating Philadelphia. Everywhere one went, every joke one heard, most of the shouting and cajoling, most of what the press recognized as good copy was about a man who, just over a month earlier, had been hard to regard seriously as a threat to the leading Republican candidates. There were the crowds of Willkie Club people, flooding the city from all over the country, responding to Root's calls to mass their strength before the delegates. It also seemed that just about everybody who couldn't attend wired or wrote. Nobody had ever seen such a deluge of telegrams, letters and petitions. Some one million pro-Willkie requests reached the delegates that week, with New Jersey's group alone receiving about one hundred thousand. It was, said the Willkieites, a spontaneous demonstration by "we, the people" for the delegates to recognize the obvious truth.

Skeptics later questioned the "spontaneity" of the avalanche. In reality, it was about as spontaneous as the proliferation of the Willkie clubs. A large segment of the public was ready to do what was needed to elect Willkie, but the activists were necessary to make their desire significant. Oren Root had shown the way by soliciting the storm of paper; but the same Kirk Landons and Donald Smiths and Bill Harmans, who had not contented themselves with forming just one local club but had spread their salesmanship and created organizations in other centers, now—despite the misgivings of those who feared an adverse reaction from annoyed delegates—regarded telegrams and letters as their most effective last-minute weapons. For example, in Eau Claire, Wisconsin, a Willkie group called "Minute Men for Freedom" sent out radio announcements revealing that form messages that read "To Willkie—For Freedom" were available at telegraph offices in the area. Anyone wishing to sponsor one had only to provide his name and cash for the wire. Throughout most of the rest of America similar efforts were being made. Many messages, therefore, had identical wording. Usually they were initiated by local businessmen, bankers, lawyers, realtors and other influential members of the community. That many of the messages that resulted were spurious cannot be denied. Alf Landon, who diligently hired a staff to acknowledge those that he had received, was later to return to Topeka and discover that eighteen mail sacks of his replies had been returned bearing a postal stamp saying "Address Unknown." Clarence Budington Kelland, a writer of popular fiction and a Willkie worker as well as a Republican national committeeman from Arizona, has left an oral memoir that speaks freely about such deception. But none of this, however, should discredit the legitimacy of the fervor that did contribute to perhaps the most remarkable outburst of popular feeling in all of American history; rather than question the spontaneity of the Willkie movement, the overriding consideration should be whether the public can ever make such feelings known without some kind of organized leadership.

That Willkie had become the favorite of many rank-and-file voters was beyond doubt. His boosters among the Philadelphia street crowds and the contents of the mails and Western Union deliveries showed that, but Dr. Gallup's pollsters also collected some solid evidence that week. Their findings, which were not published until July 7 and were thus unknown to the delegates, were, however, based on a sampling that was taken between Tuesday and Thursday of convention week. The figures showed, in effect, the complete success of Willkie's drive for favor among Republican voters. He had become their first choice, with 44 percent preferring him and only 29 percent still liking Dewey. From less than one percent on March 24, his upward climb had been spectacular.

Although news had come about eventual support from some Pennsylvania delegates, a special caucus of the state's delegation confirmed their plan to cast all seventy-two votes for "favorite son" Arthur James on the first ballot. The state was under the firm, conservative domination of Old Guard oilman Joseph N. Pew. Pew was anything but friendly to a candidate like Willkie; but his overwhelming desire to dump Roosevelt prepared him to accept anybody who looked like a winner.

Less flexible was the Texas delegation. The state's Republicans were as boss-dominated as any big-city Democrats. Their leader was National Committeeman Colonel R. B. Creager, who was unwilling to share his power with anyone else. Facing Texans at the Robert Morris Hotel, Willkie received a warm reception, but Creager remained determined to deliver his twenty-six votes to Taft.

Even at that late hour there continued to be no sign that anybody could dominate the convention. For Dewey, his inability to gain a majority on an early ballot would mean almost certain defeat, and when the convention opened he looked far weaker than he had earlier that spring. There was a growing reluctance to choose him during so grave an international crisis, and the loyalty of Dewey delegates on subsequent ballots was known to be doubtful. More and more, Taft seemed to be the man Willkie would have to beat. Making the outcome even more uncertain were the rumors that former President Hoover had people canvassing delegates for him. Many thought Hoover's big chance would come after his Tuesday-night address to the convention, and they thought it significant that, unlike his departure from Chicago after he had spoken at the 1936 convention, he intended to remain in Philadelphia. Some even regarded the "favorite son" movement in Iowa for Hanford MacNider that was led by Cedar Rapids *Gazette* publisher Verne Marshall as a holding action for the ex-President, who was a native of that state. Whether or not Dewey could actually get four hundred votes at the start of balloting, as he had claimed, he could no longer be regarded as the most likely winner.

2

There were empty seats in the galleries and not all delegates were present that Monday morning when the twenty-second presidential nominating convention of the Republican party came to order. With the news photographers eager to record the official opening and with the delegates still milling around and crowding the aisles, National Chairman John Hamilton struggled to establish order in the huge hall. At 11:17 A.M. he first gaveled to start the proceedings; but ten times he had to repeat his motions as photographers kept demanding reruns. Finally, at seventeen minutes before noon, the first session was ready to begin.

After the invocation the delegates were welcomed to Philadelphia by its Mayor, Robert E. Lamberton, who declared that not since the Republicans nominated Abraham Lincoln, when the nation was about to divide in 1860, had a convention met under more ominous circumstances. "The nation needed the Republican party then," Lamberton reminded them. "The Republican party saved the Union. There are many of us who feel that the nation needs the Republican party even more today, in order that the American system of government may be saved. There is a heavy responsibility resting on your shoulders. You have a great patriotic duty to perform."

The first session was brief. As expected, Governor Stassen was nominated and elected as the Temporary Chairman. The other officers and heads of various committees were chosen and their meeting schedules announced. Then, at 12:33 P.M., little more than an hour after it had begun, the convention was recessed until 4:30, when the Republicans were scheduled to reconvene for an Americanism-patriotism session at Independence Square.

The evening meeting began with an invocation by the Archbishop of Philadelphia. Then Ray Middleton and the Lynn Murray Chorus sang John LaTouche's "Ballad for Americans," with the accompaniment of a thirty-four piece band from the Philadelphia Symphony. It had cost ten thousand dollars to stage the inspiring piece before the convention, and the delegates and guests showed their appreciation with a standing ovation.

The real highlight of the session was Governor Stassen's keynote speech. The "boy governor" was not a particularly inspiring speaker, but it was a highly partisan account that included everything faithful Republicans wanted to hear, such as the call for Americans to "keep burning brightly the light of liberty" and a castigation of big government, demands for protection from subversives "boring from within," and a call for allowing free enterprise to do a more efficient job of bolstering the nation's defenses. Appeasing the isolationists, Stassen argued that our real interests "lie in this hemisphere" and called for appropriate defenses.

The cathedral-like atmosphere evaporated as delegates cheered wildly and stood on chairs waving hats and small American flags. The Temporary Chairman then recessed the convention at 11:26 until eleven the next morning.

3

Joe Martin of North Attleboro, Massachusetts, fifty-six years old and a member of the House of Representatives since 1925, was also the party's minority leader. A thorough party stalwart, Martin could hardly become enthusiastic about the prospects of nominating a renegade Democrat. It was no less difficult for Joe Martin than for many other experienced observers to believe that the president of Commonwealth and Southern was a serious candidate for the nomination.

After all, there was mostly just a flock of amateurs around the man and very little help from any real pros. He didn't even have a floor leader. Martin, himself a favorite-son nominee, had come to Philadelphia ready to await the collapse of the Willkie enthusiasm. When Tuesday's first session was held late that morning, the delegates approved the nomination, by the Committee on Permanent Organization, of Joe Martin as the convention's Permanent Chairman. Then he addressed the delegates on the need to maintain a constitutional republic and the urgency of removing from office the extravagant, free-spending Administration of Franklin D. Roosevelt. That session adjourned at 1:30 P.M.

But that day's real drama was taking place outside the auditorium. In every hotel and eating place of the city, the word was the same: Dewey was slipping. His lead would dissipate rapidly after the first two or three ballots. Reports circulated that the Willkie forces were continuing to puncture whatever loyalty the DA could command on later ballots and that Willkie, although not expected to look strong at first, had increasingly great reserve power that was enough to make him the man to beat. There was renewed talk that Dewey and Taft would have to combine to stop the Hoosier, but Dewey countered such notions with the comment that "The story of negotiations between myself and Senator Taft is a phony, and you can take it from me."

Senator Taft, meanwhile, had begun to emerge as the man most likely to hold what he already had against the overtures from the Willkie forces. Charles P. Taft, his brother, and campaign manager David S. Ingalls even reported gains from midwestern delegations. Their candidate made a late-afternoon visit to the Connecticut delegation, which was the only one ready to go with Willkie from the outset. Taft was hoping that the desire of the professionals to stop Willkie was enough for them to rally around him as their last hope. But many doubted that Taft had the warmth and color to campaign against Franklin D. Roosevelt.

Nobody denied that Willkie did. And the Hoosier was working hard meeting delegates. Visiting those from Indiana, he declared that the utility argument being used against him was invalid because he could not be pictured as an unscrupulous businessman. "If you can find any successful accusation against me," he told them, "I want you to be against me." His sixteenth-story Ben Franklin suite overflowed with a steady stream of delegates as he met with group after group, answered their questions and requested their support.

At the same time, there was growing excitement about another possible candidate: Herbert Hoover. Many were convinced that he now wanted the nomination and that, unlike in 1936, he could have it. After all, FDR had trounced him in 1932, but this was 1940. He was the party's only living ex-President, an elder statesman and, at the age of sixty-six, still ready to carry on his fight against what he regarded as the New Deal's dangerous threat to personal liberties. Furthermore, no one could doubt his Republican loyalties. Even if he did not become a serious candidate, he could still help to influence the final choice. His word would be particularly great precisely because he had made no alliances. By Tuesday afternoon, wrote Mark Sullivan, "there was almost a Macedonian cry to Mr. Hoover" calling on him to provide the wisdom to help decide which candidate would be the best choice under the prevailing conditions. Speculation increased all day that a Hoover boom might be touched off after his speech at the night session. Only the former President and Taft seemed to offer a real possibility of preserving the nomination for a real Republican.

That night, Tuesday, June 25, there was not a vacant seat in Convention Hall. While proceedings were obviously awaiting the nationwide radio hookup time to come at nine-thirty, many delegates were able to exchange visits with members of other delegations. The most recent rumors were swapped. Finally, at twenty minutes after nine, Joe Martin pounded the gavel and called for order. "Delegates will take their seats," he ordered. "The sergeant-at-arms will clear the aisles." Then the entire convention joined in the singing of "God Bless America."

Suddenly the band played "California, Here I Come" and delegates and spectators jumped to their feet as Herbert Hoover walked down the center aisle. John D. M. Hamilton, at the head of the Committee of Escort for the former President, introduced him as simply and directly as possible. "Mr. Chairman," said Hamilton, "it is a very great pleasure and honor to present the honorable Herbert Hoover."

And then came moments of agony for the Willkie people. The delegates were applauding, whistling, stamping their feet and cheering for the only man with enough prestige to tell them how to avoid a deadlock. Or, if Hoover gave the word, he could possibly win

the nomination for himself after so many had worked and fought for
so long. Not since they had come to Philadelphia had it appeared that
the wonderful Willkie crusade that had been moving steadily upward
might suddenly fizzle out and disappear.

Such thoughts were undoubtedly shared by most of those who
watched the pack of photographers flash their bulbs at the rostrum.
Hoover, at the center of all the lights, looked somewhat grayer but
otherwise unchanged from his White House days and waved to all
sides of the auditorium. Finally, Joe Martin intervened with his gavel
and reminded everybody about the radio networks waiting to carry
the speech. Another volley of applause followed, and then Hoover
spoke.

"Almost everywhere in the Old World the light of liberty for which
men have struggled and died has gone into a long night," he reminded
his audience. "Men and nations have lost their moral and spiritual
moorings. . . . The whole world is in confusion." The one surprise of
his speech came with his statement that "There is no such thing as
our isolation from wars which envelop two-thirds of all the people in
the world." He was cheered as he denounced the German aggressions
and left no doubt that we should aid the Allies without becoming
direct participants. But then, as Stassen's keynote address had done,
he made a concession to the other side by saying, "Every whale that
spouts is not a submarine. The three thousand miles of ocean is still a
protection. The air forces, tanks and armies of Europe are useless to
attack us unless they establish bases in the Western Hemisphere," he
pointed out, virtually restating Charles Lindbergh's position. Then,
summarizing what had become everybody's argument, he demanded
stronger national defenses as the best way to avoid war.

Most important, however, was his statement that Republicans
would like nothing better than to have FDR as a rival in November
and that the quest for a third term was in violation of tradition and
fundamental restraints. He did not actually say so, but few doubted
his personal readiness to respond to the challenge he was describing.

Just as Hoover was concluding, Edith Willkie walked into the hall
with Roy Howard and Westbrook Pegler. They heard the cheers and
applause as the former President took his seat. However enthusiastic
the response, it did not match the reaction to his Chicago speech of
four years before, when there was no thought of his candidacy, and it

certainly gave no evidence that his words had sparked a great pro-Hoover rush. "Well, he didn't make it" was how Edith Willkie's escorts reacted.

The next day, however, Hoover held a press conference that removed any doubts about his intentions. He urged the delegates to reach an open decision and alluded to the early-morning, smoke-filled conference room that had given the 1920 nomination to Warren Harding. When asked directly whether he would accept the nomination, the former President replied curtly: "I have no further comment." The press accepted that as a virtual declaration of his candidacy.

As helpful as Hoover had been in perking up the convention, the delegates were, actually, stalling for the Resolutions Committee to complete its work. For nearly two weeks a subcommittee appointed by chairman Herbert K. Hyde had been struggling with the task of drafting a foreign-policy statement. Alfred Landon, heading the task force, wanted a version that would be acceptable to all groups, but, most of all, one that would nevertheless offer the possibility for some form of aid to the Allies while avoiding direct military involvement. Day-and-night meetings had occupied them. Finally, word had it that the party's official position on foreign affairs would be a forthright recognition of the importance to America of the survival of the Allies and particularly Great Britain, which could then refute the prediction by the *Times* of London that the final version could contain "a half pennyworth of aid to 'oppressed peoples' and an intolerable deal of isolationism."

But there was another interested party, one that felt its own vital interests very much involved in the performance of the Republicans at Philadelphia. That was Nazi Germany. Through their *chargé d'affaires* in Washington, Dr. Hans Thomsen, the Hitler government was continuing efforts that had been started earlier in the year not only to defeat Roosevelt but to strengthen the isolationists. Only with the American publication after World War II of seized German documents was the full extent of Nazi interference in the election of 1940 revealed.

Representative Hamilton Fish spent three thousand dollars and invited fifty "non-interventionist" Congressmen to Philadelphia so they could testify before the Resolutions Committee in support of a "keep out of war" platform. With this group Fish formed an *ad hoc* committee as a pressure lobby. On June 25, the second day of the convention, the day of Hoover's appearance before the delegates, Fish's committee was represented by a full-page advertisement that appeared in a number of leading newspapers, including *The New York Times.*

"TO THE DELEGATES TO THE REPUBLICAN NATIONAL CONVENTION AND TO AMERICAN MOTHERS, WAGE EARNERS, FARMERS AND VETERANS," read its heading; and in large print immediately below: "STOP THE MARCH TO WAR! STOP THE INTERVENTIONISTS AND WARMONGERS! STOP THE DEMOCRATIC PARTY." The finely printed text below was devoted to quoting from several Senators on the advisability of keeping out of war. At the bottom of the page appeared the names of the sponsoring organization, the National Committee to Keep America Out of Foreign Wars. Aside from Fish, who was listed as its chairman, others designated as vice-chairmen were Harold Knutson, a primitive reactionary from Minnesota and one of the eight signers of the anti-Willkie resolution that was issued on Monday morning; John J. O'Connor, the purged Democratic ex-Congressman from New York; Samuel B. Pettingill, a former Democratic Congressman from Indiana, now the chairman of a New York group called the National Committee to Uphold Constitutional Government and about to become better known as the author of *Smoke Screen,* a hysterical diatribe that depicted the New Deal as the start of a Fascist corporate state in America; and Walter L. Reynolds, who was listed as secretary-treasurer.

On that same day, just as it looked as though the Landon point of view would mold the foreign-policy plank, such active isolationists as Henry Cabot Lodge of Massachusetts and C. Wayland Brooks of Illinois included a statement that read: "The Republican party stands for Americanism, preparedness and peace. We accordingly fasten upon the New Deal full responsibility for our unpreparedness and for the consequent danger of involvement in war." It was no advance at all over the original Glenn Frank report; and, considering the trend of international developments since that document had been presented in February, the new statement was a retreat from responsibility. It was becoming a standard tactic to accuse Roosevelt of preparing to lead the nation to war and, at the same time, condemn him for not providing adequate defenses. The most vociferous isolationist, or non-interventionist, could support that position. In preparing the final platform for submission to the delegates, however, Alf Landon was able to salvage something with a passage that declared: "We favor the extension to all peoples fighting for liberty, or whose liberty is threatened, of such aid as shall not be in violation of international law or inconsistent with the requirements of our own national defense."

Nevertheless, the British press concluded that German and Irish-American voters had been satisfied. H. L. Mencken wrote that the plank was "so written that it will fit both the triumph of democracy and the collapse of democracy, and approve both sending arms to England or sending only flowers." After the platform had been adopted by the convention, Hans Thomsen cabled his government that the foreign-policy plank was "taken almost verbatim from the conspicuous full-page advertisements in the American press, which were published upon our instigation."

There is no evidence that either Fish or the Resolutions Committee were aware of the Nazi involvement. No newspapers noted it. Nor can it be determined whether or not they knew about the nature of their financial backing. Fish was, however, the same Congressman who provided the use of his office for the mailing activities of Nazi agent George Sylvester Viereck. Years later, when acknowledging the German role in the affair, Hamilton Fish's only regret was that the Nazis had not spent more to ensure American non-participation. After all, he reasoned, America's neutral position entitled the Germans as well as the British to finance propaganda in the United States however they saw fit, just as both powers had done before Congress had declared war in 1917.

4

All the candidates were continuing to receive delegates. Vandenberg hardly left his hotel room as the visitors kept coming. Taft went out to visit delegations. In the Dewey camp there were still differences over what the New Yorkers would do. Reports circulated that only six New York County delegates, including Allen W. Dulles, would vote for Dewey on the first ballot. His delegates were continuing to be bombarded by pro-Willkie telegrams. William F. Bleakley, the County Executive of Westchester and chairman of the state's delegation, reported that he had received 7,500 telegrams at Philadelphia and that another fifteen thousand had piled up at his White Plains home. In other states, Willkie clubs were continuing to contact their supporters in person or by wire to spur the flow of telegrams. From Phoenix, Arizona, a club chairman informed Root that "prominent businessmen are very gladly doing the same thing."

Willkie himself spent another busy day. He had breakfast with a group of Ohio delegates, who were pledged to Taft, and that produced rumors that he was trying to raid the Senator's home delegation. But he had been invited to attend; and when he addressed the more than seventy-five who were present, he said he admired and respected Taft and asked for their support only if and when Taft was no longer a contender. He also met with a group of Massachusetts delegates, who wanted to know when they should stop voting for Joe Martin and turn to him.

At a press conference Willkie revealed the day's big news. Harold E. Stassen had agreed to serve as his floor manager. After his keynote address, Minnesota's young governor had met with his delegation and informed them that Willkie's recognition of America's need for a more responsible foreign policy had convinced him to vote for the Hoosier on the first ballot. When the news reached Willkie, Stassen was telephoned and invited to become his floor manager. Stassen, somewhat surprised, observed that the hour was rather late to start changing managers. Willkie then informed him that none had even been chosen but that the other governors behind him—Vanderbilt, Baldwin and Carr—had all agreed that Stassen was the man for the job. Furthermore, Charlie Halleck and Congressman Frank O. Horton, as well as Walter Hallanan of West Virginia, Sinclair Weeks and Sam Pryor, were all ready to serve as floor leaders. Their plans were discussed at a 2 A.M. conference in Willkie's hotel suite. As a first step they made what they considered a realistic estimate of Willkie's first-ballot strength; and, from that tally, as Stassen has since explained, "We decided to hold some in reserve, since starting in this weak position we knew that any slippage between balloting would be very adverse in its psychology."

5

Wednesday's first session was brief because Herbert K. Hyde's Resolutions Committee was not ready with its report, and the meeting was adjourned only twenty-two minutes after its start, until 4:45 that afternoon.

Finally, before the eagerly awaited roll call of the states, Hyde led the afternoon's first piece of business by reading his committee's recommended party platform. Appropriately enough, in addition to its ambiguous wording on foreign policy and standard denunciations of what the New Deal was doing to America, it included an endorsement by the party's twenty-second convention of what would eventually become the federal Constitution's Twenty-second Amendment, a limitation of the President's tenure of office to two terms. After brief seconding speeches by Henry Cabot Lodge and Hamilton Fish, who repeated the desire "to appropriate billions of dollars for adequate national defense but not one single dollar to send an American soldier to fight in foreign lands to fight other people's battles," the platform was adopted by a unanimous voice vote.

Then began a roll call of states, not for the purpose of placing names in nomination but merely to determine which delegations would offer candidates. Alabama yielded to New York, which would have the honor of nominating Dewey. Arizona also yielded to New York, but for Frank Gannett; and Arkansas gave Ohio the privilege of making the third nomination, which would, of course, be for Taft. But when Indiana simply passed, there was consternation. Charlie Halleck was still evidently undecided whether to risk political suicide by placing Willkie's name before the convention. The matter was resolved, however, at the end of the roll call when Arch N. Bobbitt of Indiana announced that his state had reconsidered and would nominate Willkie. Only then was Halleck's contribution certain, and it meant that Willkie would be the fourth entry. The ensuing eruption of approval equaled the ovation given the previous night to Hoover. But the uproar stilled after a few minutes and the official business continued.

John Lord O'Brian of Buffalo delivered a long nominating speech for Thomas E. Dewey. "Fellow Republicans," he said pointedly, "it is our equally good fortune that this man is a lifelong Republican."

He recited the DA's career and assured the convention that, "above all, he can be trusted to keep us out of war."

When he finished, there was cheering throughout the auditorium, including the balconies. Delegates stood in the aisles with little standards that had Dewey's picture, and then began the traditional parade as Dewey banners were held aloft. "Dewey can beat Roosevelt," "Tom Dewey is a vote-getter," "Nominate a winner, Tom Dewey," they proclaimed. Dewey umbrellas were also carried through the aisles. At 7:15, after the demonstration had gone on for more than twenty minutes, Joe Martin rapped the gavel and called for the four seconding speeches.

Arizona's yield to New York signaled James W. Wadsworth to nominate publisher Frank Gannett, whose campaign to head a return to reaction in American life had cost him half a million dollars. For that, as three live elephants he had brought to Philadelphia stood outside the hall, he too was seconded by four speeches and was honored by a two-minute outburst of handclapping and whistling. "Hardly a ripple" was the way the *Times* described it. And hardly his money's worth.

Arkansas followed with a yield to Ohio. Grove Patterson, editor of the Toledo *Blade,* then nominated Senator Robert Alonzo Taft, son of a former President and increasingly the hope of old-line Republicans eager to keep the party out of the hands of those with mixed blood. "Fellow delegates," Patterson concluded his speech: "Ohio's candidate comes to us from one of America's most distinguished families, famed for the preservation of all that is finest in home and national life. He presents a program. He is equipped to face the tragedy of a war-blasted world. He has imagination and courage. He is an amazing vote-getter."

The standards were ready to be waved. Banners were rising higher, about to be carried by excited demonstrators. But Patterson first had to deliver his final lines, which were: "Above all, ladies and gentlemen of the convention, he has woven for himself and wears, through life's sun and storm, the durable fabric of character. Ohio, Mother of Presidents, brings to this convention its distinguished son, a great American, Senator Robert A. Taft."

Delegates jumped from their seats. Horns blared. Balloons dropped from the ceiling. Taft's picture filled the auditorium. "Taft Will Win," read the banners. "As Ohio Goes So Goes the Nation."

"Taft the Statesman." "Out of the Wilderness with Bob Taft." Then, from the middle of the Ohio delegation, Congressman George Bender of Cleveland called for "Three cheers for the winner!" "Three cheers for our next President," which was, in turn, repeated by the marchers, who then followed with explosive cries of "We want Taft! We want Taft! We want Taft!"

Joe Martin asked the delegates to be seated so the program could continue and called for the aisles to be cleared. In a mood of complete confidence, R. B. Creager of Texas spoke out. "Ladies and gentlemen of the convention," he said, "will you please be quiet. Let us give the other fellow a chance, not that it will amount to anything but let us give him a chance. Please sit down." The Taft people had wanted to end their performance rather than have it taper off gradually for lack of continuing enthusiasm.

Senator Warren Austin of Vermont then seconded Taft's nomination, and he was followed by other Taft speakers from Washington, Kentucky and Missouri.

With state after state passing, the roll call proceeded from California to Indiana, whereupon Archie Bobbitt asked the chair to recognize Representative Charles Halleck. That was at about 9:15. Loud applause and excited cheers came from the balconies, but booing and catcalling could be heard from the floor. For Halleck, it was a nervous moment. At the age of thirty-nine he had placed his political career in danger by stepping forward as the principal advocate of the former Democrat. Never before had he faced such hostility. Martin had to call for order. Then he reaffirmed Halleck's standing as a loyal Republican by placing his arm around the Congressman's shoulder; the boos diminished, and he began.

Instead of the approach that had become so traditional for such speeches, the tantalizing delay of the nominee's name until the very end, seconds after he began to speak he said: "If anyone were to ask me what job in this convention I would like best to have, I would choose the job I have right now. I would say, I want to place in nomination before this independent body the name of the next President of the United States, Wendell Lewis Willkie."

A burst of boos again came from the delegates. Some tried to wave him off the rostrum. Rushing to his support, at the same time, were the cheers from the balcony. Halleck, countering the controversy he had created, persisted with even greater determination, making it clear to them that whether or not they wanted to, they would have to listen to what he had to say. Then they laughed with him when he declared that "It will be better to have a public utility president than a president who has no public utility." Pointedly, he recalled Willkie's Elwood background, even the rise and decline of the natural-gas boom, and depicted his candidate as an American who should not now be penalized for having fought his way to business prominence in the best American tradition.

"Are we to understand," Halleck asked, "that any man is barred from our deliberations who has been an American success?"

Cries of "no" came from the audience. Then, addressing himself to one of their chief objections, he argued that the Republican party was not run according to seniority. "Let it never be said," he urged, "that we bar from our deliberations a man who is one of us—a man who believes in us—a man in whom millions of our people, members of our party, already fervently believe. Now let's get down to business here! You know, and I know, that Wendell Willkie can win next November!"

The end of his speech brought demonstrations that overwhelmed everything that had gone before. The Indiana standard was lifted from its place and carried around the hall. A struggle broke out to wave the New York standard for Willkie. Syracuse Mayor Marvin seized the standard, but it was grabbed by a Bronx delegate. Finally Marvin, a powerfully built six-footer, managed to pull it away from the man and then ran with it to the head of the Willkie procession. Bronx district leader Peter Wynne made another attempt to retrieve it from Marvin. The two men wrestled until they were separated by a flying wedge of police. Then William F. Bleakley told the officers to let Marvin have it, and the Mayor held aloft the New York standard at the head of the Willkie parade. Eleven other states joined the line.

The galleries, meanwhile, were in complete pandemonium.

"The Chair must remind the occupants of the galleries that they are guests of the convention," shouted Martin. "The Chair must recognize delegates for seconding speeches. If you desire to hear them I advise you to come to order."

But the response was in the form of more "We want Willkie!" chants. Some of the delegates listened impassively; others turned and booed back.

Outside the hall the furor was being duplicated. Broad Street was filled with marching brass bands and drum and bugle corps. Hundreds of Willkie volunteers, particularly from the Northeast, staged a foot and automobile parade with "We want Willkie!" cries dominating the downtown shopping district, a mile from Convention Hall. On the street in front of the auditorium, Frank Gannett's three elephants were almost ignored as the sounds of glockenspiel and piccolos playing the "Beer Barrel Polka" and "God Bless America" entertained the crowds.

Not before the sergeant-at-arms had cleared the aisles was the convention able to continue so the three seconding speakers—Representative Bruce Barton, Miss Ann Stuart of Minnesota and Governor Baldwin—could be heard. That ended the session, which adjourned at eleven.

When the delegates returned to their hotels that night, exhausted and hot after the six and a half hours they had spent in the hall, the Willkie mailing committee confronted them with additional bundles of petitions, and even chain letters, showing how many thousands in their own districts were behind the Willkie drive.

6

On that Thursday morning, the day for which the balloting was scheduled, Ogden Reid's New York *Herald Tribune* came out with a front-page editorial announcing formal support for Willkie. "Extraordinary times call for extraordinary abilities," it said. "By great good fortune Mr. Willkie comes before the convention uniquely suited for the hour and for the responsibility." Expressing the paper's confidence in Willkie's ability to direct the nation's national-defense preparations, the editorial praised him as "heaven's gift to the nation in time of crisis. Such timing of man and the hour does not come often in history. We doubt if it ever comes twice to a political party."

Edith Willkie anticipated that it would be a big day. She sent a friend to buy her the biggest hat she could find in Philadelphia. Then, wearing the hat at an angle to conceal her face from prying photographers, she put on a new dress, which was also unfamiliar to the press. She went to lunch with Mrs. Roy Howard, Mrs. Will Hays and the wives of other prominent Republicans, but refused to join them to observe the rest of that morning's session.

It had begun at 10:45 before half-empty galleries and sleepy delegates. During the next four hours six additional names were entered. Cedar Rapids *Gazette* editor Verne Marshall was not a delegate, but the convention nevertheless gave him its unanimous consent to nominate Hanford MacNider and, joining in the stop-Willkie sentiment, he declared that "this is a Republican convention." MacNider, a past commander of the American Legion, thus became a possible means of holding Iowa's twenty-two votes for Herbert Hoover. After three seconding speeches, Representative Roy O. Woodruff of Bay City, Michigan, nominated the convention's fourth major candidate, Senator Arthur Vandenberg.

Woodruff, at first denouncing the stop-Willkie feeling but then extolling Vandenberg as "the tried and trusted veteran of all the recent wars that have been fought in our behalf," presented his man as the one most likely to attract the Jeffersonian Democrats. Delegates and alternates rose to their feet at the mention of Vandenberg's name and waved small American flags and then led the convention in singing "God Bless America" and "The Battle Hymn of the Republic."

Then came the last four names to be placed in nomination: Styles Bridges of New Hampshire; Senator Charles McNary of Oregon, who seemed to be a liberal where Willkie was a conservative and a conservative where Willkie was a liberal; Pennsylvania's Governor Arthur James; and, last, Governor Harlan J. Bushfield, South Dakota's favorite son. By the time Bushfield's seconding speeches had concluded, the audience was ready to rest for the important session slated to start at four-thirty.

Wendell Willkie remained in his hotel room when the convention reconvened that afternoon. Edith, wearing her new hat, managed to slip unobserved into a seat in the middle of a row in the upper balcony. Oren Root, who was also up there, noted the many spectators wearing Dewey, Taft and Vandenberg buttons, showing quite clearly that all had not come to cheer for the Hoosier. Former President Hoover, who only the day before had confirmed to reporters his willingness to run, had been working since eight that morning rounding up as many delegates as possible. In his eleventh-floor suite in the Bellevue-Stratford, he also met with most of the other candidates. Each contender hoped to inherit the prestige of the former President's name by winning his support if he should change his mind. Frank Gannett went to see him twice. Senator Vandenberg, at the same time, concentrated on his cigars and said his view of the outcome was "completely fatalistic." As the afternoon session neared, the candi-

Vice President John Nance Garner with FDR at the annual Jackson Day Dinner in Washington —*International News Photos*

ABOVE: *Wendell Willkie with William Allen White*
—*Courtesy of Mrs. Wendell L. Willkie*

RIGHT: *Secretary of Labor Frances Perkins*
—*Brown Brothers*

*Willkie at Convention Hall, Philadelphia, June 28, 1940, with
Representative Joe Martin and Mrs. Willkie. Behind them (l. to r.) are
governors Harold Stassen, John Bricker and Raymond Baldwin.*

                                        —International News Photos

Oren Root, Edith Willkie and Willkie attending a performance of Life
with Father *in New York City* —*Wide World Photos*

Willkie in Washington on July 9 with senators Taft and Vandenberg
—International News Photos

Harry Hopkins, Harold Ickes and Senator Alben Barkley at Chicago
—Franklin D. Roosevelt Library

ABOVE: *Russell Davenport with Willkie at Colorado Springs*
—*Wide World Photos*

RIGHT: *Samuel F. Pryor*
—*Wide World Photos*

Wendell Willkie at Cheyenne, Wyoming
      —Courtesy of Mrs. Wendell L. Willkie

FDR signing the Selective Service Bill, September 16, 1940
          —Franklin D. Roosevelt Library

LEFT: *Father Charles Coughlin*
—Brown Brothers

BELOW: *FDR and his running mate, Henry Wallace, at Hyde Park*
—Franklin D. Roosevelt Library

WAKE UP Mr. VOTER!

DOWN THE DICTATORS

FUEHRER · DUCE · ROOSEVELT

The Three Termites

Americans interested in the "DOWN-THE-DICTATORS" movement may obtain limited copies upon request — PRINA, Grantwood, N. J.

ABOVE: *An example of one of the many vicious campaign circulars*

RIGHT: *Cover of sheet music promoted to exploit Elliott Roosevelt's "Overnight Commission"*

LEFT: *District Attorney Thomas E. Dewey and Willkie at Yonkers, New York*
—Courtesy of Mrs. Wendell L. Willkie

BELOW: *Willkie in New York City's Duffy Square. City Council President Newbold Morris (right) looks on.*
            —Franklin D. Roosevelt Library

FDR speaks in New York City, October 28, 1940
—International News Photos

ABOVE: *FDR with Governor Herbert H. Lehman and Mayor Fiorello La Guardia*
     —International News Photos

LEFT: *John L. Lewis*
          —Brown Brothers

FDR campaigning in Newburgh, New York, the day before his re-election for a third term —International News Photos

FDR at Hyde Park on election day 1940 with his mother and wife
—International News Photos

dates moved to their radios and telephones so they could communicate with their managers on the convention floor.

Philadelphia, as most of America, became attentive. Radios and television sets were in great demand. In Elwood, business virtually stopped. People headed to a radio or stood outside the offices of the *Call-Leader* to await the posting of late bulletins.

Inside the hall the scene was much more frenetic than at that day's earlier session. Bright lights filled the arena. American flags added color and served as a background for the drifting gray cloudlike smoke that was illuminated by the powerful beams. Those lights were supplemented, around the rostrum, by the additional wattage that was needed for the newsreel and television cameras. Added to the natural heat of warm days in late June, the temperature on the floor and at the rostrum must have been several degrees hotter than at the 103-ballot convention that wilting Democrats had to endure in New York's Madison Square Garden before they finally chose John W. Davis in 1924. At precisely four-thirty, Permanent Chairman Martin called for the roll of states and the start of the first-ballot vote.

Dewey picked up thirty votes from the first nine states. Considering that California had scattered votes among eleven names, it was not a bad showing. But, still, Dewey needed to move at a better rate to reach the 501 needed for victory.

"We want Willkie! We want Willkie!" chants started in the gallery. With the combination of strong lights and deafening noise, Joe Martin could hardly continue. A New Hampshire delegate complained that there was so much confusion in the hall that delegates, "who are here to attend to important business, cannot hear the votes as cast or the announcements." He asked Martin to clear the aisles and to demand order from the guests.

"I regret to have to admonish those in the galleries to be quiet," shouted Martin, "and to remind them that they are guests of this convention and must conduct themselves accordingly."

"Guests, hell," someone shouted back. "We *are* the convention!"

Throughout the subsequent balloting, Willkie votes were greeted with vigorous applause and more rhythmic chanting. They were particularly demonstrative whenever he gained votes that had been predicted for another candidate. When the first ballot was finished, Dewey's camp saw evidences of its worst fears despite his 360 votes, which were 171 more than his closest rival, Taft.

Taft had come close to being shut out in the New York–New

England–mid-Atlantic area as well as in the Great Plains and the
Northwest, but he was clearly the favorite of the South, had more
votes than any single candidate in the Southwest, and, with the help
of Ohio's fifty-two, had taken more than a quarter of the votes from
the Midwest.

Superficially, Dewey looked very strong. One hundred and forty-
one votes short of an absolute majority, he held commanding leads in
the Northeast, mid-Atlantic, Great Plains and northwestern states.
His sixty-one from New York was at the lower end of the range
previously predicted by the Dewey camp and his over-all total was
somewhat less than they had expected, but his margin over the runner-
up fit in nicely with the DA's own estimate. His weakness, however,
became more apparent when Willkie's progress was examined.

Willkie's 105 votes on the first ballot was the biggest surprise. It
was thirty more than his own most recent pre-convention prediction
and placed him ahead of Vandenberg. In fact, the Michigan Senator's
national total was only exactly twice the thirty-eight given by his own
loyal delegation. Willkie, getting all sixteen votes from Connecticut as
had been promised by Governor Baldwin, polled better than 17 percent of the total from the New York–New England region or the
Northeast. While New York gave Gannett seventeen, Willkie managed eight and was certainly a better bet than Dewey to gain from
defections from the Rochester newspaper publisher. The New Yorkers had not cooled tempers engendered by the Dewey–Simpson feud,
with its incidental alienation by Dewey of the Gannett forces. Also,
the combination of his remarkable eighteen thousand write-in votes in
the New Jersey primary and the rebellious followers of ex-Governor
Harold Hoffman enabled Willkie to take twelve from what should
have been a solid bloc of thirty-two Jerseyites for Dewey. Next to
his showing in New Jersey and the New York–New England area,
Wilkie did best in the Southwest. Helped by three votes from
Governor Carr's state of Colorado and seven out of California's forty-
four, Willkie's fifteen in that region placed him second only to Taft,
who got sixteen, and two ahead of Dewey. But the fragmentation of
the votes from the Southwest on that first ballot can best be illustrated by noting that the region gave the four leading candidates only
63 percent of its total vote.

Minor entrants and "favorite sons" were prominent, holding delegations that would undoubtedly help to decide the issue on subse-

quent ballots. California had given seven to native son Herbert Hoover, but was also generous to such outsiders as Gannett, Mac-Nider, Martin and McNary. Loyally, Oregon held all its ten votes for Senator McNary, South Dakota eight for Governor Bushfield, Kansas its eighteen for Senator Arthur Capper, Iowa its twenty-two for Mac-Nider, and all but one of the thirty-four in Massachusetts were for Joe Martin. Both New Hampshire and Maine went solidly for Senator Styles Bridges, while Pennsylvania gave Governor James seventy of its seventy-two. Then there were, of course, the sizable home-state blocs for Gannett, Taft, Dewey and Vandenberg, whose first-ballot showing left him with only the dim hope of succeeding with a dead-locked convention that refused to go along with an ex-Democrat. But then there was the newest entrant, Hoover, who picked up seventeen on the opening count.

Martin called for the second ballot as soon as the first results were announced, and tension increased as everybody awaited a possible break that could point to the probable direction of the outcome. Willkie, close by his radio, ate a steak, picked at raspberries and chatted with a small group of reporters. When Tennessee announced five votes for him, an increase of three, Willkie said, "That's where that utility fight of mine occurred."

The galleries continued to roar approval with every Willkie vote, particularly the gains. Creager, who was Taft's floor leader, had told the press on Wednesday that Pryor's Committee on Arrangements, to which the Texan also belonged, had issued thousands of standing-room tickets without the committee's authority and that they had been used to "pack" the galleries. Willkie himself had denounced the allegation as ridiculous. For the balloting, Creager said he would ask Hamilton to install new doormen in the galleries and improve the security to confine admission to legitimate ticket holders. If Creager did concern himself with how the galleries were filled that Thursday, his methods were no less helpful than Pryor's to the Willkie cause, for the spectators were more enthusiastic than ever.

While the second ballot was continuing, Creager engaged in a floor debate with Pryor, who challenged him to repeat before the entire convention what he had told to the press. The Texan then charged up to the platform, where Martin cooled him off by saying such a debate would damage the party's image before the country. Creager then dropped the matter, but his charges persisted even though they could not be substantiated, and the only evidence available, the actual attitude of the guests even after "precautions" were instituted, suggests that such a planned effort was not at all necessary.

Heavy pro-Willkie pressure was being exerted within many delegations. Nebraska, which had been committed to at least one ballot for Dewey by its primary, now decided it had already discharged its obligation and only five of the state's fourteen delegates remained loyal to the DA. Willkie, Taft and Vandenberg each received two and the other three were given to Hoover, McNary and Martin. The Missouri delegates were being influenced by Edgar Monsanto Queeny, president of the Monsanto Chemical Company of St. Louis, and thus gave the Hoosier seven additional votes. Wisconsin, however, held firm for Dewey despite efforts by its governor, Julius Heil, to persuade them to break away. When the results of the second ballot were announced, Dewey still led, but he had lost twenty-two and was down to a total of 338. Taft had gone from 189 to 203, Vandenberg had lost three and now had just seventy-three, and the Willkie surge was evident.

The ex-Democrat had gained sixty-six votes and had a second-ballot total of 171. Willkie's strength had improved in every region but the Northwest. He had picked up nine Maine votes that had been for Bridges, seven more in Massachusetts from Martin's column, and five additional New Yorkers. Maryland, which had given its sixteen en masse to Dewey, now gave Willkie four. Taft's gains were confined largely to the Midwest and Southwest, and Dewey seemed to have lost his chance. A Willkie–Taft battle was developing.

Landon then consulted with Martin about what course Kansas should take if the state's eighteen Capper votes were to be released. Martin suggested Dewey because of the New Yorker's progressivism when compared with Taft and thought that Kansas would probably be more receptive to him.

At 6:45 there was unanimous agreement to recess until 8:30 for the third ballot.

Landon was stopped by Harold Stassen. Unable to make themselves heard above the noise, they found refuge in a freight elevator. There Stassen tried to convert Landon to the idea of switching his delegation to Willkie. But the Kansan declared himself neutral toward Willkie and said he would not deliver a bloc vote to any one candidate and that, anyway, he could not decide for the entire delegation.

Perhaps the most attractive voting bloc still available was Pennsylvania's seventy-two, sixty-five of which had continued to go to James on the second ballot, five to Willkie and two to Dewey. Its delegation, however, was clearly controlled by Joe Pew, the vice president of the Sun Oil Company and the epitome of the GOP's Old Guard. Willkie persisted in his refusal to heed advice that he "make his peace" with the Pennsylvania leader as a bid for those votes, just as he had refused to have anything to do with Ohio's Governor John Bricker. He declared that it was against his principles to compromise with a man like Pew and that no consideration could sway him; thus he displayed an attitude that constantly frustrated his advisers. Pew's own opposition to Willkie was known, but Willkie's people felt that any prospect of defeating Roosevelt could sway the Pennsylvanian.

During that recess Taft decided to make the gesture toward Pew. The Senator's managers made some desperate efforts to get to the oilman, but it was all in vain. Pew was busy bathing and eating and had left his servants with strict orders not to disturb him.

The Taft forces had optimistically sensed that the changes would put their man over, with or without Joe Pew. Word even reached the street crowds that Taft had all but won. Taft's managers were working hard and had made additional gains. Earlier that day Senator Thomas H. Burke of Montana had seen Willkie and informed him that, after two ballots for Dewey, his delegation might give him some votes but needed additional assurance about how he stood on the tariff issue before they would agree to switch to him. Willkie reiterated what had become his stock response at Philadelphia to such questions, that the war had negated reciprocal trading as a factor and that, in any event, he would not press the issue. Armed with that information, Burke returned to his delegation only to find that Taft's people had already arranged for at least four Montana delegates ultimately to support the Senator.

The big New York delegation was still uncertain. Kenneth Simpson and Mayor Marvin had advanced the idea of polling its ninety-two members on the third ballot to expose the real Willkie strength. Others, however, including Stassen, argued that it would only cause resentment because of the time that would be required to go through such a large delegation and that it would be regarded as a public airing of the Dewey–Simpson feud. So the idea was dropped.

7

Convention Hall was packed again by 8:30 as Joe Martin called
for a third ballot. The galleries cheered as Willkie gained a Taft vote
from Alabama. The "We want Willkie!" chorus began to mount.
Even some with Dewey and Vandenberg buttons were joining them,
and they really burst into loud applause as Arizona quickly followed
with the announcement that her six Gannett votes had switched to
Willkie. California gave Hoover twelve, more than to any other single
candidate. Landon left Capper and threw eleven to Dewey. As the
roll call proceeded, it was evident that the switching was mainly
toward Willkie and, to a lesser degree, toward Taft. Dewey was still
ahead but falling. When New York was reached, delegation chairman
Bleakley announced seventeen for Willkie, which brought a great
response because it meant a gain of four more from that important
Dewey lode.

But one New York delegate, Walter Mack, Jr., was upset. He had
told Bleakley that unless the votes were counted on the floor before
the total was submitted, he was going to demand a public vote.
"Now, Walter, be patient," Bleakley had replied. "Be quiet. Take it
easy. We're counting them properly." Then, in defiance of the pre-
balloting decision to avoid polling the delegation, Mack rose to say,
"Mr. Chairman, I request a poll of the New York delegation."

The huge audience was clearly annoyed. Individual polling of
ninety-two delegates was time-consuming, but Joe Martin answered
the boos by reminding everybody that Mack's request was consistent
with the rules governing the convention. Not only the galleries were
booing now, but so, it seemed, was everybody in the place. But Mack,
of course, had his way.

And the polling did yield a different result. Now, twenty-seven
New Yorkers, including Frank Gannett's son-in-law, were for Willkie. That was ten more than Bleakley had reported. It was not necessarily a reflection of the chairman's veracity but, rather, a clear
response to each delegate's having to make a public announcement of
his vote. Mack suddenly became a hero and the Willkie crowd went
wild. Friends within the Pennsylvania, Massachusetts and New Jersey
delegations were advised by Mack to check up on their own chairmen.

For Taft there was frustration. During the voting, Senator Vandenberg telephoned Taft's headquarters to say he was ready to do anything to help his colleague, and visions of thirty-eight votes from Michigan brought excitement. But when Michigan's vote was actually announced, there were only two defections from Vandenberg, and both were for Dewey. Similar hopes of support from Dewey also evaporated.

One delegate was absent, so 999 votes were actually cast. The results of the third ballot showed Dewey still ahead with 315, but down by twenty-three. Pandemonium, however, greeted the announcement that Willkie had moved into second place with 259, which meant he had gained eighty-eight. Taft's rise was held to nine, giving him 212, and Vandenberg had seventy-two. Thirty-two were cast for Herbert Hoover.

Willkie's gains were made in all regions, including one vote from the District of Columbia. But his bandwagon was really being fashioned in the Northeast and mid-Atlantic states, where he had picked up nearly 47 percent of all the delegates. He even won the fifteen from Pennsylvania who bolted from Governor James. He was in first place in those two regions and also in the Southwest. Most of his gains were at the expense of Dewey and the lesser candidates. It was clear that any real hope of stopping him would have to depend on the staunch Taft support in the South and the Midwest. Taft could also stay in the race by picking up votes from Dewey and the released delegates of Gannett, James, Hoover, MacNider and Martin, most of whom were concentrated in conservative areas.

Then came the fourth ballot. Martin kept gaveling so hard, he later recalled, that the noise "merely blended in with other sounds like a kettledrum in a symphony orchestra." Politicians and reporters filled the aisles. The galleries were in an uproar. The Willkie bandwagon, which had put him in second place on the third ballot, now sent him into the lead with 302 to 254 for Taft and 250 for Dewey. The chief interest in Vandenberg's sixty-one votes was speculation about their eventual disposition, along with James's fifty-six, Hoover's thirty-one, MacNider's twenty-six, McNary's eight and Frank Gannett's four. A lone vote for Bridges was still being cast by New Hampshire. The incredible tumult that responded to the results of the fourth ballot was not at all tempered by thoughts that a substantial portion of those 187 votes could still go to Taft, let alone what Dewey still held.

Such an assumption was not unreasonable. Those votes were mainly held by conservative delegates and many of them were from the Midwest. Any coalescence of stop-Willkie forces could yet rally around Taft as the last hope to keep the Republican party Republican. While their psychological advantage may have already slipped away, the Taft people knew that the fifth ballot could provide their last chance.

There was some agitation within Colonel Creager's Texas delegation, which had continued to give Taft an automatic twenty-six votes. John W. Herbert of Fort Worth and Joe Ingraham of Houston, convinced that the majority of their delegation would welcome the freedom to support Willkie, attempted to force a caucus in preparation for the fifth ballot. But Creager's hold could not be broken, and no vote was taken.

Alf Landon now became a leading target for the Willkie people. Kansas had given Willkie just five of its votes. Eleven had gone to Dewey and Taft had won the remaining two. Winning all eighteen for Willkie would have the additional prestige of demonstrating support from one of the party's national leaders and acceptance in the Midwest. Some of the Willkie managers and William Allen White tried to persuade Landon, who was concerned about the high-pressure tactics of the Hoosier's supporters and doubted that Willkie's nomination would be the best thing for the party. It was risky to grant the possible control over the spoils of victory to one who was not a confirmed member of the faith and who might have his own claque to compete with the party's regulars for positions. Again, Landon conferred with Martin. Martin told him that Willkie appeared well on his way to victory and implied that the Kansan's wisest move would be to join the winner's circle. When Landon asked whether the convention should be recessed to prevent a stampede, Martin replied: "Alf, we agreed that this would be an open convention."

Landon, now powerless to do anything else, said, "All right, let her go the way she's going."

Thus, Joe Martin called for the fifth ballot.

8

Anticipation of the coming drama must have staved off whatever feelings of exhaustion and heat prostration would have otherwise overcome the over seventeen thousand delegates, alternates and spectators. Mrs. Willkie was still unnoticed as she sat in the upper balcony under her big hat. Her husband was in his hotel room, where he had taken some cat naps. Then he had exchanged telephone messages with Stassen, who was working on the convention floor. He smoked cigarettes and sat with the reporters near the radio. At twenty minutes after eleven that night, the fifth count began.

From the very beginning, when Alabama reported, the shape of the contest was obvious. All but one of Dewey's seven votes now went to either Willkie or Taft. Arkansas left the DA altogether and bolstered the Ohioan. As the clerks repeated the count from each state, the crowd's response was attuned to the gains made by the two leading candidates. Then came Alf Landon's state, Kansas.

"Mr. Chairman," announced the delegate, "Kansas casts her eighteen votes for Wendell Willkie."

Cheering exploded from the galleries and even many delegates joined in the applause. Willkie, in his headquarters, reminded the reporters he had suggested they should watch Kansas on the fifth ballot. There was bedlam in the hall. State after state reported delegates shifting to the two front-runners, although California still held out eleven for Hoover.

Then North Dakota provided some welcome comic relief when one delegate rose to say, "North Dakota casts four votes for Senator Taft and four votes for *V*endell *V*illkie."

"For who?" Martin fired back as the crowd roared.

"For *V*endell *V*illkie," he replied.

"Spell it," Martin ordered, but the laughter drowned out the reply.

Oklahoma gave its twenty-two to Taft, but Joe Ferguson, one of the state's delegates, demanded that his group be polled. The result delighted the galleries, as it gave four to Willkie and Taft just eighteen.

Nat U. Brown answered for the state of Washington by saying, "Mr. Chairman, Washington casts sixteen votes for a real Republican, Senator Robert Taft."

"This is a Republican convention," said the chairman, "and all of the candidates before this body are Republicans. Will the delegate again state for the benefit of the tellers the exact number of votes he has cast."

The delegate complied and the roll call continued. No one could tamper with Martin's firm and fair handling of the proceedings.

The final result of the fifth ballot, after Georgia and Wisconsin had altered their initial votes, gave Willkie 429 and Taft 377. Dewey was down to fifty-seven, and Vandenberg, with his Michigan delegation still loyal, had forty-two. James was given fifty-one from Pennsylvania, and six states gave Hoover a total of twenty, while McNary got nine, all from Oregon.

Willkie had been the big gainer in the Northeast, especially in New York, where Dewey was abandoned en masse, with only six remaining loyal. Willkie picked up forty from the big state. All of Maine's thirteen also went over to Willkie. Of the 180 votes cast by that section, Willkie had received 148 to just twenty-one for Taft. But Taft had a commanding lead in the South, Midwest, the Great Plains and the Northwest. The combined total for Willkie and Taft was 806. Willkie was just seventy-one votes shy of an absolute majority. That left the choice between the Republican party stalwart from Ohio and the ex-Democrat up to the nearly two hundred other delegates.

Edith Willkie had left her balcony seat before the fifth ballot had ended and taxied to meet her husband, who had gone over to the Warwick Hotel. "My word, Wendell," she said, "you're going to get this thing." Willkie, who until then had been the calmest man in the room, was very tense and chain-smoked cigarettes that the reporters had contributed.

It was after midnight. Everybody realized that the next ballot would be the last. Ohio's Governor John Bricker, the leader of Taft's home delegation, asked Martin to adjourn the convention and put off the sixth ballot until the next day. But Martin, who had given his private assurance to Willkie that he would not permit an opportunity for overnight deals that could reverse the trend, replied: "I can't do that. In announcing the vote at the end of the last ballot, I asked the convention to prepare for the sixth ballot. A motion to adjourn would be out of order." At 12:20 A.M. on the morning of June 28, the roll call resumed.

"Alabama," called the reading clerk.

"Alabama casts her thirteen votes as follows: For Taft, seven; for Willkie, six."

The crowd cheered the gain of one for Willkie.

Arizona again gave Willkie all six votes, and Arkansas followed with ten for Taft and two for Willkie; again, no change.

"California."

"Mr. Chairman," said the delegate, "the California delegation asks for a poll." The big state, which had given Willkie nine fifth-ballot votes, now responded with seventeen and twenty-two for Taft, while casting four hold-out votes for Hoover. Taft had a thirty-nine to thirty-one lead.

"Colorado."

"Colorado casts her twelve votes: For Hoover, one; Taft, six; Willkie, five," said Governor Ralph Carr.

Connecticut and Delaware then gave Willkie their twenty-two votes, placing him in the lead with fifty-eight to forty-five for Taft.

Florida gave Taft two and Willkie ten, a significant gain for Willkie and a loss of one for Taft, and applause followed.

"Georgia," continued the clerk.

"Georgia casts her fourteen votes: For Taft, seven; Gannett, one; Willkie, six."

"Idaho."

"Mr. Chairman, Idaho casts her eight votes as follows: For Taft, six; for Willkie, two."

"Illinois."

"Mr. Chairman, Illinois casts her fifty-eight votes as follows: For Dewey, one; Taft, thirty-three; Willkie, twenty-four."

Indiana, reported Archie Bobbitt, gave Willkie twenty-three and Taft five. Then Taft picked up fifteen from Iowa while Willkie got seven.

"Kansas."

Alf Landon was at the microphone. "Mr. Chairman," he said, "Kansas casts her eighteen votes for Wendell Willkie." There was appreciative applause, and Willkie had a thirty-five-vote lead.

But Kentucky followed with twenty-two for Taft.

"Louisiana."

"Louisiana casts her twelve votes for Senator Taft."

Willkie's lead had been cut to just one. Maine passed.

"Maryland."

"Maryland casts her sixteen votes: one for Taft and fifteen for Willkie."

"Massachusetts," called the clerk.

Governor Leverett Saltonstall replied: "For Taft, two; Hoover, two; and Willkie, thirty."

"Michigan."

Howard C. Lawrence, Vandenberg's manager, came to the platform amid deafening applause. "In fairness to all of you I want to say that Senator Vandenberg has authorized me to release the Michigan delegation, and, subject to that release, the Michigan delegation has taken a poll. The chairman of the delegation has asked me to announce the result of that poll as follows: For Hoover, one; Taft, two; Willkie, thirty-five."

The "We want Willkie!" chants broke out as the galleries were jubilant. Martin again had to remind them they were just guests. Michigan had helped to give Willkie a 228 to 152 lead. But, more important, the psychological advantage was now all with him.

From that point, Willkie continued to move toward his goal. Minnesota gave him ten and Taft eleven. Mississippi, reflecting the Taft appeal in the deep South, contributed nine to the Senator and two for Willkie. But Missouri gave Taft only four and twenty-six to Willkie. As that showed a loss for Taft and a gain for their man, the gallery excitement continued at a high pitch. Montana then gave each man four, Nebraska passed, and Nevada gave Willkie four of its six votes. New Hampshire gave the Hoosier six more and two for Taft, and New Jersey followed with all thirty-two votes for Willkie. New Mexico added five more to his total and just one for Taft. Bleakley of New York was cheered as he announced seventy-eight for Willkie, with seven for Taft, six for Dewey and one for Hoover. Willkie had 395 votes and Taft only 192.

The roll call continued. Ohio remained firm and gave Taft her full fifty-two. But then Walter Tooze of Oregon, the man who had questioned Willkie about tariffs when the candidate had first arrived in Philadelphia, announced that Senator McNary had released his votes and the state's ten were cast for Willkie. The big Pennsylvania delegation, which had given Willkie twenty-one on the fifth ballot, passed. Creager's Texas organization remained with the Senator and continued to give him its full twenty-six votes.

With Willkie in front with a vote of 435 to 275, Governor Bricker of Ohio came to the platform and was greeted by a tremendous wave of cheers. But Martin signaled for the roll call to continue. David A. Reed of Pennsylvania then announced that his state, which had passed, was ready to report. All of Pennsylvania's seventy-two votes were then reported for Willkie, which brought him up to 507 and more than enough to clinch victory. Bricker, then recognized as Martin attempted the impossible task of maintaining order, moved that the Willkie nomination be made unanimous. Martin pointed to the convention rules and said the motion must await the end of the roll call but would recognize that Ohio had changed her fifty-two votes from Taft to Willkie.

The inevitable followed. State after state joined the winner. Even Nat U. Brown of Washington, who had previously announced all of his state's votes for "a real Republican, Senator Robert Taft," now gave Washington's sixteen to Willkie. By the time Bricker was able to make his motion of unanimity, it was completely extraneous, as Willkie had been backed by all the delegates present. Nevertheless, the ritual was accomplished for the record, and Joe Martin then made public a message from Hoover to Willkie.

"My congratulations," it said. "The result of a free convention and a free people will carry you to victory."

The Permanent Chairman also revealed that Willkie had telephoned his thanks to the delegates and had vowed a fight for the principles of the Republican party. The long session thus ended at 1:57 on the morning of June 28.

9

Only three hours later the phone rang in room 510 of the Bellevue-Stratford. Sam Pryor picked up the receiver and heard an agitated Wendell Willkie. He wanted Pryor to hurry over to his room at the Warwick.

"Sam, I'm in a jam," said the party's new nominee, "and you've got to help me. Roy Howard, Helen Reid and a whole lot of others all think I ought to balance out the ticket with a Western man, and that McNary would be the best man in the West, and not pick an Eastern man because they all say I'm looked upon as an Eastern man, not from Indiana."

"Wendell," said Pryor, "I don't agree with you. And what's more, you've given your word. The only thing you can do is to get Ray Baldwin over here, and you tell him. He's a big man. But only you can do it. I'll call him and say you want to see him; then find out what Joe Martin thinks about the McNary idea."

Baldwin accepted the expediency with all the grace and manliness that Pryor had predicted. How he really felt can only be conjectured.

Martin reached the Warwick at sunrise, listened to Willkie and agreed that the McNary move was good. The political differences between Willkie and the popular Senator from Oregon, and particularly the Senator's support of Monday's futile attempt to stop Willkie, however, made his acceptance doubtful. Agreeing to Willkie's request, Martin phoned the Senator, who had already returned to Washington.

But McNary's quick response was, "Hell, no. I wouldn't run with Willkie."

"You've got to consider the Republican party," Martin told him. "You are in a position to do the party a great service. Your presence on the ticket would give it strength. We'd have a better chance to win."

McNary agreed to run with a man who was a political and personal stranger.

When the convention reconvened in midafternoon, great applause greeted Martin's announcement that Willkie would arrive later to express his thanks in person. Moving off, then, with a feeling of satisfaction, the convention rebuffed a vice-presidential bid from the one declared candidate, Missouri's Representative Dewey Short, aptly called by Marquis Childs a "reactionary isolationist" and the "Ham Fish of the Ozarks," and chose McNary by a vote of 890 to 108. A political and geographic balance had been achieved.

Soaked from that afternoon's rainstorm, Wendell and Edith Willkie walked down the center aisle at 4:35 as delegates, alternates and spectators waved hats, handkerchiefs and flags. Now, as Colonel Creager must have noticed, the whole place seemed "packed" with Willkieites. The nominee bowed to all sides en route to the rostrum. Mrs. Willkie got her own warm ovation as she was introduced by Joe Martin. Never very outgoing, usually preferring the quiet background, she was a trim and attractive figure who was overwhelmed by what was going on, and the crowd loved her, especially when she managed a shy smile and said nothing. A storm of confetti then descended on the couple whom everyone in the auditorium, as well as millions listening on radio, hoped would be America's next First Family. Martin introduced the "next President of the United States."

It was not a formal acceptance speech, just a brief extemporaneous statement of appreciation, the award for their days of deliberation.

Willkie immediately praised Martin's handling of the convention, a widely shared judgment. After emphasizing that he had made no private deals, he promised to conduct a "crusading, aggressive, fighting campaign to bring unity to America, to bring the unity of labor and capital, agriculture and manufacturer, farmer and worker and all classes to this great cause of the preservation of freedom."

Concluding his short address, he must have made some people wince as he said, "So, *you* Republicans, I call upon you to join me, help me. The cause is great. We must win."

The "you Republicans" had certainly been a blunder, one that appeared to confirm the fears of those who had tried to stop an "outsider" from taking over the party. But the crowd was with him that afternoon as he said, "We cannot fail if we stand together in our united fight. I thank you." His final words were, "Now I'm going to sleep for a week!"

One of the most unusual conventions in American history thus adjourned at 4:55 that afternoon. The tired delegates prepared to leave Philadelphia, after having participated in a political miracle. Yet, if the Willkie forces had won, as the stories later said, by "blitzing" the convention, they had been curiously unable to storm the entire Republican party. Willkie's real strength had been in a powerful nucleus that drove outward from the northeastern and mid-Atlantic states. As late as the fifth ballot, the last that can be used to reveal anything with accuracy, he had won a majority of all votes in only that eleven-state area. Elsewhere, he had a slender plurality in the Southwest and was far behind Taft in the great center of the country. The galleries, the letters, the telegrams and the petitions had certainly shown evidence of the popular support that Dr. Gallup later confirmed. His victory, however, was also manufactured by a Republican unwillingness to unite around any other candidate. Mr. Hoover had all but announced his own desire to run only the day before balloting took place, and, as many had already guessed, he had wanted to badly. He would, however, have been better able to preserve the nomination for a "real Republican" by throwing his support and influence behind Taft. It would have helped deprive Willkie of the psychological advantage. Such, however, was the risk involved in holding an open, unbossed and democratic convention.

There was no doubt, too, that the deepening international crisis, which reached a new height just as the delegates were settling down at

Philadelphia, had also made the miracle possible and had enhanced the temptations tossed out by Oren Root, Russell Davenport, Charlton MacVeagh, Sam Pryor, Sinclair Weeks, Harold Talbott, Harold Gallagher and many others, mostly amateurs working more competently and energetically than professionals. The Bill Harmans and Don Smiths and Kirk Landons had helped to provide the needed "pressure from home"; their overtures made additional sense to those fearful about going with Dewey in the face of disastrous news from abroad. More than a gang-buster was needed.

And Dewey's own ambitions had been destructive, producing a serious schism in his own home delegation. There was also little reason, by June, for much excitement about Vandenberg. He was dignified and almost pompous, but his isolationism was becoming obsolete and his desire to avoid participating in the war was no different from every other candidate.

Watching this significant convention closely, along with the rest of the world, the *Daily Express* of London stated the feeling of all Englishmen about the Republican choice: "Great Britain can feel confident today that America is going to remain her active friend." Herr Hans Thomsen agreed. "From the standpoint of foreign policy," read his telegram to the Nazi ministry in Berlin, "Willkie's nomination is unfortunate for us. . . . neither his membership in the American Legion nor his pure German descent have so far had any influence in diverting him from his pro-Allied stand."

But Alf Landon had misgivings about it all. When he returned to his hotel room early that Friday morning, after the sixth ballot, his wife noted that he looked "so white and scared."

When she asked why, the 1936 candidate replied: "I wonder what I've done to my party and to my country."

CHAPTER SEVEN

The President Decides

1

THE PRESIDENT had pretended to ignore the Republican convention, and, after it had ended, he gave it only one public reference. When he arrived late for a press conference, he explained that the power for his elevator had been turned off. With a laugh, he expressed the hope that the incident had no connection with what had happened the previous night in Philadelphia.

The Willkie fervor of those early post-Republican convention days is difficult to exaggerate. Even Herr Thomsen, in a melancholy telegram to his bosses in Berlin, acknowledged that the opposition party had chosen "a distinct leader personality on the political stage," a choice that greatly enhanced their chances of winning. Harold Ickes confided in his *Diary* that the GOP candidate might be too much for the President because Willkie would "force the fighting all along the line." Another Democrat and future Secretary of War confessed in a letter to a Willkie aide: "I may have to vote and work against him;

but just between you and me, I don't think he would make such a bad Chief Executive." Columnists Drew Pearson and Robert Allen declared that the Democrats were "scared stiff" of the Willkie–McNary ticket. Its strength might point up the weakness and divisiveness of the Democrats, whose party, said Pearson and Allen, had been without a functioning national committee for months because of the Farley–New Deal split. Speaking for many enthusiasts, Vermont's Senator Warren R. Austin declared that if his "party cannot win with this ticket it ought to be liquidated." Father Coughlin's *Social Justice* caught the spirit by running a portrait of Willkie on the back cover of its July 1 issue and indirectly giving him its highest praise by pairing it with a picture of Colonel Charles A. Lindbergh instead of the Senator from Oregon. Other isolationists, including John L. Lewis, explored the possibility of a third party.

Some Willkie admirers wrote to the White House to suggest that the President should go along with the tide by convincing the Democratic convention also to nominate Willkie. Wrote a lady from Atlanta, Georgia: "Hitler will be answered. The Democratic party will have united the country. America will gasp for an hour then ring all its bells and blow all its whistles. America needs you." A New Rochelle, New York, lady appealed to Eleanor Roosevelt to urge Franklin that "a cohesion of forces" had become necessary because of the foreign situation. Others claimed to have received "confidential" information that Roosevelt was planning to rock the Democrats at Chicago by asking for Willkie as a bipartisan candidate. "This act will make you the greatest man in our history," he was assured by a telegram from Nantucket Island. "It will be a deadly blow for Hitler for United we Stand and Divided we Fall."

But the realities of partisan politics in a democracy were not so simple. An extreme view, held by some members of the Administration, was that Willkie's election would be an opening wedge for fascism in this country. In the Senate, Claude Pepper of Florida launched a fifty-one-minute attack upon the Republican nominee, scathingly denouncing his selection as the result of "blitzkrieg tactics" and calling him a "colorful figure from Wall Street," one who was clearly associated with such figures as Thomas W. Lamont, a senior partner of J. P. Morgan & Company. Pepper referred to the pending addition to the Hatch Act of 1939 that would extend to state and local government employees limitations on political activities similar to those imposed on workers for the federal government, and limit individual contributions to $5,000 and the income of any one political organization to $3,000,000 during any calendar year. Representative John Rankin of Mississippi called for an additional provision. He wanted to "get at these utilities henchmen," saying that it would be outrageous "to close the mouths of every employee of the federal and state governments, and then turn all these hired henchmen of the utilities loose on the country."

In Elwood, however, there were no party lines. Everybody seemed to be a Willkie fanatic. Sightseers came from hundreds of miles away just to get a glimpse of Willkie's birthplace on South A Street; and on the night of July 2 there was a celebration with flags, banners, a torchlight parade and a speech at the high school by the chairman of the National Americanization Committee of the American Legion. The highlight of the evening was a telegram from their famous native son. It confirmed what he had told the press that afternoon—that he would deliver his formal acceptance speech from the front steps of the Elwood High School.

John Stout, a seventeen-year-old high-school football player from Handley, Texas, heard about Willkie's plans for Elwood and became inspired. John's father had gone to school with the Republican candidate. Willkie's nomination, therefore, had provided the Stouts with more excitement than the routine Democratic primaries in that one-party town; and the lad, having digested his father's stories about Willkie and hoping to strengthen his leg muscles to prepare for football at Texas A. & M. College, decided to bicycle the 1,025 miles to Elwood. He equipped his bike with special balloon tires and a number of rear-wheel sprockets, each with a different gear ratio, and took along his pet frog in a specially built cage. "Some unknown friend named H. L. Hunt of Dallas who had become quite interested in what I was going to do" made it possible for Stout to hand out Willkie buttons to all takers by arranging to have his supply replenished at rural post offices all along his route. On the bicycle was a cloth banner donated by the Fort Worth Chamber of Commerce that said: "Fort Worth Says Howdy." Determined to pedal at least ten hours each day, John left Handley on July 8. As he moved northward, press notices alerted towns of his arrival and crowds turned out to cheer and wave encouragingly as he passed through.

For Willkie, meanwhile, important decisions had to be made be-

fore he could retire to some quiet place with his advisers to prepare
the acceptance speech, at a date yet to be determined, and plot the
campaign. He had returned to New York from Philadelphia on Roy
Howard's yacht and then spent the first week in July winding up his
Commonwealth and Southern affairs, meeting with the press and con-
ferring with his personal advisers. The voters, he predicted, would
divide on "certain basic beliefs" rather than on party labels and
would carry him to victory no matter whom the Democrats might
choose. He also said he would not have a "brain trust" and was
determined to present his position in speeches that he would write. "I
have never in my life delivered a speech which I haven't written
myself and I am not going to change my habits now," he declared. He
named an impressive personal advisory committee of twelve that was
headed by Harold Stassen and included Martin, Baldwin, Carr, Root
and, significantly, Mrs. Ruth Hanna Simms of the Dewey campaign
committee. He also reached McNary by telephone and arranged to
meet with his running mate later that week in Washington.

His most serious problem during those early post-convention days
concerned John Hamilton. To many in the party, as well as to Sam
Pryor, retention of the national chairman was a necessity. As the title
also customarily meant doubling as the campaign manager, they felt
that Hamilton had the respect and confidence of the party regulars
that was needed to win their enthusiasm for a renegade Democrat.
Hamilton, as national chairman, had managed to liquidate the party's
debts from the 1936 campaign and had been converted by Charlton
MacVeagh and Sam Pryor to the Willkie cause. The most logical
move, it seemed, would be his reappointment.

An executive session of the party's national committee, held in
Philadelphia on June 28, listened to Willkie's own views. Willkie
wanted a new chairman. Hamilton's identification had been with the
Old Guard, and even in his home state of Kansas he had opposed the
progressive forces that had included Landon. Retaining him, believed
Willkie, would tarnish his own chance to present himself to the voters
as the leader of a freshly updated Republican party unblemished by
associations with past leaders and doctrines.

Politically, as the candidate and the party's new titular head, Willkie needed no further justification to drop Hamilton. He had the
right. Its wisdom was another matter. Willkie, however, seems to have
had what he considered an additional justification. In a letter that he

wrote to Henry Luce four years later, he made the following cryptic explanation: "I didn't appoint him because fifteen advisors unanimously agreed that to do so might produce a national scandal under the facts then existent."

Willkie was en route to New York from Philadelphia when a subcommittee of the Republican party decided to leave the problem of selecting officers up to the candidate. From New York, during the first week in July, Willkie named Joe Martin as the new national chairman and, to reduce the blow to Hamilton and the affront to the party regulars, named the former chairman to a newly created post as executive director of the Republican National Committee. Hamilton and Harold Stassen were assigned to operate out of the campaign's national headquarters, to be located in Chicago; both men would handle the campaign in the western states. As national chairman Martin would continue as the House minority leader. Understandably, Martin was reluctant to accept the additional responsibility. Many agreed that it was an unwise burden, one that would leave him with too little time to do justice to either.

Anticipating Martin's attitude, Willkie arranged for the application of pressure. Once Martin was established at his Cape Cod retreat, he was contacted by Landon, Helen Reid and even by Colonel Robert McCormick. He was, they pointed out, the only man who could unite the party. Nevertheless, Martin did not capitulate until he was brought to New York and cornered in Willkie's apartment by the candidate, Sinclair Weeks and Sam Pryor. Of the persuasive powers of Willkie, Martin later wrote, "I have never known a man so hard to say *no* to. He had a great midwestern simplicity and enthusiasm. . . . As he talked on, I became conscious of the fact that I *liked* Willkie."

The change became one of Willkie's most controversial moves. Hamilton, claiming his behind-the-scenes efforts had been instrumental in Willkie's success, became embittered. He attributed the move to the "liberal wing of the party" and to the *Herald Tribune*'s distress that he had denounced Knox and Stimson for having joined the President's Cabinet.

Sam Pryor was placed in charge of managing the campaign for the Eastern Division, which gave him a seventeen-state area that would be run from a New York headquarters. Russell Davenport was appointed to be Willkie's personal representative. In recognition of the need to attract Democrats and independents, the decision was made to continue Oren Root as the head of the Associated Willkie Clubs of America. Root promptly asked club leaders in the various states to continue their work, which they were eager to do.

On July 8, before leaving New York, Willkie submitted ten resignations, as president of Commonwealth and Southern as well as director and chairman of its facilities, and as president and director of the General Corporation of New York City. Late that afternoon he arrived in Washington, where he held his first meeting with McNary. Then he went on to vacation headquarters, at the Broadmoor Hotel in Colorado Springs. A letter from Alf Landon told him that he had "caught the imagination of the American people" and that a sampling of voter sentiment in the Democratic section of Missouri had shown heavy pro-Willkie sentiment. Meanwhile, the House of Representatives beat back Rankin's amendment and voted by 243-122 to extend the Hatch Act to limit financial contributions as a safeguard against pernicious political activities, and the Senate Campaign Expenditures Committee, led by Guy Gillette of Iowa, decided that there was insufficient evidence to justify an investigation of reports that a high-pressure "telegram drive was employed in the campaign" to nominate Willkie.

The President knew that he had a formidable opponent. Apart from the Hoosier's brash statement that he hoped FDR would run for a third term, the Republican presented new and solid problems. Since Willkie had never held office, he had no public record that could be attacked; and the manner of his nomination was intimidating. His political amateur enthusiasts had already achieved the impossible. Most disturbing, perhaps, was that Roosevelt was finally faced with an attractive antagonist. Glamour had, in the past, been a Roosevelt prerogative. And although FDR thought it a "godsend to the country" that Willkie was not an isolationist, he knew that, consequently, the issues must concern domestic matters, and the Republican's criticism, he felt, would have to center on the New Deal. Privately, Roosevelt had said that if he should run against Willkie without a continuing European war, his opponent would be elected. An important question now was whether, since there was general agreement that a Dewey, Taft or Vandenberg might have been stopped by Cordell Hull or someone else, Willkie presented a mandate for four more Roosevelt years.

2

Since the Charlottesville policy had been stated, the rapid deterioration of the war situation for the Allies only added to the President's feeling of uncertainty. The diplomatic picture was both sensitive and many-faceted. The Soviet Union was assuming an actively defensive role toward Hitler. The Vichy government required cautious handling. The problem of the French fleet's disposition caused constant anxiety, and it was crucial that the French government be discouraged from full collaboration with the Third Reich. Also, the United States was the link between Great Britain and her former ally, France. With adroit manipulation, rifles, machine guns and ammunition were sent to the British Home Guard so that they could hold back the expected invaders. Roosevelt's advisers were frantically opposed to his efforts to give this personalized aid to Britain. They named it political suicide and exactly what the President's opponents needed to provide them with the argument that Roosevelt was indirectly helping the enemy of the United States. Since England must fall, they argued, anything sent to her would eventually fall into German hands.

Very conscious of the Roosevelt Administration's hostility, Germany had an intense interest in the choice of the Democratic presidential candidate. For many years the Third Reich had equated FDR with anti-Nazi American foreign policy. *Chargé d'Affaires* Hans Thomsen had written, "The *leitmotiv* of Roosevelt's policy is America's participation in another war of annihilation against Germany." Therefore, it was most important for the Third Reich, he insisted, that Roosevelt's possible candidacy be stopped.

Thomsen's initial step, taken in the spring of 1940, the publication of the German White Paper, had failed to discredit the President. Consequently, additional Nazi money was assigned to a projected literary campaign. Twenty thousand dollars was disbursed to encourage five projects whose objective was Roosevelt's defeat. For many years the German Embassy had recognized that, rather than the silly posturings of Fritz Kuhn and his German-American Bund, it was the isolationists who were potentially most useful to the German position. If they could be supported and encouraged to continue their anti-interventionist stand, Germany would be free to pursue her conquest of Europe unimpeded and Roosevelt would be effectively stopped.

The Nazi government had been trying to influence American voters since early that year. Working through a New York publisher, German money backed offers to several isolationist writers. Care was taken to conceal the source of the funds, and, through this method, such writers as Theodore Dreiser, Kathleen Norris, Burton Rascoe and George Creel turned out anti-interventionist literature.

Americans responded with horror to the bombing of Britain and the growing danger of Nazi domination of Europe. Therefore, Thomsen pressed harder for the policy of allowing the isolationists to support German aims. The Nazis maintained discreet contacts with several Congressmen to reach large audiences. The attaché reported to his superiors that three anti-interventionists' speeches were introduced into the *Congressional Record* and that, thanks to the franking privilege, about one hundred thousand citizens would receive free copies. "The cost of this large-scale propaganda can be kept disproportionately low," he rejoiced.

As the time for the Democratic convention drew near, Thomsen wired a full analysis of FDR's pre-convention status. On July 4 he predicted that Roosevelt's prospects for re-election had declined. His optimism was based on the swift defeat of France, the President's underestimation of German power, the nomination of Willkie and the election campaign activities of John L. Lewis and Senator Burton K. Wheeler. Furthermore, he said, the Democratic party was disunited and John L. Lewis, in control of eight or ten million votes, was opposed to the war lest it lead to American fascism. In conclusion, Thomsen told his superiors, "the psychosis holding America in its grip today will make way for a saner approach to German-American relations. If Roosevelt is defeated in the election [this] can be regarded as certain in the light of all past experience."

Citing successful German influence in achieving isolationist language in the Republican foreign-policy plank and congratulating himself that "nothing has leaked out about the assistance we rendered in this," Thomsen proposed similar action in Chicago. He assured his home office that "several reliable Congressmen went to Chicago in order to exert influence on the delegates with the purpose of including, at least formally, in the Democratic platform, as well, a pledge of non-participation in a European war."

Just before the convention started an additional forty-five hundred dollars was allotted for "travel assistance" to the several unidentified Congressmen and for a full-page advertisement in the Chicago *Tribune* similar to the one in *The New York Times* of June 25. The advertisement, signed by John J. O'Connor of New York, Samuel B. Pettingill of Indiana and Martin L. Sweeney of Ohio, was sponsored by The National Committee to Keep America Out of War. Addressed to the delegates of the Democratic national convention, American mothers, wage earners, farmers and veterans, its plea, in large letters, was to "Stop the March of War" and, in slightly smaller letters, to "Stop the Interventionists and the Warmongers." The big issue at the convention, the notice cautioned, was a referendum on war. "The Republican party at Philadelphia deliberately struck out of its platform a declaration against sending our boys to fight on foreign soil. Don't let the Democratic party make the same mistake. It will be fatal in November." Quotations from isolationist Democrats such as Senators Wheeler and Champ Clark criticizing the appointments of Stimson and Knox filled the page.

In retrospect, it could be questioned why the German government, if it really believed so much to be at stake, did not spend more money to achieve its aims.

3

Senator Wheeler regarded Roosevelt's commitment in his "stab in the back" speech as little short of participation in the European war. Wheeler said, "I want everyone who is interested in the matter to know that I am not going to support any candidate for President of the United States of America, no matter who he may be, who is going to try to get us into this war." The danger for the Democrats now, he thought, was that it would be regarded as the war party.

But others looked at the situation more realistically. Congress voted to postpone its scheduled adjournment because of the gravity of the war crisis. And Hitler's latest success had resulted in a sharp increase in favor of the incumbent.

The appointments of Stimson and Knox puzzled some commentators who observed that, politically speaking, this might mean that FDR would not seek a third term. Otherwise, logically, would he make a first move toward a coalition government so close to convention time?

Nevertheless, Roosevelt was still adding to his pre-convention strength. The Michigan Democrats unanimously endorsed him. Colorado and Minnesota voted their support. The executive vice president of labor's Non-Partisan League resigned because of Lewis' opposition to a third term. In spite of the official stand, he said, the majority of the members of the League support FDR. By the end of June the unofficial scoreboard estimated 707½ votes for the President at the forthcoming convention. He was far ahead of the contenders who were still being mentioned, such as Hull, Garner, McNutt and Farley.

James Farley's autobiography states that his own final decision to become a candidate was made on June 28, 1940, after a Cabinet meeting which offended him because politics was discussed rather than the foreign situation. Farley was "disgusted with the political situation." As in Hull's case, he had not been told in advance of the Knox–Stimson appointments, which he would have opposed simply because of their Republican affiliations. For a long time Farley had sought an interview with Roosevelt to have a serious talk about party matters.

On Sunday, July 7, Farley arrived at Hyde Park just before the President returned from church. He was greeted by Mrs. Sarah Roosevelt, who immediately commented on the morning newspaper stories that revealed Farley's intention to leave politics to head the New York Yankees. The President's mother said, "You know I would hate to think of Franklin running for the Presidency if you were not around. I want you to be sure to help my boy."

As soon as FDR returned, lunch was served. It was a quiet meal with conversation ranging from a discussion of the French surrender to speculation on the legality of Andrew Jackson's wife's divorce. After lunch the two Democratic party leaders retired to the President's study for the confrontation.

Just as the year before, the discussion of the important subject was long in coming. Roosevelt foundered in small talk for about half an hour, and Farley did nothing to help him. Finally, the President launched into a summary of his past year's political activity.

Though a seemingly excellent report, the only account of the conversation between Farley and Roosevelt is Farley's own. FDR appeared to be defending his failure to decline a third term, an action that he had assured the Postmaster General the preceding summer he would take no later than February. The war in Europe was given as his reason for changing his mind. "It would have destroyed my effectiveness as the leader of the nation," he observed.

Throughout the long interview the President chain-smoked, puffing through his familiar long holder. Farley listened and fought against being overwhelmed by the Roosevelt charm.

"Jim, I don't want to run and I'm going to tell the convention so," Roosevelt asserted.

"If you make it specific, the convention will not nominate you," answered Farley. These were his first words and enabled him to expand on his opposition to the third term as a matter of principle, his own and the Democratic party's.

The President's smiles were turned off as Farley discussed the other possible Democratic candidates who could be nominated and elected if the convention were free to act. However, at this late date, commented Farley, everyone but Garner and himself seemed to be out of the running. Farley believed that Roosevelt knew and everyone else knew that he would run again. And furthermore it was Farley's belief that this conversation had been deliberately delayed until one week before the convention because otherwise Secretary Hull, for one, might have prevented the renomination.

It was a relief to their mutual discomfort when the conversation shifted to the other major problem, the vice-presidential nominee. They mentioned the touchy subject of Garner and then quickly dismissed Senator Scott Lucas of Illinois and Governor Lloyd C. Stark of Missouri. Roosevelt made no comment about Farley's criticism of Henry Wallace. The Postmaster General's observation that Wallace would not get the farm vote and would lose votes in the East was ignored, as was the comment that it would be a mistake to have in such an office someone whom people regarded as a "wild-eyed fellow." While Farley talked he became convinced that FDR had made up his mind to choose Wallace but would keep a canny silence in order to retain the support of the other vice-presidential contenders.

For the first and last time in the Roosevelt–Farley relationship, the President mentioned his physical disability. He said that the Vice President must be healthy because "a man with paralysis can have a breakup anytime." He pulled up his shirt, unbuttoned it and displayed a lump of flesh and muscle under his left shoulder. This, he said, was due to polio and having to sit all the time.

Many vice-presidential potentials were mentioned and rejected:

Jesse Jones, a presidential unfavorite; Garner; Rayburn; James Byrnes; Paul McNutt and others. After this review Farley announced abruptly that he could not run the 1940 campaign because of his opposition to a third term and because of his financial obligation to his family. Roosevelt was visibly concerned. He tried to figure out ways in which Farley could remain as national chairman, conduct the campaign and hold down a job. One suggestion was that Farley assign the heavy work to a campaign manager. Both men agreed that the only serious difference that would develop in the writing of the party platform would be the foreign-relations plank. Roosevelt had a number of suggestions for the wording that would be acceptable to all: "We do not want to become involved in a foreign war," or "We are opposed to this country's participation in any wars unless for the protection of the Western hemisphere," or "We are in favor of extending aid to democracies in their struggle against the totalitarian powers, within the law."

A false heartiness punctuated the conversation. Roosevelt surely disliked having to defend himself, and Farley was working hard to control his temper. The chairman was certain that FDR had decided long before to break the third-term precedent because of his belief that only he was qualified to fill the office of President of the United States at this time. It is possible that it was during this exchange with his party's voice and self-appointed conscience that FDR decided to run again.

Farley now knew definitively that he would not have Roosevelt's endorsement even for Vice President. When he left the study he was in a rage. Steve Early, who said that he was "the maddest white man I've ever seen," drove him around the countryside to cool him off before the reporters got at him. It was a grim-faced national chairman who finally informed the press that "I have full knowledge of the President's thoughts and what he has in mind on the subject of the third term, but I will not discuss it with any individual."

4

Roosevelt had great ambivalence about his decision to accept or to reject a third term. He wanted the New Deal to continue, and he thought it imperative for the safety of the world that his foreign policy prevail. His superb political sense told him that he alone, of all the Democrats, could be reasonably certain of success. But it is equally certain that the acceptance of a third term constituted a genuine personal sacrifice. Granted that FDR enjoyed power, felt that no one could do the job as well as he, was accustomed to the White House routine and would miss the excitement of office. Nevertheless, there was another side of him that craved other things. Roosevelt wanted to be a country squire just as his mother always pictured him, raising trees and improving his working farm. He wanted to be an elder statesman issuing brilliant solutions of complex problems from his Hudson River retreat. He wanted to be a scholar going over his papers and writing the definitive history of the New Deal from the lovely Memorial Library. He wanted to be an influential editor, sending his regular copy to *Collier's,* as he had contracted to do.

More personal was the urge to give in to the nagging physical fatigue that seven years in office had turned into a chronic complaint. The city of Washington was very bad for Roosevelt's sinus condition. He said that what he really needed was a month in the hospital to clear up the condition, but such a move would upset the country, perhaps the world. And he was a man imprisoned in a wheelchair with little outlet for the tremendous pressure that presidential office carries with it.

As powerful as was the intensive strain of his work, more difficult was the loneliness that Roosevelt had endured. Responsibility cannot be passed on any farther than the Executive Office. Rexford Tugwell said that was why FDR had to think of himself as "God's servant" going about his "Father's business with no doubts to torment him." His family was not much help. The children were scattered all over the country, and Mrs. Roosevelt was involved in many activities and many commitments. The companionship of friends was not always feasible. It can be uncomfortable to be too close to the throne. Harry Hopkins, who lived in the White House for several years, said that he was often flooded with appeals for help from office-seekers and people down on their luck, which he found embarrassing. But whenever he told the President that he would like to leave, FDR would ask him to stay so that, as Hopkins put it, he would have "someone to talk to when he wants to—or not to talk to."

Most of the Roosevelt children privately opposed a third term because they could see clearly that their father had aged considerably on the job and that, probably, his health was beginning to decline. Elliott Roosevelt tried to head off a third term from his radio station in Texas, saying that many opposed the New Deal. FDR defended his son's action with the statement "Mr. Elliott Roosevelt is an American citizen—free and of adult age. He, therefore, enjoys among other things the right of free speech and is entitled to the exercise of that right." James Roosevelt admitted that he had one of his few serious arguments with his father when he tried to talk him out of running a third time. Apart from a belief that the tradition should not be broken, the President's eldest son felt that his father had done his job beautifully and deserved a rest. "We did not want to lose him," he said. Mrs. Eleanor Roosevelt was disturbed at the idea of another term for all of the reasons already stated and some personal ones of her own. But she made no attempt to dissuade her husband because it was her policy not to try to interfere with the President's major decisions.

Any attempt to pinpoint accurately the precise date when Roosevelt made up his mind to be the Democratic candidate for 1940 is presumptuous. Contemporaries, including the President's closest friends and advisers, differ sharply on this matter. Most agree, however, that it was after Hitler's resumption of the war in the spring of 1940. James Farley and Ed Flynn believed that it was after the seventeenth of May. Frances Perkins indicated the beginning of 1940. Judge Rosenman reported that up to April 8, 1940, Roosevelt had decided not to run and that by the time of the invasion of France, on May 10, he was still uncertain. It was not until after the evacuation of the British at Dunkirk that his mind was made up. Tom Corcoran set the date back a few months. "The Democratic convention was held in Copenhagen," he said. Arthur Krock placed the date very much earlier. By 1938, he said, Roosevelt believed that he was indispensable, that the security of the country depended on his continuance in office because of the European war, which he predicted could not be avoided. Harry Hopkins, however, told Paul H. Appleby that the President did not definitely decide until late in the day following the actual voting at the Democratic convention. However, Pearson and Allen, by writing that Roosevelt made his definite decision on July 10, point to its connection with Willkie's nomination. Whether or not it actually occurred on that day, it seems that Roosevelt had indeed kept his options open for just such a contingency.

The President had to weigh very carefully the reasons for and against acceptance of the nomination. Objections included the danger of challenging the tradition, exposure to the charge of dictatorship, personal considerations such as health both physical and mental and the postponement of other activities such as farming and writing. He did not need to be a wartime President to achieve fame. These arguments, all valid, break down on one point—a successor. Who was the liberal New Dealer able to continue the delicate international program and capable of capturing the labor vote and the support of minorities? The names of Farley, Hull, Garner and the many others revolved endlessly in his mind when he thought about the dilemma. No one, and certainly no one at that late date, fitted the part. Although *The New York Times* observed that because there was no clear difference in attitude toward foreign affairs between Willkie and FDR, therefore "It is now that President's clear duty" to withdraw and support a candidate with his own principles, the *Times* didn't have a Democratic candidate to offer. And all indications showed that the electorate wanted FDR. Of 5,450 letters that were received at the White House by convention time, the third term was favored 89-1.

Many admirers of Roosevelt's political genius were disappointed and puzzled by his seemingly haphazard handling of this difficult and important maneuver. He was accused of displaying only a casual and intermittent interest in planning the convention. In part, this attitude might have been an unconscious wish to fail to get the nomination or, at least, to postpone a conscious acceptance. Roosevelt knew that he was tired and older and that the years ahead promised to be even more trying than those that had gone before. Self-preservation might have been at work. But, on the other hand, practical genius that he was, he knew that the vacillating technique worked well. Maybe it was the master plan after all. Except for a weak conservative opposition, there was no real competition to the President as the Democratic delegates prepared to travel to Chicago.

CHAPTER EIGHT

Shattering a Tradition

1

As THE DEMOCRATIC delegates started to converge on Chicago for the business of choosing a presidential candidate, Franklin Roosevelt invited Judge Samuel Rosenman to join him at the White House. Rosenman, who had been with the President during the convention weeks of 1932 and 1936, sent his family on ahead to Montana for their vacation and obeyed the summons. Most observers immediately concluded that Rosenman's presence meant that he was there to help write the third-term acceptance speech.

Washington was particularly hot and humid that July, a discomfort that the President did not have relieved by air conditioning. He said that refrigeration irritated his sinuses, and he permitted only a floor fan to be placed far away from him in a corner of the study. He made himself as cool as possible by wearing seersucker trousers, removing his jacket and tie, unbuttoning his collar and rolling up his sleeves. He looked uncomfortable as his clothes wrinkled, and he perspired heavily. But he would just mop his brow and claim not to mind the heat. This was, of course, a trial to those who worked with him. Some of the other White House rooms were air-conditioned, but anywhere that the President received was not.

Roosevelt saw to it that conversation about the imminent convention was avoided, particularly at mealtime. He went to bed early and succeeded in giving the appearance of being completely unperturbed by the approaching event. Judge Rosenman spent his time reading the rough drafts of the platform and notes for the acceptance speech. The decision to run had not been made, nor had the nomination been tendered, but, realistically, a speech would have to be ready. Some conversation with the President revealed that he preferred Henry Wallace for Vice President and was rather stubbornly opposed to all other contenders.

Roosevelt had made up his mind that under no circumstances would he go to Chicago. His duties at the Capitol were only part of the reason for his decision. He felt that his presence there would be tantamount to forcing the votes of the delegates. But his strongest advocates at the convention were disappointed. His appearance, they reasoned, would please the delegates and spark enthusiasm. Nevertheless, FDR told his wife, who was at her Hyde Park cottage, that neither of them should go to the convention city. Rather more abrupt than usual but cheerful and in seemingly excellent health, Roosevelt informed the press of his decision to remain in Washington.

On Saturday, July 13, the presidential party took a weekend cruise down the river on the *Potomac*. Roosevelt loved the sea. The quiet atmosphere aboard the ship and the fine meals prepared by his Filipino chef were a respite from the hectic White House pace. His stamp books were carried on board so he could spend some time arranging his stamps, and there was an opportunity to fish.

Serious conferences about political matters took place in the dining cabin. Roosevelt believed that Farley would make a fight on the floor and therefore particularly wanted the delegates to realize that he was not exerting the force of his prestige to capture the nomination. What he really wanted was a message that would carry to the Democrats just that nuance of thought. Hopkins had been given a presidential message to take to Chicago but it was not precisely right. Rosenman took his own version out of his briefcase and presented it to the President. In longhand, FDR wrote a message that integrated both versions. He added a sentence that clearly released his delegates.

About four P.M. Sunday afternoon the ship docked in Washington. Dinner at the White House again skirted political talk. Oppressive heat sent Roosevelt to bed early, but Rosenman continued to work on the acceptance speech in his air-conditioned bedroom. Very late, Attorney General Robert Jackson and Frank Walker telephoned from Chicago. They warned that the consensus was that the President should not send a message that released his delegates nor should he announce that he did not wish to be a candidate. They said that Chicago, just before the convention, seemed to be feeling Farley strength.

2

About a week before the start of the convention the Garner offices were opened. The mezzanine of the Sherman Hotel, where the headquarters were established, was transformed to look like a little corner of Texas. A Texas steer head was hung on the wall and cactus plants replaced the hotel's potted palms. The climax of the opening festivities was Manager Eugene B. Germany's ride into the lobby mounted on a bronco. The horse carried a valuable saddle and bridle. The rider wore a white satin shirt trimmed with black braid, khaki cowboy pants, high-heeled boots and the traditional ten-gallon hat. "Go with Garner" banners were unfurled to the accompaniment of rousing cowboy yells. A free-lunch counter and bar completed the opening of the offices. Proudly, Campaign Manager Germany claimed Texas' forty-six votes for Vice President John Nance Garner.

"Wheeler for President" headquarters were opened much more quietly at the Congress Hotel on July 9. Wheeler had stated his position clearly: opposition to Stimson and Knox, whom he called warmongers, and a liberal peace movement, outside the two major parties, if necessary. Wheeler had supported Roosevelt's measure for an appropriation of four billion dollars for defense right before the convention, but he had done this only after the President had assured the country that he would not send American troops to Europe. However, it was clear that Wheeler planned to be a candidate at the Democratic convention.

The most interesting headquarters in Chicago was not at the Stevens Hotel, where the Democratic national staff was domiciled, but at Harry Hopkins' daytime suite at the Blackstone Hotel and nighttime quarters at the Ambassador East. The real status of this amateur FDR stronghold was difficult to assess. For all practical purposes, it was conducted as if it had full presidential approval. Such ardent New Deal supporters as Robert Jackson, James Byrnes, Mayor Ed Kelly of Chicago, Mayor Frank Hague of Jersey City and Frank C. Walker spent most of their time with Hopkins. And those who were not full-blooded New Dealers received cool treatment. For further security from anti-Rooseveltians, the headquarters was manned by members of the Commerce Department whom the Secretary had brought with him.

FDR denied to Eleanor Roosevelt that Hopkins was his direct representative. Hopkins, most observers said, believed that he was. And the direct telephone line to the White House that was concealed in the Hopkins suite seemed to verify that impression. Paul Appleby, who was Hopkins' lieutenant in his official assignment, which was to support Roosevelt's choice for Vice President, declared that before that mission Hopkins was not the President's manager but strictly on his own.

At least two of the most prominent Democrats refused to recognize Hopkins' role. Party Chairman Farley said testily that if Harry Hopkins wanted to see him, "he can see me in the office of the Democratic National Committee, where everybody else sees me." Harold Ickes was particularly peeved because he thought of himself as the keynoter of the third-term movement. He, claimed Ickes, was advocating a third term when Hopkins was still "nurturing his own sick and absurd boom." But the presence of Hopkins meant the same thing to all the delegates—that Roosevelt planned to run again.

The Hopkins pseudo-headquarters was typical Roosevelt behavior. Chicago was bustling with professional politicians, but the President preferred a personal pipeline for his information. Hopkins was bypassing officialdom in much the same manner as did Sumner Welles on his European mission earlier in the year.

3

Bright red was the dominating color at the Democratic convention. The banks of seats covered in red gave a festive look to the Chicago stadium. Three thousand yards of red, white and blue bunting covered the tiers, and six hundred and twelve American flags were hung about the hall. Suspended from the west-end balcony was a huge sketch of FDR's head, on which a spotlight played at appropriate times during the sessions. A picture of Vice President Garner hung from the opposite end. The Speaker's rostrum was decorated with a great golden eagle with a six-foot wing spread. Into this patriotic scene trooped thirty-five hundred delegates and alternates and seventeen thousand visitors. The heat generated by the people and the million-watt lights was counteracted by an attempt at air conditioning. Twenty-four hundred tons of ice were placed in thirteen hoppers while fans threw fresh air over them and fed the cooled air into the stadium.

The beautifully planned, well-organized convention had provided adequate housing for the delegates and all kinds of provisions for their comfort. Television had been banned because of the heat that the lighting would have caused. And for seating the delegates, four hundred college men, each one at least six feet tall, were employed as ushers. Dressed in blue and gold, they too added sparkle to the proceedings.

In spite of all this, it was an unhappy convention, even before it started. The excitement was missing. If the delegates were there to renominate the President again, they really had nothing to do. The joy of battle would be absent. It would not be easy to bring this crowd to life.

The first session met on Monday, July 15. James A. Farley presided and declared the convention open. A bombastic, pithy speech was delivered by Mayor Edward J. Kelly. Harold Ickes thought that his delivery had improved considerably. The Mayor praised Chicago and mocked the Republicans. "Chicago's environment will help you to ward off any telegraphic bombardments from Wall Street," he said. "You will not find here any Morgan shadows ghost-walking at your heels, those who would corner the market, even on humanity. . . ." He then suggested that though the President was not a candidate, "We must overrule his comfort and convenience and draft Roosevelt." There was applause but no spontaneous outburst.

In the evening session Farley spoke and was received with great enthusiasm. Though he talked of the achievements of the Administration, not once did he mention the President by name. Speaker of the House William Bankhead of Alabama was presented as the Temporary Chairman. His speech was an uninspired summary of Democratic achievements and Republican shortcomings. It was surprising, however, that he also failed to mention FDR by name.

The first round would have to be awarded to Farley. Even the band selections favored the anti-New Deal wing. Most frequently played was "Take Me Out to the Ball Game," to remind the delegates of Farley's determination to leave the Cabinet and the party for the Yankees, and "The Eyes of Texas" for Garner. The atmosphere was cold and indifferent. Roosevelt supporters feared that the convention might turn hostile.

One key to the situation was Mayor Kelly's report that he had received only 10 percent of the visitor seats instead of the customary 20 percent allotted to the Mayor of the convention city. Ickes, learning about this, suspected that Farley meant to pack the galleries with anti-Roosevelt people. A hasty conference of New Dealers, including Ickes, Jackson, Byrnes and Hopkins, came up with the idea of shortening the convention by holding nominations earlier than scheduled. This tactic, they thought, would thwart any renewed interest in other candidates. Ickes was rather suspicious of Hopkins' easy acquiescence to his plan, but it was arranged that the stampede take place on Tuesday night. Roosevelt, after being informed of the scheme by phone, vetoed it. He preferred to take his chances and to continue the convention procedure as planned.

At the White House, Roosevelt had been in touch with Hopkins and the others over the direct line. He absolutely would not be persuaded to change his mind about the message to the convention because he wanted his nomination to come freely and openly from the delegates and he wanted it clear, for the permanent record, that he was not actively seeking a third term. He was equally adamant about having the message read as early as possible, by Bankhead, at the first evening session. However, when it was pointed out that, because of the difference in time between Chicago and New York, it would be midnight there before Bankhead could deliver the President's message, Roosevelt changed his mind. In order to be certain that more people would hear the statement, he agreed to its delay until Barkley's speech, which was scheduled for early Tuesday evening. He wanted the message to reach as many listeners as possible.

Meanwhile work on the acceptance speech continued. Archibald MacLeish contributed some passages. The break between the Tommy

Corcoran–Ben Cohen team and the President, which had been rumored for some time, became apparent over this speech. The President answered with a cool "No" when Rosenman asked him if he
wanted them to collaborate on the drafts.

Roosevelt was convinced that the advice of his Chicago advisers
had been correct after he heard the tone of Bankhead's speech. He
must have been relieved to know that his message was in Barkley's
hands instead. After the speech, Harry Hopkins called to complain
that Farley and his friends were spreading the story that the President
had promised Farley the nomination. It was clear that Farley was still
after it.

4

The low point of the convention for the Roosevelt backers was
Tuesday morning, July 16. The atmosphere in the Chicago stadium
was leaden and depressed. The New Dealers felt overwhelmingly
that the President should come to Chicago but were afraid to ask
him. Ickes, whose brashness was legendary, finally agreed to send a
telegram to the White House. It was a long, dramatic statement.
"This convention is bleeding to death . . . your reputation and prestige may bleed to death with it," Ickes wired. He said that the "nine
hundred leaderless delegates milling about like worried sheep"
needed the President's "personal appearance." Ickes predicted that
the result of the tactics of the "Farley–Wheeler" clique could be a
ticket that would "assure the election of Willkie, and Willkie meant
fascism and appeasement." The telegram was never acknowledged in
any way.

But that night the atmosphere at the convention changed. Alben
Barkley accepted the permanent chairmanship of the convention with
a vigorous speech that attacked the Republicans and, most important,
paid personal tribute to Franklin D. Roosevelt. The effort of the past
seven years to remold "the faith of our people in their own brand of
democracy," Barkley said, has been under "the leadership of one of
the world's greatest and most outstanding Democrats, Franklin D.
Roosevelt." Barkley's words awakened the somnolent delegates. They
rose to their feet, cheered, applauded, poured into the aisles carrying
their standards high. After a brief struggle the Massachusetts banner

was wrested from its holder and carried into the parade. The chairman tried to restore order but was answered with cries of "No, No!" and the cheering continued, interrupted only by shouts of "We want Roosevelt" and "We want Roosevelt now." After addressing the convention as "My friends," which was received with bursts of laughter, Barkley was allowed to continue his denunciation of the Republicans and recapitulation of New Deal achievements.

"Now, my friends," said Barkley, "I have an additional statement to make on behalf of the President of the United States." Once more he was interrupted by cheers and applause. He paused for a moment, then went on. He informed them that Roosevelt had "no wish to be a candidate again, that he had not influenced the selection of the delegates" and that "all of the delegates to this convention are free to vote for any candidate."

After a brief moment of uncomprehending silence the convention seemed to go mad altogether. As shrieking delegates waved stuffed donkeys and surged toward the platform, the chant "We want Roosevelt" was resumed. State chants followed: "Florida wants Roosevelt," and so on from coast to coast. Completely carried away, one delegate roared, "Willkie wants Roosevelt." Throughout the uproar the organ played the Roosevelt theme song, "Happy Days Are Here Again." Even the most unlikely were involved in the demonstration. Someone spotted Sumner Welles involved in a snake dance in the aisles, looking determined but vastly uncomfortable. Barkley was handed a picture of FDR which he waved from the rostrum, evoking more and louder cheering. From 11:10 P.M., the demonstration continued for fifty-three minutes.

Mrs. Roosevelt listened carefully to Barkley's speech from Hyde Park. Earlier, the President had phoned her to turn on the radio. On the whole, she thought the speech a good one. But she knew now that Roosevelt would not turn down the draft, and, as the demonstration raged, she shook her head resignedly.

London also interpreted the statement as tantamount to renomination of the President. The British were greatly relieved, as David Low's cartoon, published the next day, reflected. He drew FDR and Willkie sitting on some steps flipping a coin. Hitler watched from behind a pillar. The caption read, "Heads we win, tails he loses."

The New York Times continued to be disapproving. An editorial chided Roosevelt for failing to honor the third-term tradition and for the release of his delegates. The newspaper pointed out that this move had no meaning in practical politics other than an invitation to a draft.

A number of postponements had delayed the presentation of the Democratic platform by the Committee of Resolutions, whose chairman was Robert Wagner, senior Senator from New York, until Wednesday night, June 17. The difficulty had been over the language of the foreign-policy plank, just as Roosevelt had predicted. Isolationists, interventionists and the independent voter all had to be satisfied with the statement. Disagreement centered about the statement which said: "We will not send our army, naval or air forces to fight in foreign lands outside of the Americas." Roosevelt protested that no human being could guarantee such a promise. After discussion over the telephone with Hopkins and Byrnes, who, in turn, talked with Wheeler and other isolationists, Roosevelt solved the problem himself. He added the phrase "except in case of attack," which was adopted by all the factions.

At the convention the presentation of the platform went smoothly until an amendment was introduced by Congressman Elmer J. Ryan of Minnesota stating that "no man should be eligible for a third term of the presidential office." It was overwhelmingly defeated by a voice vote and, just as overwhelmingly, the platform was adopted.

The climax of the convention, the selection of the presidential candidate, was about to take place. Almost everyone in the country, even in the world, assumed that Franklin D. Roosevelt would be renominated. It was the main reason for the general lack of enthusiasm that characterized the disgruntled delegates. They did not oppose the President. On the contrary, most of them supported him. But as professional politicians they chafed uncomfortably at the prospect of four more Roosevelt years. They had been subjected to the introduction of strange figures such as professors, economists—all sorts of amateurs—and had been deprived of patronage. The abortive "purge" frightened some, the Supreme Court fight alienated others. Many had been by-passed for men who supported FDR but were either brand-new Democrats or, often, not Democrats at all. In brief, they were tired of the New Deal and longed for an end to it, a return to the familiar field of partisan politics.

Representative Lister Hill of Alabama had been given the privilege of nominating "the valiant American," Franklin Delano Roosevelt.

He did so in a most undistinguished speech. Nevertheless, from 9:15 to 10:17 P.M. the crowd almost repeated the performance following the Barkley speech. At Hill's mention of FDR's name, the band burst into "The Song of Franklin D. Roosevelt Jones." The California delegation led the eruption into the aisles, followed by Iowa, its delegates waving bunches of corn leaves. Marching delegates thronged the corridors shouting and waving standards. Virginia, Texas, Oklahoma and most of New York, however, stayed out of the general rejoicing.

Many were annoyed to read, later, accounts of the activities of Thomas D. Garry, Mayor Kelly's loyal Superintendent of Sewers. To make up for the Mayor's curtailed power in the balconies, Garry was stationed in the basement with a microphone through which he roared "We want Roosevelt" and other appropriate messages that would spark the delegates' enthusiasm. By the second day some of the delegates suspected that something was going on. On July 18 the newspapers had published the story. Honors for arranging the strategy must be shared by Mayor Frank Hague, who was credited with starting the parade of states, after Barkley's announcement of the President's message, by carrying the New Jersey placard into the aisles. It was, realistically, a critical moment. The mayors and others feared that the message might be used as the excuse to start an anti-third-term defection that would cause an immediate swing to another candidate that could not be stopped.

When the state of Arkansas was called by the clerk, its chairman yielded to Virginia. Senator Carter Glass, frail, old and sick, made his way to the platform while the crowd cheered. Employing two emotional gambits—the third-term tradition, which he hallowed by using the name of Thomas Jefferson, and religious equality—the aged Senator said: "I have come from a sickbed to present to this convention the name of a great Democrat, James A. Farley of New York." There was a five-minute demonstration.

The roll call of states continued without incident except for the nominations of Millard E. Tydings by Edward J. Colgan, Jr., of Maryland and, later, John Nance Garner by Wright Morrow of Texas. The delegates from the Lone Star State paraded enthusiastically to the tune of "Round-Up Time." After the roll call of states was completed with its nominations and seconds, the first ballot was called.

There were 1,100 votes. Roosevelt received 946 13/30; Farley, 72 9/10; Garner, 61; Hull, 5 2/3.

Action moved fast. Sam Rayburn of Texas rose to declare that it was the wish of Vice President Garner and the unanimous desire of the Texas delegation to withdraw its forty-six votes for Garner and to cast them for Roosevelt. Farley then got the floor and moved to suspend the rules and to declare President Franklin D. Roosevelt nominated for President of the United States by acclamation. Applause and cheers met this proposal. Millard Tydings withdrew from the race. Governor Prentice Cooper of Tennessee told the convention that Cordell Hull authorized him to say that he was not nor had he ever been a presidential candidate.

There was no wild demonstration when the decision was reached. Entertainer Phil Regan led the band in the song "When Irish Eyes Are Smiling," which seemed more of a tribute to the popular Jim Farley than to the victorious candidate.

5

Roosevelt stayed close to the radio and the telephone during these proceedings. Stephen Early stood guard to answer any political questions with "No news." The nomination was not in the form that the President had ordered. He had wanted a genuine draft, a spontaneous wave of acclamation that would carry him into the White House free of any accusation of political self-seeking. It had been only partially achieved. Wheeler, avowedly satisfied with the foreign-relations plank, withdrew, but Farley, Tydings and Garner spoiled the show.

So far the New Deal was triumphant, but the hardest task was yet to be accomplished. Roosevelt did not address the convention nor did he change his mind about going to Chicago. He waited to see whether his personal power could achieve the nomination of his choice for Vice President, Henry A. Wallace.

FDR wanted the Secretary of Agriculture on his ticket because he believed him to be honest, a hard worker, a good administrator, a New Dealer, right on the war question, and, furthermore, he told Farley when he telephoned the party chairman on the morning of July 18, "He's the kind of fellow I want around." That Wallace was a relatively new Democrat, shy and often out of contact with the party, was perfectly well known to Roosevelt. Also, he was aware of Wallace's interest in the occult, which frightened many Rooseveltians, particularly those who had seen the letter in which Wallace told FDR that he could be "the flaming one." Roosevelt could strip away such a personality quirk by dismissing it as Wallace's interest in some kind of philosophy. He knew him, much more importantly, as knowledgeable and hard-hitting when he wanted his agricultural policies adopted. And his colleagues and subordinates admired him.

The President's insistence on Wallace for Vice President was not loss of political perspective in the handling of the convention, as Ickes charged. He wanted Wallace for what he considered to be excellent reasons, meant to get him and, with characteristic optimism, was ready to stake his future on it. Grace Tully said that when Harry Hopkins called the President after his nomination to tell him that the convention might not go for Wallace, Roosevelt shouted: "Well, damn it to hell, they will go for Wallace or I won't run and you can jolly well tell them so."

The vice-presidential aspirants had been subjected to the same ruthless Roosevelt guillotine as the presidential hopefuls. Farley estimated the number of possibilities at seventeen. They included a range of personalities from Garner, who was now *persona non grata* with his chief, to James Byrnes, a presidential favorite but considered an impractical candidate because he had changed his religion from Roman Catholic to Episcopalian.

Ed Flynn worked with the delegates to try to stir up support, if not enthusiasm, for Wallace. Meanwhile, Secretary Ickes enjoyed a gratifying "boomlet" that never quite got past the talking stage. Ickes believed, rightly, that the President would have blighted it if it had ever grown into anything serious. Actually, FDR said later when he heard about the suggestion, "Dear old Harold, he'd get fewer votes even than Wallace."

Ickes had another Chicagoan to suggest for Vice President, Robert Maynard Hutchins, the youthful, dynamic president of the University of Chicago. In a telegram to Roosevelt sent on July 18, Ickes offered his own name and that of Hutchins. Ickes called Hutchins a liberal, imaginative, new, attractive and energetic enough to trail Willkie around the country. He was also well able to take care of himself "in a free-for-all fight" with the Hoosier, if necessary. Everything that Ickes said about Hutchins was true. But it was also a fact that Chicago University's president was an isolationist, which made him an odd choice for near-interventionist Ickes. Furthermore, Hutchins was completely without political or governmental experience of any kind. "Pa" Watson, at the President's instigation, had a very uncomfortable phone conversation with Ickes during which he delivered the message that FDR considered Wallace the strongest candidate because of the farm vote, the labor vote and the foreign situation. Roosevelt used a familiar subterfuge to avoid telling his Secretary of the Interior directly that he was turning him down.

6

But if a sullen convention had to be roused by the "voice from the cellar" for a tremendously popular President, how could Wallace, a prime example of the non-politician, be put across? The Rooseveltians understood the problem. They understood also that there was no alternative.

Secretary of Labor Frances Perkins, a veteran campaigner and close to FDR's ear, after persuasion from all sides, phoned the President at the White House to beg him to come to the convention. She told him that the atmosphere in Chicago was depressing and the delegates cross and bitter. He refused.

"I know I am right, Frances," he said. "It will be worse if I go. People will get promises out of me that I ought not to make. If I don't make promises, I will make new enemies. If I do make promises, they'll be mistakes. I'll be pinned down on things I just don't want to be pinned down on *now.*"

However, they found a solution.

"How would it be if Eleanor came?" FDR asked. "You know Eleanor always makes people feel right. She has a fine way with her."

After her husband urged her and she cleared it with Jim Farley, who agreed to delay the vice-presidential nomination until she got there, Mrs. Roosevelt consented, reluctantly, to go to Chicago. She flew down from Val Kill Cottage to New York, where she met her son, Franklin D. Roosevelt, Jr., who had been at the White House with his father. The President had urged his family to stay away from Chicago. But Elliott Roosevelt was there with the Texas delegation and, it was rumored, planned to support Jesse Jones's candidacy for Vice President. This was another matter with which Mrs. Roosevelt was burdened.

The First Lady explained to the reporters at La Guardia Airport that her mission was to do whatever Jim Farley requested of her and then to turn around and come right back. In Chicago, Farley was at the airport with a cordial welcome but bad news about the Wallace nomination. Farley asserted that other candidates had to be nominated. He informed her that he was going to nominate Jesse Jones and that Elliott Roosevelt would second him. Mrs. Roosevelt agreed to call her husband, not to tell him what to do but to advise him of the situation in Chicago. The President's answer was that Jones would not do. "He doesn't speak our language," he told his wife. Again the roster of possibilities was reviewed. Barkley was called loyal but without backbone, Byrnes splendid, but again the religious problem was mentioned. It must be Wallace and, the President threatened, if Wallace did not get the nomination, the Democrats would have to find another presidential candidate.

Mrs. Roosevelt was in an ambiguous situation. She was not "happy" about the nomination, yet she was placed in the position to assure it. For a few feverish hours she worked industriously, shaking hands with thousands, generally sweetening the convention. Seated on the platform, she waited her turn to speak.

The first name placed in nomination for the Vice Presidency was that of William Bankhead, "Alabama's gifted, brilliant, tested, tried, beloved, illustrious" Speaker of the House. Congressman Henry B. Steagall of Alabama's presentation of Bankhead's name set off a fifteen-minute demonstration. Jesse Jones was nominated. And then the name of Henry Wallace, "the outstanding exponent of agricultural rights in America," was offered to the convention by Frank O'Connor of Iowa. The seven-minute demonstration that followed was mixed with boos and catcalls. On the other hand, the nomination of Paul V. McNutt was accompanied by excessive cheering. It was revealed later that about 3,500 unofficial admission tickets had been distributed by the McNutt faction, and, with the cooperation of an acquiescent gateman, they were honored. The McNutt supporters hoped that the gallery enthusiasm would infect the floor and carry their man to victory. It did not work and McNutt refused the nomination.

Sam Rayburn's seconding speech for Wallace seemed to reflect the feeling of many of the delegates. He said, "I can do none other than follow what I believe to be the wish of our great leader. . . ." Jesse Jones withdrew his name, saying that it had been presented without either his knowledge or his consent. Other nominations were made: Prentiss Brown, Bascom Timmins, Alva Adams, Scott Lucas, Jim Farley, Joseph Mahoney, Alben Barkley, Louis Johnson and Davis Walker. Much of this excessive activity merely reflected the frustration of the delegates, their need to keep the convention in their own hands. Most of them were prepared to vote for Wallace after their little rebellions. There was a resurgence of despair at the thought of the same Administration again.

In the midst of this charged atmosphere, Eleanor Roosevelt rose to speak. There was applause and cheers, perhaps the most genuine expression of good will of the entire week. Then there was the tribute of silence so that all could hear her. The talk was brief, simple, high-minded, brightly sincere. Its theme had been introduced at the airport when a reporter asked, "Are you happy about the nomination?" Mrs. Roosevelt's answer had been, unsmiling, that it was a tremendous responsibility. To the convention she spoke of dedication—the President's and theirs. Candidacy, today, is a "very serious and a very solemn thing," she told them. "You cannot treat it as you would in an ordinary time." Therefore, she continued, this year the candidate who is President of the United States cannot make a campaign in the usual sense of the word. He must be on his job. So it is the party that must rise above narrow and partisan considerations and carry on. This must be done "by a united people who love their country and will live for it to the fullest of their ability, with the highest ideals, with the determination that their party shall be absolutely devoted to the good of the nation as a whole and to doing what this country can to bring the world to a safer and happier condition." The applause came from a sobered house. Eleanor Roosevelt's lofty words had a calming effect on the over-emotional scene.

The balloting that followed gave Wallace 626 votes; Bankhead, 329; McNutt, 68; Jessie Jones, 59; and the others less than a dozen each. A motion to suspend the rules and nominate Wallace by acclamation was accepted, ending the convention on a somewhat false note of unanimity. Business was over. The chair announced that the President would address the assembled delegates from the White House.

Henry Wallace had been present all through the proceedings. He sat alone and neglected until the results of the roll call were tallied. Then friends and well-wishers thronged around him offering congratulations. But he was told firmly that it would be best if he refrained from delivering an acceptance speech at this time. The delegates were not in the mood for further triumphing by the Administration.

7

A card table was set up in the Oval Room at the White House on the night of July 18 so that the President could play solitaire while he listened to the convention over the radio. Judge Rosenman, the Watsons, Dr. Ross McIntire, Missy LeHand, Grace Tully, Steve Early and Dan Callaghan sat around silently listening and watching the boss. Roosevelt's face was disturbing. It expressed the fear that they all had that something would set off a stampede for Bankhead or McNutt.

Calling for a note pad and pencil, Roosevelt put aside his cards and became absorbed in writing. After he had covered several pages, he said to Judge Rosenman, "Sam, take this inside and go to work on it; smooth it out and get it ready for delivery. I may have to deliver it very quickly, so please hurry it up." He then resumed his game of solitaire.

The manuscript was Roosevelt's speech to the convention if they failed to nominate Wallace. "Pa" Watson and Missy followed the Judge out of the room. Missy approved of Roosevelt's action but Watson suggested, "Sam, give that damned piece of paper to me—let's tear it up." Rosenman answered that FDR would read it if Bankhead got the nomination "and nobody on earth is going to stop him." After the papers were returned, Roosevelt accepted the typed suggestions, added a paragraph, reread the manuscript, said, "This will do" and again returned to his cards.

The gist of the speech was that the Democratic party had the support of the electorate because it had championed progressive and liberal governmental policies. The Democratic convention seemed to be divided on this fundamental issue. "Under the circumstances, I cannot, in all honor, and will not, merely for political expediency, go along with the cheap bargaining and political maneuvering which have brought about party dissension in this Convention." The fight must take place now. "The party must go wholly one way or wholly the other." The conclusion read, "By declining the honor of the nomination for the Presidency, I can restore that opportunity to the Convention. I so do."

Although his mind was made up, Roosevelt was tense as the vote was being taken. He set aside his cards to keep the score. Immediately after Wallace's victory was announced, Chicago was informed, for the first time, that Franklin D. Roosevelt would accept the nomination.

The President looked tired; his face was lined, his clothes wrinkled. He was wheeled into the bedroom to freshen up and, in a short time, reappeared smiling, cheerful and jaunty. The group in the Oval Room was all happy except for Missy, who was in tears because FDR had not been nominated by acclamation. They all accompanied Roosevelt to the radio broadcasting room for the delivery of the acceptance speech.

In a very calm, paternal voice, the President told the members of the Democratic convention that "Lying awake, as I have, on many nights, I have asked myself whether I have the right as Commander-in-Chief of the Army and Navy to call on men and women to serve their country . . . and, at the same time, decline to serve my country in my own personal capacity." He asserted that it was the danger of the times that robbed him of his personal choice. "I had made plans for myself, plans for a private life . . . but my conscience will not let me turn my back upon a call to service." There was an intimacy about his recital that sounded as if FDR were telling each delegate, individually, why he had to make his decision. Thus he dismissed the two-term tradition as irrelevant to the greater consideration, which was his patriotic obligation to remain available.

While Roosevelt spoke, a blue-white spotlight played on the tremendous portrait of the President that hung in the Chicago stadium. Mrs. Roosevelt and Henry Wallace sat on the platform listening. At the conclusion of the speech, united momentarily at least, the delegates rose to their feet and roared their approval of their thrice chosen candidate.

CHAPTER NINE

"The Rich Man's Roosevelt"

1

CENTRAL CITY, forty miles west of Denver, had suddenly become the liveliest "ghost town" in the West. Its little opera house was offering a lusty production of Bedrich Smetana's opera *The Bartered Bride,* but there was more interest in a spectator named Wendell Willkie. Outside, people were waiting for him to make his appearance on the street during intermissions. United Press newsman Paul T. Smith had been delegated to remain back at the Teller House to listen to the latest news about the Democrats in Chicago.

The first intermission came and Willkie went to the street, where a loudspeaker was mounted on a truck and everybody could hear the seconding speeches for the President's renomination. "Well, boys," said the Republican candidate to the appreciative newsmen who surrounded him, "This is a good deal different from that night when we listened to the balloting back in Philadelphia." When Willkie returned to the site during the second intermission, balloting had already

begun. Roosevelt had about 390 votes and the Massachusetts delegation was being polled. Willkie paused for a while to listen to the
individual roll call, satisfied some autograph hunters and returned to
the theater.

The last act had about fifteen minutes left before the final curtain
when Paul Smith's figure could be seen scouting the aisles of the
darkened theater, looking for one of those most interested in the
proceedings at Chicago. Willkie thanked Smith for the news and then
sat through what remained of the opera. The familiar "Willkie! We
want Willkie!" cheer erupted as he left the opera house. When a
crowd later gathered under his window at the Teller House, Willkie
waved back and said, "The battle's on." Nobody could doubt his
satisfaction with the opportunity of being able to counter "the
Champ" directly.

The President's renomination was hardly seventy-two hours old
when Willkie began to talk about a "revolt" of Democrats becoming
strong enough to maintain the two-term tradition. And his reasoning
seemed to have an impressive basis. "It is a sad reality for one who
was rocked in the cradle of Jeffersonian democracy," wrote a North
Carolinian, "and I bow my head in silence and respect for the great
Democratic leaders who have gone on before." Other Democrats,
equally perturbed by their party's disregard for the unwritten law,
sent Willkie messages of support. Two of them, John W. Hanes and
Lewis W. Douglas, ex-New Dealers, had backed Willkie even before
the Philadelphia convention; they wired him the "support of Democrats who believe with us that loyalty to country takes precedence
over loyalty to party." With Alan Valentine, on leave from the presidency of the University of Rochester, Hanes and Douglas were later
given the responsibility for heading an organization called Democrats
for Willkie. Also joining the dissenters was Democratic Senator Edward R. Burke of Nebraska. Burke, recently defeated for renomination in his party's primary because of a voting record that apparently
antagonized everybody but Adolph Hitler, now lamented his party's
desertion of the two-party tradition. He was joined by a Representative from his own state, Harry B. Coffee, and a parade of other
apostates which included a long list of notables, scholars, college presidents, writers, entertainers and, perhaps most welcome to Willkie,
Alfred E. Smith. New York's former Governor was thus continuing
his by now well-known opposition to the New Deal. Willkie called

him "the first citizen of New York" when he learned about Smith's declaration that the Chicago convention had "sounded the death knell of the Democratic party," with the third-term nomination piling the "last straw on the camel's back." Smith urged his admirers to "march under the banner of Wendell L. Willkie, a lifelong Democrat."

The daily volume of messages reaching the Broadmoor from all over the country was so great that a telephone switchboard with two operators was installed in the Willkie suite. In addition, to handle the six hundred letters coming in every day, there were secretaries Fred Rahter and Grace Grahn and a supplementary staff of eight men and women and four volunteers.

With the formation of Democrats for Willkie, besides the Willkie clubs and the regular channels of the Republican party, there was an interesting question about the applicability of the revised version of the Hatch Act, which Congress passed on July 19. A legal opinion by Henry Fletcher, general counsel to the Republican National Committee, was that the three-million-dollar financial limitation that it imposed was a restriction on any one particular campaign agency or committee and that the various groups being set up could each spend that amount. More simply, Fletcher's judgment revealed the obvious inability of the new law to cope with the reality of the situation.

Willkie, however, was determined to eradicate from the public mind the stories of how his nomination had resulted from massive spending by shadowy financial Wall Street moguls. His was to be a crusade that would be carried by the indignant American people and not by the usual political or vested interests. One of his most appealing attributes was his lack of conventional political ties. From Colorado Springs, then, he announced that he expected all three committees promoting his candidacy to total not more than the three-million-dollar limitation. To show his own enthusiastic support of the Hatch Act's intentions, he offered two additional amendments. One would require the President, members of Congress and officials of federal regulatory agencies, as well as all members of their immediate families, to file detailed listings of their personal assests on assuming and leaving office. The other amendment would prevent any member of their immediate families from receiving compensation for any services for representing "outside interests" before any government body or agency. He added that, although they were not part of the law, he and his family would nevertheless comply with the suggested restrictions. Thereupon Ernest Weir, the financial chairman of the Republican National Committee, immediately threatened to resign. In his view Willkie was writing off the lavish contributions that the party could usually expect to get from several wealthy families.

At Colorado Springs Willkie secured the additional assistance, for the first time, of a press secretary. He was twenty-nine-year-old Lem Jones, a former New York *Herald Tribune* newsman, who had been serving as Thomas Dewey's press liaison man. Gardner Cowles had convinced Willkie that the chaotic paperwork, which had grown quite out of hand even at the mountain retreat, needed to be coordinated. And although Willkie had fully intended to author his own speeches and had Russell Davenport for assistance, the realistic demands of a campaign eventually forced him to increase his research and speech-writing staff to twenty. Such people as financial writer Elliott Bell were ultimately added. But the big writing project at Colorado Springs, meanwhile, which had to go on despite all the forays to the surrounding country and meetings with various people, was the preparation of his acceptance address. Charlie Halleck had been placed in charge of planning the physical arrangements at Elwood, and when the Congressman conferred with Willkie on July 22 they announced that the speech would be delivered on Saturday, August 17; but instead of from the high-school steps, Willkie would face a much larger crowd by speaking from a platform in Callaway Park. The park, at the northern edge of Elwood, was a forty-acre tract, and the town planned to clear additional space to expand the acreage to 350.

On the day that these plans were announced, John Stout pedaled into Elwood. A large contingent of fellow bicyclists joined him for the last ten miles, and music from a band filled the downtown business district as they entered the festive town, which seemed determined to celebrate until August 17. Old shacks and abandoned buildings were cleared away, streets were repaved, railroad station repainted and tricolor markers installed to direct visitors to the high school and to the sites where the young Wendell had lived. There was a great demand for souvenirs. For local merchants and restauranteurs, Willkie had already restored prosperity.

A *Fortune* poll, conducted for the magazine by Elmo Roper, then showed that the enthusiasm had become a most serious threat to FDR's third-term hopes. Roper reported a sharp national trend to

Willkie; even though the President's popular percentage was still some three and a half points higher, Willkie was ahead in every region but the South and Rocky Mountain states. Not only would that surely give him a majority of the electoral votes, but when Roper analyzed his results further he concluded that Roosevelt could not even be sure he would get most of the popular votes. A few days later Dr. Gallup, in substantial agreement with Roper, said that Willkie was leading with 304 electoral votes to 227 for FDR.

2

The Democratic delegates returning from Chicago had misgivings about their historical assent to a third term. Many muttered about having been "bossed" by the President or by his chief aide, Harry Hopkins; and some blamed it all on such expert politicians as Ed Flynn of the Bronx and Mayor Kelly of Chicago. Nothing that had happened at Chicago had convinced the doubters that any man was indispensable, and even those closest to the Administration were pessimistic about the outcome of the contest.

It was immediately apparent that the classic New Dealers, who, as a group, had failed to generate the necessary enthusiasm for the coming emphasis on preparedness, were no longer in FDR's favor. Even worse, many of the Westerners among them were isolationists with views indistinguishable from those Republicans who wanted to concentrate on building up the home-front defenses without jeopardizing American neutrality.

The President's acceptance speech had publicly stated the rules for the campaign. Roosevelt would attend to the country's needs and devote little time, if any, to the struggle. Nor would he mention his opponent by name. Such chores would be left to other spokesmen, particularly acerbic Harold Ickes, who deplored the re-election of Farley as national chairman for one more month. It was an odd reward, thought the Secretary, for a man whom Roosevelt himself had termed disloyal. Farley, however, had been boosted by loyal party members, some of whom were grumbling that FDR was dropping all his close friends.

Wallace's nomination was another difficult decision to accept. Many Democratic party workers deplored the by-passing of stalwarts for the mystic who was still, they believed, part Republican. Robert Hutchins, the president of the University of Chicago, prophesied that Wallace's name on the ticket would cost the party four million votes. Even Lowell Mellett, the President's faithful executive assistant, was gloomy about the vice-presidential candidate.

Farley was present, along with Roosevelt and Wallace, when the Democratic National Committee met to choose his successor. Speculation had included the names of Federal Deposit Insurance Corporation chairman Leo T. Crowley, James Byrnes and Paul McNutt. Roosevelt, however, was determined to have another Irish Catholic. The job was, therefore, given to Ed Flynn. The "boss of the Bronx" had been closely associated with Roosevelt in New York State politics, was an experienced political practitioner and was, at the age of forty-eight, a trim, elegantly dressed figure. Although he had been a national committeeman, he was, nevertheless, unknown to thousands of party leaders throughout the country who had been close to Farley. Flynn's reluctance to accept the position was overcome by the natural appeal to his vanity and the strength of Roosevelt's persuasiveness.

One loyal Republican informed Sam Pryor that the Irish voters were threatening to revolt because of Farley's being eased out as national chairman and that they "seem to believe the New Deal crowd is Communist." Then he added: "Those who have expressed their views that Communists control the New Deal crowd I have never disputed. Let them labor under such illusion—it means more votes for Willkie."

Flynn had definite opinions about his role. As the President's choice he would be expected to deliver an election victory; but any man with that kind of responsibility had to have the authority to plot the campaign. So the dedicated party stalwart informed the President that he could not be hampered by New Deal amateurs who would only further antagonize the regulars, the permanent officers on the battlefield. To overcome the problem he suggested that the non-professionals maintain their own headquarters and thus have the freedom to conduct their own kind of campaign. Even when Roosevelt subsequently by-passed party channels and appointed a New Dealer as the federal district attorney of New York, Flynn held his ground. The new chairman phoned the White House and threatened to resign. He was, however, placated by renewed assurances that, if he remained, the battle would be fought on his own terms.

Roosevelt was pleased with his appointee. Flynn, he felt, had many of Farley's qualities and was still one of his close friends. And, as a Northerner, he should prove particularly effective in the critical eastern and midwestern states. Even Ickes, who had viewed Flynn as a liability and as a potential butt of newspaper attacks, revised his opinion on meeting the new chairman. He found that Flynn was, after all, a New Dealer and was genuinely attached to the President. Their bond was actually a mutual distaste for Harry Hopkins. According to Ickes, part of the terms extracted from FDR by the Bronx leader was that Hopkins would have no power over the direction of the campaign. Flynn then set up headquarters at the Biltmore Hotel in New York and went ahead with plans to persuade Mayor Fiorello H. La Guardia to head an independent group of liberals, former Republicans and laborites to work for Roosevelt.

As the Washington heat drove Roosevelt to Hyde Park during the first week in August, dissension among the Democrats continued to grow. Earlier, Roosevelt had scoffed at the pro-Willkie stance of people like Burke, Hanes and Douglas; but now others, led by Vice President Garner, were refusing to participate in the campaign. Their ranks included "Cotton Ed" Smith, Millard Tydings, Carter Glass and Harry Byrd, all prominent southern Democrats. Nevertheless, the squire of Hyde Park coolly made his own analysis of the election. He saw a chance to carry Massachusetts and probably Connecticut, but figured he might have to fight for New York, which was certainly a valuable prize. Pennsylvania, he felt, was doubtful but possible. He could count on the solid South, California, Washington and Illinois. Knowing this, he would not waste time and money on states that were automatically Willkie's.

Hyde Park would be the jumping-off place for sorties to inspect defenses at Watervliet and Buffalo, both in New York, and perhaps New London, Connecticut—a decision that started a continuing controversy over the definition of a "political" and a "non-political" speech. To the President, unless he was disputing issues directly with his opponent in open battle, he was engaging in non-political activity. Republicans, naturally, scoffed at his dubious rationale. They complained, with obvious justification, that every presidential appearance had political significance. Every speech was an opportunity to extol his accomplishments, to demonstrate the President in action and to woo a captive audience with his charm. Budget-conscious Republicans, a category that included just about every member of the GOP, resented the free time and exposure that such forays gave the President; but that, of course, is the normal advantage of the incumbent.

Those who analyzed the strategy saw it as the work of the Roosevelt team, sometimes called the "New Brains Trust." Ed Flynn's bogey, Harry Hopkins, worked underground to realize a viable Democratic structure. Robert Jackson, endowed with the honesty, brains and ability to interpret and apply New Deal law, was particularly valuable. Francis Biddle, who was famous for sending anti-Willkie memos; Harold Ickes; Sam Rayburn of Texas, a dependable political aide; Cordell Hull and Assistant Secretary of State Adolph A. Berle, strong anchors in the realm of foreign policy, were all key figures in the third-term attempt. Old and loyal friends were Secretary of the Treasury Henry Morgenthau and Judge Samuel Rosenman.

3

For Great Britain, Roosevelt's renomination was equal to an important military victory. Churchill, believing that the future of American aid to his country depended on the choice of candidates, had waited for the outcome of the Democratic convention before replying to Germany's peace offer. Once that decision had been reached, the Prime Minister advised the British Foreign Office to make a firm reply to Hitler as the best hope of getting a reasonable proposal. Englishmen were generally sure that Roosevelt's re-election was inevitable. Harold Laski, writing in the *New Statesman,* predicted that labor would vote for FDR despite the obstreperous behavior of John L. Lewis and that Henry Wallace would get the farm vote.

The nightmare Nazi air assault, which came to be known as the "Battle of Britain," had started on July 10. Until early August, however, the Germans concentrated on industrial objectives, convoys and harbors. The bombardment had a disastrous effect, particularly on merchant shipping, which had to go unprotected, for destroyers had to be reassigned from convoy duty to home ports because of fear of invasion. The Nazi U-boats inflicted heavy losses on the British merchant marine. Therefore, Hitler wanted Britain beaten, not in a year or two but promptly. On August 1 a directive from *der Führer* ordered the German air arm "to overcome the English Air Force with all means at its disposal and in the shortest possible time." Herman

Goering translated this into a lightning timetable. There was to be complete air supremacy in four days, total destruction of the Royal Air Force in one month. This was a very optimistic schedule, because German air supremacy was not double that of England's and daylight bombing, which was essential to blitzkrieg warfare, required additional fighter escorts.

On the target date, August 13, waves of planes swept over Britain. By the seventeenth, the Nazis claimed air control. Coupled with the raids were devices to assault British nerves. For example, on August 14, forty-five empty parachutes were discovered on the Scottish lowlands, the Midlands and other deserted spots. Along with them were found maps, wireless transmitters and lists of addresses of prominent people. After a complete investigation the British government assured the public that the objects had been planted as an enemy hoax.

Americans responded to the latest German atrocities with sympathy and admiration for the victims. Roosevelt, who was attending First Army maneuvers in northern New York State, and Canadian Prime Minister Mackenzie King discussed the problem of joint defenses at a meeting on the Canadian border. The two leaders decided that a Permanent Joint Board on Defense would be set up by both countries, and studies immediately relative to sea, air and land problems, including personnel and materiel, would commence at once. The defense of the northern half of the Western Hemisphere would be the scope of the board's interest.

The American maneuvers that had brought the President and his staff up to the North Country revealed distressing shortages and a dangerous degree of obsolescence. General Hugh Drum told FDR that broomsticks were being used for guns and rain pipes for mortars. Roosevelt answered glibly that "everyone seemed to be in the same boat." Privately, however, he was most concerned.

4

Oren Root had his problems, too.

The Associated Willkie Clubs of America were continued with a clear purpose: to provide an outlet for independents and doubtful Democrats who would support Willkie by contributing their time and money to an organization that had nothing to do with the Republican party. A more direct benefit was the higher-purpose appeal that could be generated best through a grass-roots movement. For the most part, the plan was to have the pre-convention clubs continue and also add new units for the real campaign that would start in September. Until then, Root notified the leaders, they should utilize the slow summer months by keeping a skeleton organization intact and establishing a framework for new clubs as quickly as possible. Meanwhile, there would be perhaps a dozen field representatives who would each canvass a territory consisting of a group of contiguous states and work to initiate and activate additional clubs as, for example, Root's friend Thomas H. Barber had done that spring. The entire apparatus could then be ready for action immediately after Labor Day.

Victory, according to every mathematical calculation, could not be achieved without appealing to more than just party loyalists. Some anti-third-term Democrats would, of course, be accommodated by the organization that was being set up by Lew Douglas and Johnny Hanes; but the Root people had already shown what they could do, and, of the two groups, they were more likely to attract non-ideological types. At the same time, Root knew that there were serious dangers, mostly in the form of resentment from the regulars, who wanted no infringements placed upon their prerogatives and no competition from the amateurs for the prizes that could come with victory— patronage, power, influence. Such was the risk in continuing the Willkie clubs.

Pressed by National Chairman Joe Martin, Root moved to minimize such conflicts. In his mid-July instructions to state club leaders he stressed that while they must appeal to those who wanted no part of the Republican party, political prudence demanded that they adhere to certain procedural advice. This involved clearing their intentions with state party leaders. Accordingly, a San Francisco Willkie club man was able to report on July 19 that "At Oren Root's suggestion we have cleared pretty well with William Knowland, who seems to approve our objectives, our personnel, and our plan to raise funds." Knowland, who later became a well-known United States Senator, was then the California national committeeman and, therefore, the person the San Francisco leader needed to consult before he could establish his "non-partisan" group. Before the convention Knowland had been a Taft supporter, and he was still unconvinced about the wisdom of continuing the Willkie clubs. But he was placated by assurances that their only purpose was to conduct a unified Willkie campaign and that they would disband after election day. Nor would good Republicans who happened to join the clubs be discouraged from also working through regular party channels.

Root took further precautions. His own headquarters, which had recently opened offices at 100 East 42nd Street in New York City, retained the power to approve policy matters that affected all clubs. Even more important, in some cases, was his authority to confirm the appointment of the statewide chairmen of the movement. Joe Martin had been particularly adamant on this point. In no case should Root give such status to anyone who was unfavorable to the party's state committee. A considerable number of clubs subsequently appeared without Root's sanction; exactly how many will never be known. But only those that complied with Root and were recognized by the Associated Willkie Clubs of America were eligible for financial aid from the New York headquarters.

On July 20 Root announced that the Associated Willkie Clubs would finance themselves by collecting twenty-five-cent fees from each member. No campaign funds would be solicited, he added, and he stressed that the membership dues would be spent exclusively in the states where they were collected. All that was consistent with Willkie's stated determination to rely on small contributions rather than risk the onus of being financed by wealthy individuals, whom so many suspected of being the sinews of his drive. When Stanley Resor, of the J. Walter Thompson advertising agency and treasurer of the Willkie Campaign Fund, subsequently initiated chain letters requesting contributions of from twenty-five cents to one dollar, which provoked indignant protests, Root's organization was able to disclaim any responsibility for such improprieties.

By the end of July the club movement seemed to be progressing. Root had already recognized some 560 clubs, 168 in New Jersey alone, and hundreds more were being formed. Chairmen had been cleared by the regular organizations of their states and thus appointed by Root in Pennsylvania, New Jersey, Massachusetts, Connecticut and the District of Columbia.

But the inevitable problems were already plaguing their efforts. Kirk Landon, who was in the process of setting up thirty-one additional branch clubs in Maryland, began to fear that his troubles were just beginning. As a fight deepened among two party factions for control of the Republican City Council in Baltimore over who would collect and be able to supervise campaign funds, Landon feared that his clubs would be the only groups in the state doing anything for Willkie. Robert Bonnell, president of the Public Bank of Baltimore and chairman of a group called the Maryland Committee to Foster Truly Democratic Institutions, was determined to maintain control over both the City Committee and the financial role that had been given to him by Ernest Weir, head of the Weirton Steel Company and finance chairman of the Willkie campaign, despite the protests of the former governor and the national committeeman.

Pennsylvania was being organized by Bill Harman in the face of hostile regulars led by the reactionary triumvirate of Governor Arthur James, Joe Pew and State Chairman James F. Torrance. Torrance, people complained, was more concerned with building his own machine to prepare for a gubernatorial race in 1942. Root was warned to provide Harman with a few political strategists before Pew and Torrance "take him for a ride."

In Kansas, Jay Scovel, a lawyer from the town of Independence, was learning that, with the party's convention over and the regulars behind his candidate, he was no longer wanted. The party machine that was headed by Alf Landon and national committeeman Harry Darby expected to be in full control. Root was in a predicament. Originally he had sent Tom Barber as a field representative to get Scovel to organize clubs in the state, a task accomplished by the lawyer in May. Scovel assumed that he would thus have important status in the coming campaign. Shortly after the end of the convention, with the aid of Topeka banker Henry A. Bubb, he began building a statewide organization, assuming, as Donald J. Smith had been able to do in New Jersey and Bill Harman in Pennsylvania, that Root would confirm him as the Kansas chairman. In mid-July Scovel informed Barber that he was, in fact, the chairman, and he announced the news to others as an established fact. The local press reported it that way, Scovel's letterheads said so, and he acted as chairman. But that was not the way Harry Darby saw it, and he protested to Joe Martin.

Root, obligated to heed the organization's desires in such matters, then sent a letter that was hard for him to write but even more difficult for Scovel to digest. While the clubs must remain as independent as possible, he wrote, "the leadership of the Willkie Clubs has to be generally acceptable to the regular organization because the two must be able to sit down together behind the scenes and work together toward their common goal." As to confirming the small-town lawyer as chairman, Root added, "I will not reach any decision until I have got in touch with you," which was clearly a "don't call me, I'll call you" situation. An indignant friend of Scovel's complained to Sam Pryor bitterly: "Understand Joe Martin has given orders no one from Kansas goes to work for the committee (or gets a job later)—without Harry Darby's okay *(which is Alf Landon)—This is not* the way to carry *Kansas for Willkie* and is a *hell of a way* to *show appreciation to we loyal ones.*"

The volume of correspondence on the Kansas situation alone was practically large enough to require Root to increase his office staff. The real political battles had already begun, even before the candidate could begin to battle "the Champ." The squabbling was largely motivated by the fact that, for the first time since 1928, it looked as though there might be prizes to share.

5

Joe Martin reached Colorado Springs during the last weekend of July and had some advice for Willkie. The national chairman was voicing the fears of many Republican Congressmen that the candidate would embarrass their legislative position. Foreign-policy matters were the major concern. Republicans had been the strongest advocates of the neutrality laws and the most unyielding opponents of defense spending, and Willkie's internationalism could well leave the impression that the GOP was unwilling to follow its own leader. Martin, therefore, reminded him that he was not yet the President, that such legislative issues should be left to the incumbent and that he should not provoke unnecessary conflicts by indiscriminantly volunteering his opinion.

Martin was either clairvoyant or had secret intelligence on what was about to happen, for his advice was timed with precision. Only two days before he had gone to see Willkie, the Century Group, a select club of prominent people, many of whom were members of William Allen White's committee, had met in New York and drafted a memorandum to the State Department stressing that Great Britain's survival was of paramount importance for American security and that her ability to resist a German invasion could be improved by placing more destroyers in the English Channel as soon as possible. Moreover, continued the memo, "these destroyers should be offered to Britain in exchange for immediate naval and air concessions in British possessions in the Western Hemisphere."

As early as May 16 Churchill himself had issued a request for destroyers. Roosevelt, however, had doubted his own authority to comply without Congressional action. Then, in late June, Congress had apparently closed the issue by forbidding the disposal of any military equipment that was not certified by the Chief of Staff or the Chief of Naval Operations as non-essential for American defenses. Since the spring, however, the number of destroyers that were available for Britain's home defenses had been reduced to a fraction of what was needed in the English Channel to deter a Nazi invasion. Furthermore, requesting bases in British possessions off American waters was, politically, a master stroke designed to appease isolationists who were emphasizing the need to improve hemispheric defenses. The Century Group, believing that the June law meant that new legislation would be necessary to permit the transaction, agreed that Willkie's endorsement might help to avoid the possibly fatal effects of solid Republican Congressional opposition.

Immediate action was taken. Archibald MacLeish, the Librarian of Congress, acted on his own and contacted his friend Russell Davenport to sound out Willkie. In Colorado Springs on August 1, Willkie had lunch with William Allen White, who used that opportunity to advance the plan. On that same day, in Washington, three Century Group members placed the matter before the President. When the Cabinet met the next day, the idea won general approval, and Jim Farley was enthusiastic about finding out whether Willkie would agree to go along. It was also suggested that the best man to act as liaison for the Administration with him was White. The President then phoned the Kansan and asked him to return from Colorado. Then, stressing that whatever Willkie felt about the issue was less important than his willingness to use his influence to persuade Republican Congressmen to go along, the President asked White to contact Willkie again, which he did.

Willkie could hardly have forgotten Martin's advice. Even so, he was fully aware of the differences between his party's record in Congress and his own position and had a realistic idea of how effectively he could lead before he had the authority of the presidential office. His public statement, then, which finally came on August 9, was understandable. He repeated his recognition of what the international crisis meant to the United States. "As to specific executive or legislative proposals," he continued, "I do not think it appropriate for me to enter into advance commitments and understandings." He pointed to Roosevelt's unwillingness to commit himself to Hoover's requests for assurances about economic policy in November 1932. "Much doubt was expressed as to the wisdom of that statement by a President-elect," said Willkie. "None can doubt its correctness when taken by a candidate for President." He also made clear his freedom to comment whenever the Administration took a public position on a specific matter.

Before Roosevelt could be discouraged for very long he received a telegram from White. "It's not as bad as it seems," said the message. "I have talked with both of you on this subject during the last ten days. I know there is not two bits difference between you on the issue pending. But I can't guarantee either of you to the other, which is funny, for I admire and respect you both."

6

The wisdom of having Willkie spend his vacation in Colorado eventually produced a flurry of controversy. Sam Pryor often said that it was "the worst possible place for Willkie to have taken that vacation" and that a secluded spot in the Maine woods would have assured a more complete rest. "All the 'screwballs' in the United States visited him while he was out there," said Pryor. "He was mentally fagged out before the campaign started and didn't recover from it until the day he died." Others have repeated that theme. But Pryor did not arrive at Colorado Springs until August 3, and then for merely an organizational conference of party leaders. Lem Jones, who was with Willkie daily after July 22, felt that he did get enough rest.

Pryor's real complaint seems to be implicit in his statement that Willkie was "completely out of touch with the real party leaders." But he was, as Pryor himself stated, an "unorthodox candidate." It was no more realistic to believe that Willkie could be secluded for one month than to think the issue of war and peace could have disappeared from the campaign. He was, in addition, too gregarious and flamboyant to discourage self-appointed advisers from besieging him. The trips Willkie made from his Colorado Springs base, such as the one to speak before farm leaders in Des Moines on August 5, were the necessary functions of a candidate, particularly one who was still striving to acquaint his party with him. Perhaps Jones was closer to the truth when he said, "We spent too much time in Colorado. We let what was the hottest thing in the world get cold."

As the date set for the acceptance speech neared, and the Willkie party was preparing to leave Colorado Springs, Republicans from all over the country began to head for Elwood. Among loyal party members, making the trip was somewhat of a pilgrimage. "I'll see you in Elwood," was the usual greeting. One hundred left by a special motorcade from New York. A Willkie-for-President train carried others from Pennsylvania Station. Private parties organized their own expeditions. One group that was called "Working Girls Who Save Nickels to Elect Willkie" was started by eight young ladies who wanted to travel together to Elwood for the speech. Elwood, Indiana, itself was being billed as "the center of the United States" and the "political capital of the world." All the major radio networks and a vast array of newspapers prepared to cover Willkie's acceptance speech.

Willkie's departure from Colorado Springs was at noon on August 16. The next day, Saturday, was hotter than it usually is when the sun bakes the prairies. The mid-morning temperature was over ninety and was continuing to rise.

Willkie's special train brought him to the town at 12:30. He wore a dark-blue suit and blue tie and had on his familiar straw hat. The band played "Back Home Again in Indiana" as his motorcade went to the high school for a brief nostalgic ceremony. The crowds almost smothered their hero.

Joe Martin, getting his first look at the completed speech that Davenport had written, was astonished to find it a conventional double-spaced typescript in ordinary pica instead of triple-spaced in large block letters.

"Where's your reading copy?" Martin asked.

"This is it," said Willkie.

"Well," said the national chairman, agitated but helpless, "this isn't the way we do it in Washington."

Possibly as many as two hundred thousand people filled Callaway Park, where the sun's heat, relieved by only a few trees that were near the platform, brought the temperature up to 102 degrees. The extreme weather and his tangle with the crowds had obviously affected Willkie. He was perspiring and his clothes were wilted. Then Charlie Halleck introduced Joe Martin, who delivered the official notification of the nomination, and the candidate began.

Reading Davenport's prose, Willkie spoke in restricted and even tones. Pryor and Martin, standing on the platform behind him, each learned with consternation that the other had not read the speech in advance. The text was but in its early stage of development when Martin saw Willkie at Colorado Springs. Willkie, then, was launching his effort with a statement that would reflect his own principles, regardless of whether its contents would please fellow Republicans.

"Party lines are drawn," he declared and presented himself as a "liberal Democrat" who had found more democracy in the Republican party than in his own. And, as the leader of that party, he declared, "We shall go into our campaign as into a crusade."

He alluded to the two major foreign-policy decisions that were being formulated, the draft and destroyers for England. Referring to the Burke–Wadsworth Bill, then being opposed by most Congressional Republicans, he said he could not ask the American people to believe in his leadership unless he told them that "some form of selective service is the only democratic way in which to secure the trained and competent manpower we need for national defense." He immediately went on by pointing out the threat to our defenses that would follow the loss of the British fleet and quoted at length Roosevelt's statement about extending to the "opponents of force the material resources of this nation" and gave his own "wholehearted support to the President in whatever action he may take in accordance with these principles." What he had said so far had been a complete endorsement of FDR's foreign policy, but then he declared that the President was risking war by dabbling "in inflammatory statements and manufactured panics." Such a conflict, Willkie charged, would be "a war for which the country is hopelessly unprepared—and which it emphatically does not want."

His discussion of domestic policies included what was virtually a point-for-point endorsement of the New Deal, with statements about the need to regulate the "force of free enterprise," federal assistance for farmers, collective bargaining for labor and wage and hour standards, federal regulation of interstate utilities, securities markets and banking, as well as pensions, old-age benefits and unemployment allowances. He then returned to his earlier charges that, rather than make the promised improvements, the government had discouraged productivity despite its spending programs and that "only the productive can be strong." He drew parallels, as many Republicans were wont to do, with France's prewar Popular Front regime of Léon Blum, which, he said, had weakened that nation's structure so that its collapse was inevitable.

The crowd showed its greatest approval when, near the end of the speech, he proposed that "the President and I appear together on public platforms in various parts of the country to debate the fundamental issues of the campaign." He followed the dramatic challenge by saying: "And I would also like to debate the question of the assumption by this President, in seeking a third term, of a greater degree of public confidence than was accorded to our presidential giants, Washington, Jefferson, Jackson, Lincoln, Cleveland, Theodore Roosevelt and Woodrow Wilson."

The speech had been delivered in tones that were far more subdued than his usually effective and dynamic oratory. Most of the professionals blamed Davenport for having written an essay rather than words that could arouse an audience. They were also disturbed because so much of its content had been a virtual endorsement of the New Deal. Sam Pryor commented that the words could have been spoken by FDR himself and lamented Willkie's failure of his opportunity to reach such a large number of people in a manner that was more characteristic of his style and tone. It would have been better, Pryor felt, to have given a fifteen-minute speech of Willkie's rather than something Davenport had written. "His performance was flat," Joe Martin later wrote.

Within a few hours the White House received two hundred telegrams congratulating FDR. Willkie "certainly can't put the soul into his voice," a Minneapolis man wrote to the President. "When you speak, it *rings* true." Socialist party presidential candidate Norman Thomas said: "He agreed with Mr. Roosevelt's entire program of social reform and said it was leading to disaster."

Yet it would be unfair to ignore the wide praise that did follow for a speech that had, for the most part, been an honest expression of the convictions of a man who felt that his party had a constructive destiny. Raymond Moley wrote that it had "revealed a big man and an honest, shrewd, courageous and practical one." Newspapers were almost unanimous in their praise. Within the next forty-eight hours the Cleveland *Plain Dealer* and Navy Secretary Knox's Chicago *Daily News* endorsed his candidacy. Telegrams of support came from President-emeritus A. Lawrence Lowell of Harvard and President Dixon Ryan Fox of Union College.

Roosevelt, adhering to his campaign policy of silence, chose Harold Ickes to reply. The Secretary spoke on Monday night over a nationwide radio hookup and delivered his most effective and, in many ways, his most vitriolic speech. He called Willkie a "simple, barefoot Wall Street lawyer" and the "rich man's Roosevelt." Observing that the Republican had denounced intolerance, he hoped he "will have the courage to tell the Coughlinites, the Bundists and other Fascists who are rallying to his support that he does not wish their favors." Attacking what had been perhaps Willkie's most unfortunate comment, he asked whether the Republican candidate thought that the bombing of London was a "manufactured panic" and likened him to the European appeasers of Hitler. He then charged Willkie with being an opportunist who would rather "join 'em" than fight, even though it meant becoming part of a political machine as unsavory as Tammany Hall.

Willkie promptly wired Joe Martin to say that the speech was "unworthy of answer" and that he didn't think any radio time should be obtained for a rebuttal. "The only truthful reference to me in his whole speech," Willkie told Martin, "is that I rent a small apartment at 1010 Fifth Avenue about a mile away from Mr. Roosevelt's town house off Park Avenue." When he appeared at a Rushville, Indiana, dinner the next night, the candidate said his Indiana heritage had taught him that "when you have a blow to strike you do it yourself, and we don't strike foul blows through stooges."

The campaign was on.

CHAPTER TEN

The Candidate Joins His Party

1

WITH THE INTENSIFICATION of the Battle of Britain, Roosevelt became even more reluctant to engage in political controversy. When answering the inevitable question about accepting Willkie's challenge for a debate, he recalled that, at Chicago, he had said that "things are in such shape this year that it is, of course, perfectly obvious that I cannot do any campaigning, as you all know." And, with a laugh, the President suggested that the answer be mimeographed by the press for future reference.

In Edith Willkie's home town of Rushville, where Wendell Willkie was using the Lollis Hotel almost as he had the Broadmoor in Colorado, the Republican candidate renewed the challenge. The President's inspection trips, Willkie pointed out, could be delegated to specialists. That would enable the Chief Executive to fulfill his democratic function by discussing the major issues.

Ickes, in replying to the Elwood speech for the President, had, of course, hit low by saying that Willkie's campaign was a vehicle for the Coughlinites, Bundists and other native Fascists, but he had not been entirely inaccurate. By marrying into the Republican family, Willkie had forsaken one collection of odd relatives for a motley array of stepchildren. Before long both the German-American Bund and the Communist party announced that he was their man. So did such maniacal extremists as Mrs. Elizabeth Dilling of Chicago, whose 1934 book *The Red Network* named such a wild list of American "Marxists" that, as Arthur Schlesinger, Jr., has noted, it was "more Groucho than Karl." But Mrs. Dilling was unable to become an enthusiastic supporter of the Hoosier and continued to have doubts about his dedication to truly "American principles."

More embarrassing were the followers of the Radio Priest of Royal Oak, Father Charles Coughlin. Benjamin Namm, a Brooklyn merchant, was particularly indignant to see men wearing Willkie buttons distributing, in front of Namm's store, copies of Coughlin's anti-Semitic paper, *Social Justice*. And there were other instances of Coughlinites peddling Willkie along with bigotry. One that persisted was at the intersection of the Grand Concourse and Fordham Road in the Bronx, in front of a department store that "belonged to a Mr. Alexander" on a prominent business corner in the middle of a predominantly Jewish neighborhood. "Vote for Willkie," said the signs. "He is pro-Christian." Local Republicans demanded an investigation to learn whether it was just another trick perpetrated by "Boss" Flynn.

It was hardly suitable for Willkie to have such "friends," particularly as the Jewish newspaper *The Day* came out on August 23 with his article about how his father had fled from the Prussian Junkers, "who were the spiritual ancestors of the present-day Nazis." Further, a number of prominent Jewish lawyers like Samuel Proskauer and Benjamin Javits, as well as Rabbis Abba Hillel Silver and Michael Aaronsohn, who had delivered an invocation at the Philadelphia convention and was a blind war veteran, had also declared for Willkie.

The candidate was in New York for a short visit when the August 26 issue of *Social Justice* appeared with the statement that Willkie had sounded a "Call to a New Nationalism" and a full-page editorial of endorsement. At a press conference, just before returning to Rushville, Willkie quickly disavowed the support with a statement that has since become a classical example of a political repudiation.

If *Social Justice* was anti-Semitic, as he had heard that it was, Willkie said, "Not only am I not interested in that kind of support, but I don't want it." Then he added: "There is no place in my philosophy for such beliefs. I don't have to be President of the United States, but I do have to keep my beliefs clear in order to live with myself."

Coughlin himself immediately followed with a statement denying that he had written anything for the weekly for six months. He had not, in fact, decided whom to support, and thought he might "prefer to keep silent." But Willkie's statement produced a rash of protests from suddenly aroused bigots. One caller said it was a "goddamned lousy trick of Mr. Willkie to throw out the big Irish vote in such a way." A representative of Queens Borough President George Harvey's office reported that Harvey was a strong admirer of Coughlin and that people to whom Willkie buttons were distributed were turning them back. Protests came from spokesmen for such organizations as the Lady's Auxiliary of the Ancient Order of Hibernians, Silver Star Mothers, Lady Lafayettes, South Brooklyn Mothers' Club and the Lady Pioneers of America. A Kansas City attorney informed Willkie that he hoped "Hitler does not stop until every Englishman and Jew have their snouts kicked out of continental Europe." Another man wrote that "a few more remarks like the ones you made about Father Coughlin and then after the election you can look for a different position or go back and manage your five farms."

The most interesting reactions came from those who protested the charge that the priest was anti-Semitic. "If Father Coughlin were anti-Semitic," claimed one man, "he would not have millions of real Americans behind him." Even more typical was the Mt. Vernon, New York, man who informed Willkie that he had not found "where in one single instance he [Coughlin] has ever been guilty of being in favor of any form of prejudice . . . if I could be convinced that he was different I would turn on him as quickly as you would, never-the-less it would take more than all of the atheistic jews in the world to convince me that he is anything other than one hundred percent American."

Willkie's position did receive support from a number of Roman Catholic and Protestant clergymen. But his statement revealed the existence of widespread anti-Semitism and injected a deeper element of controversy among many who had so fervently enlisted in his crusade. He had betrayed them. On September 2 *Social Justice* declared: "Old-fashioned Americans know not for whom to vote. They have no candidate."

2

The Willkie campaign had been at a high point at the time of the Elwood speech. A Michigan judge wrote confidentially to tell presidential assistant Stephen Early that the situation in Michigan was "hopeless" for FDR, according to a survey he had just made, because Willkie's strength in the smaller cities and towns was sure to overwhelm the Democratic vote in Detroit. Gallup reported that Ohio, which "has been a good barometer of national political sentiment since the turn of the century," was giving Willkie 53 percent of its vote. He was also narrowly ahead in New Jersey. From even the deep South came reports that the Republican candidate was being cheered by moviegoers when he appeared in newsreels. *Editor & Publisher* reported that Willkie was being backed by 66³⁄₁₀ percent of the daily press. Alan Valentine of Democrats for Willkie proudly announced that another bolter, Representative Robert G. Allen of Pennsylvania, had joined the dissidents as treasurer.

Gradually, however, even before his repudiation of Coughlin, sentiment began to change. Gallup still showed Willkie ahead, but with a reduced electoral lead, as four western states slipped from his column, while the President had 51 percent of the popular vote. Some suggested that the Republican candidate should do more to pick up the blue-collar vote and even urged those with expensive cars to hide their Willkie buttons and signs. A Virginia friend advised Willkie that his biggest weakness, however, was an evident inability to control "the Republican obstructionists in both Houses of Congress, who are doing everything within their power to delay passage of the conscription bill." More reliance on such practical politicians as Martin or Vandenberg, he suggested, would be better than being guided by "amateurs like Davenport."

Senator McNary delivered his own acceptance speech at Salem, Oregon, on August 27 and spent almost his whole time discussing the farm problem and public power projects. About the only specific words devoted to foreign policy were a denunciation of reciprocal tariff agreements. He said nothing about the draft.

Martin himself told reporters that Congressional Republicans were under no obligation to follow Willkie's leadership when they voted on the Burke–Wadsworth bill. The measure, designed to bring the first peacetime draft in American history, was passed by the Senate on August 28. Despite Willkie's repeated statements backing conscription, during and since the Elwood speech, only eleven of the twenty-three Republican Senators approved it. McNary loyally went along with Willkie's leadership, but the opposition included Vandenberg and Taft. It was a poor demonstration of authority for a man who was saying that his election would improve the nation's defenses. Only two days earlier he had blamed the President for having delayed the national defense program and had repeated his support for the draft law.

Then Willkie compounded his problems. The bill contained an amendment introduced just before the vote by Senators John Overton of Louisiana and Richard Russell of Georgia. It authorized the government to seize and operate any industrial plant or facility that refused to cooperate with the defense program. No doubt it seemed plausible and fair to most Americans, who could not understand why business should be excused from such obligations while their sons were being conscripted. But Willkie immediately saw it as a threat of government intervention that would frighten away potential investors and weaken productivity. He reacted by saying that "It may be that the American people want to Sovietize or socialize (you can take your choice of terms) American businessmen. If they do, it's O. K., but I want to present the issue." In a prepared statement he said, "I cannot understand what we are undertaking to defend" if the government can assume such powers. He also challenged the President to state his own view.

From Hyde Park, Roosevelt said he did not want to be drawn into a "political discussion" of the Overton–Russell amendment; and Willkie, realizing that most Republican Senators had approved the amendment, giving him a double setback for that day in party consistency, issued a clarifying statement. But it was of little help. It was too feeble to say, as he did, that he would support the Overton–Russell amendment if it didn't give such arbitrary powers to one man. Those who believed his major concern was for the interests of business had their evidence. Willkie kept after Roosevelt to comment, but the artful dodger counted his gains in silence.

Alf Landon, then, tried to be helpful. On August 31 he warned Willkie that he could avoid clashing with his own party's Congressional leadership by confining his statements to generalizations in support of national defense. Four days later Landon followed with another letter. This time he pointed to his own Warrensburgh speech of May, in which he had tried "to spike the attempt of the Government to nationalize American industry." He suggested that Willkie "Slip the word to two or three of your good friends among the newspaper men" to show that "your position is entirely in accord with the titular head of the Republican party in the last four years." But Willkie, who had always maintained that he would be his own brain trust, ignored both points.

3

The Democratic campaign, if it can be so called, was a uniquely odd one. The President seemed thoroughly disinterested in the subject. What actually did take place was being directed by Ed Flynn from his Biltmore Hotel headquarters in New York. On the fifth floor of the same building, Franklin D. Roosevelt, Jr., led the Young Democrats. At Des Moines, on August 29, Henry Wallace opened his part of the campaign with an acceptance speech that charged the Republicans with being the party of appeasement. By the end of that month, however, the President began to become involved. He went over plans for the western portion of the campaign with Senator Scott Lucas, who had been charged with directing the third-term drive in a thirteen-state area from headquarters in Chicago.

Roosevelt, however, continued to resist Republican pressure to debate with Willkie. When the GOP candidate persisted in calling on him to comment on the Overton–Brooks amendment, the President replied that it was his established rule not to talk about pending legislation. The Willkie camp, however, responded with a list showing seventeen different occasions since the first of the year when Mr. Roosevelt had violated his own "rule."

On September 3, as FDR headed back toward Washington after having dedicated a TVA dam in Tennessee, in an atmosphere that was strongly reminiscent of his campaign trips of 1932 and 1936, he again exercised one of the prerogatives of his high office by revealing to the newsmen a decision that he termed was "probably the most important thing that has come for American defense since the Louisiana Purchase." Reading in advance to the press his message to Congress, he reported that an exchange of notes between the British Ambassador in Washington and the Secretary of State had resulted in this government's acquisition of the "right to lease naval and air bases in Newfoundland and on the islands of Bermuda, the Bahamas, Jamaica, St. Lucia, Trinidad and Antigua and on British Guiana." The Newfoundland and Bermuda bases, he explained, were gifts, "Generously given and gladly received." They and the leases, which were for ninety-nine years, had been acquired in exchange for fifty of our over-age destroyers. He maintained that the move was not inconsistent with America's nonbelligerent status but was, rather, an act of preparedness and continental defense. The reference to the Louisiana Purchase suggested how he would use historical precedent to justify the decision. William Allen White's committee and the Century Group had won an important objective.

The deceptively casual announcement was the result of weeks of intensive negotiations and arduous questioning. The old American destroyers would be of tremendous aid to the British cause. At the suggestion of Attorney General Jackson and other leading lawyers, including Dean Acheson, the President accepted an interpretation of his powers that obviated the need for obtaining enabling legislation from Congress. Fearing the reaction on Capitol Hill, FDR told Grace Tully that "Congress is going to raise hell about this but even another day's delay may mean the end of civilization."

For the most part, the public was enthusiastic. However, few wanted actually to get into the war, as Dr. Gallup showed; Americans were, nevertheless, overwhelmingly behind the British. Isolationists, however, clearly regarded the deal as an act of war. The St. Louis *Post-Dispatch* editorialized that the leases "might not be worth the paper they are written upon in a month's time"; and, the paper declared, "Mr. Roosevelt today committed an act of war. He also became America's first dictator." A member of Boston's University Club quickly wrote to Willkie: "All that is left is for the President to likewise casually announce that *he* has declared war on Germany and so we are at war!" At the same time, a San Francisco man hurriedly wired the Republican candidate to urge his endorsement of the move. "Your support is very important," the telegram stressed.

As he had indicated to William Allen White in early August, Willkie supported the deal and said it would not become a political issue. He did, though, call it "regrettable" that FDR had acted on his own without any prior public discussion and approbation by Congress. But there was also no question about his agreement that Britain needed the help; certainly his attitude had relieved the President of an important obstacle.

"Just what do you challenge when you seem to be in accord with everything!" complained a St. Louis lady to Willkie. From Beverly Hills, California, came a telegram that read: "David used his own ideas when he met the Champ."

In the view of many Republicans, their candidate was fumbling all the good opportunities. When the Selective Service bill was passed by the House on September 7, 112 Republicans voted to kill it, while only fifty-two gave it their support. That minority included a reluctant Joe Martin, undoubtedly as a gesture toward the man whose campaign he was managing. But, at the last minute, Hamilton Fish successfully inserted a damaging provision. It put off the start of mobilization for sixty days and also limited the military increase to four hundred thousand men. The two-month delay was to be used to secure a considerable portion of that expansion by voluntary enlistments. On this amendment Republicans went along by a vote of 140-22. Joe Martin joined them. Three days later, their presidential candidate said: "I hope that, as a result of the conference between House and Senate conferees, the Fish amendment is eliminated."

And it was. Willkie met with Stassen, Martin and McNary in Indianapolis and sold them his point of view. But when the Burke–Wadsworth bill was finally passed, only forty-six of the 134 House Republicans who voted approved, and it was supported by just seven of the seventeen GOP Senators who participated. Willkie had undoubtedly helped to secure the legislation and in a form that kept it from being impotent, but as many people, including Walter Lippmann, were asking: "How can he accomplish anything when he can't even control his own party?"

4

Throughout the summer the Nazis watched the Democratic campaign with great interest. In vain they awaited the formation of an isolationist third party. Lacking that, they hoped for a Willkie victory; for all of official Germany and even the underground assumed that Roosevelt's re-election would bring America into the war. Nazi sympathizers, though rejected by the Republican candidate, noisily urged the President's defeat.

Hans Thomsen was disappointed with the quality of the people who had attached themselves to the Nazi cause. He said that they were often well meaning but uniformly without influence, and therefore no political importance could be attached to their proposals. One American, the radio commentator Fulton Lewis, Jr., suggested that Hitler address a short telegram to FDR pointing out England's responsibility for having started the war and urging him to agree to a peace treaty under the threat of having total war launched against the British Isles. Lewis predicted that Roosevelt would make a "rude reply" but that the American people, and those of Latin America, would respond favorably to the appeal. The suggestion, of course, was ignored.

However, the full-scale attack on Great Britain did raise hopes for Roosevelt's defeat, for the Nazis believed that the war would be won by election day. Consequently, their cooperation with the isolationists was reduced. Evidence that connected the German legation with Roosevelt's opponents was destroyed and the copies of such reports to the British Foreign Office were burned. Only the capture of the Nazi archives revealed the story of German complicity and explained why they failed to step up their activities against the man they portrayed as a Jew, a member of the "International Jewish Conspiracy," whose real name was Franklin "Rosenfeld," President of the "Jewnited" States and Governor of "Jew" York.

5

By the latter part of the summer the Battle of Britain had reached its height. Americans saw a series of banner headlines with news of still more waves of Nazi planes. London was hit by fifteen hundred of the Luftwaffe's force in its single largest raid. Fire raging from the constant assaults helped to guide Nazi raiders back to the city on successive nights. Invasion was feared to be very near.

For a brief time, during the nights of September 7 and 8, parts of London were in near panic. Authorities feared that the hysteria would be contagious and precipitate the type of mass-evacuation movements that had occurred in France and Belgium. But within forty-eight hours, even though the bombs still fell, the people rallied and the danger was over. The working-class districts in the East End, particularly near the docks along the Thames, had been getting most of the bombs; so there was a macabre equality when, several days later, the posh West End of London and Buckingham Palace were hit.

As the bombing was endured and as the Royal Air Force took an increasingly greater toll of enemy planes, fear of England's collapse began to diminish.

Coinciding with Britain's "finest hour," General Hugh S. Johnson made a national broadcast that launched an organization known as America First. It was to become the nation's most powerful non-interventionist group. General Robert E. Wood, board chairman of the Sears, Roebuck Company, had agreed with some reluctance to serve as its national chairman.

From the start, the organization, which also included such prominent people as Mrs. Alice Roosevelt Longworth, Mrs. Burton K. Wheeler and Oswald Garrison Villard, held that America must build impregnable defenses as the best way of being able to stay out of the war. It attracted unsavory support, although many of its members, such as advertising executive Chester Bowles and college student Sargent Shriver, were simply against the idea of war. But anti-Semitism plagued the organization, despite all attempts to dispel such a taint. Coughlinites joined. Finally, the German-American Alliance, a Bund-type Chicago group, urged its followers to contribute to America First. The nature of the organization made it impossible for it to reject either the extreme left or the extreme right.

The Battle of Britain, and particularly its successful course, seemed to make Americans even more determined to remain at peace. A Gallup poll showed quite conclusively that most Americans would vote for Roosevelt if the country became involved in the war by election day, but the overwhelming majority wanted no part of the European conflict.

6

Willkie's stay in Rushville was part of his effort to identify himself with rural mid-America rather than with the Wall Street "interests" that were usually credited with having won his nomination. For the same reason, he planned to deliver his first major campaign speech at Coffeyville as a reminder of his brief teaching career there. In Rushville during the first week of September he worked on the speech, planned an extensive seventeen-state western campaign trip and conferred with party leaders and national committeemen.

Much dissatisfaction had already accumulated. From many areas had come reports that the Willkie spark was dying out. His inability to influence Republicans in Congress was offered as a major reason. Lack of coordination with regular party leaders, insufficient time for Joe Martin to fulfill the requirements of being the national chairman, amateurish and inexperienced assistants and the suspicion that he was helping big business by his opposition to the Overton–Russell amendment were all working against him. Hugh Johnson wrote that if Willkie "doesn't get in there and pitch pretty soon he will tangle himself in his own stretch, and the ball game will be all over." H. L. Mencken and editor Harold Ross of *The New Yorker* dined together and agreed that Willkie had to stop "yessing" Roosevelt. Walter Tooze of Oregon suggested that the candidate could help himself somewhat by announcing that he would rely largely on McNary to deal with agricultural problems. Sam Pryor also agreed that the campaign had bogged down in "most parts of the Eastern Division" during the last ten days or so.

On September 5 leaders from twenty-one midwestern and eastern states met with Willkie at the local Masonic Lodge in Rushville. The candidate reminded them of their need to arouse enthusiasm among local leaders, and he emphasized that he had joined the Republican party for the duration of his stay in the White House and not merely for the campaign, a matter that had been of concern among many leaders. To further placate them he gave assurances that while Root's work would be encouraged, it would not interfere with the regular organization and that the patronage would go to the local clubs and not to the Willkie Club people nor to Davenport. He even repeated his statement for sound recordings that could be played in clubhouses throughout the country. He literally captivated the professionals, and even such skeptics as Jaeckle and Sprague were able to go home satisfied with their candidate.

Significantly, the very next day Oren Root appeared as a speaker to help open the campaign for a Republican county committee at Binghamton, New York. The committee members were so enthusiastic that its chairman suggested that Root should be used more often.

On the night of September 7 Willkie was called on to speak at an outdoor meeting in Rushville and he made a significant statement. He repeated his advocacy of "aid to Great Britain short of war" and emphasized that when saying that he meant "short of war," and the four thousand people applauded. Two days later Henry Ford, wearing a red, white and blue Willkie button in his lapel, and Robert R. McCormick were both visitors in Rushville. They could only have praised the candidate's most recent pronouncement; and when Ford returned to Detroit he gave his endorsement of Willkie as a "businessman" who "understands what the country needs first and needs most."

Better news for Republicans also came on September 9, when Sumner Sewall was elected governor of Maine in that state's early election by the largest plurality the party had won there since 1928. Sewall took 63.9 percent of the vote. Ralph Owen Brewster, who was also elected as a United States Senator that day, pointed out that no Democratic President had ever been elected when the Republicans had carried Maine by such a large margin in the state elections.

On September 12, as Willkie prepared to leave for his 7,200-mile western trip, he paused to listen to a radio speech by Fiorello H. La Guardia. The fiery little mayor of New York, nominally a Republican, gave Roosevelt strong support. He called the President a natural leader who had made America the hope of the world. He said that the President had been turning great turbine wheels for the public service while Willkie had been "working the little wheels of the stock ticker." Willkie, amused, noted that the mayor, who had recently appointed the discredited James J. Walker to a $20,000 job, had thereby joined hands with Flynn, Hague and Kelly "in a righteous cause for the benefit of the public."

That night Willkie left Rushville, his train taking him toward Coffeyville and then the Pacific Coast, as Elmo Roper was reporting in *Fortune* that the Hoosier had declined in popularity after his fantastic rise.

7

The *Fortune* poll was considered by many presidential advisers as more reliable than the widely publicized Gallup survey; and Roosevelt's reaction to its latest report was to emphasize that the hardest work should be done where his chances were best. He thought, for example, that the three states of lower New England were bound to be more favorable than Ohio, which he considered practically hopeless. He also wanted to put up a fight in Indiana, Illinois, Iowa, Wisconsin and Minnesota.

The death of Senator William Bankhead on September 14 was the occasion for Roosevelt's trip to Jasper, Alabama, four days later to attend the funeral. Great dignity and decorum were observed. The crowds that met the Chief Executive at the stations along the way did not cheer. Nor did the President greet them. Nevertheless, he had asked his entire Cabinet to attend, and the opportunity it gave him for public exposure was not without its political overtones.

Another public appearance was at the University of Pennsylvania, just two days later, when fifteen thousand attended the two hundredth anniversary ceremony of the university that was held in Philadelphia's Municipal Auditorium. His purpose for being there was to receive his latest honorary degree. En route he had visited the Navy Yard, from which many of the destroyers shipped to England had been refitted, and other military installations. As he drove to the university with Senator Joseph Guffey and John B. Kelly, the Democratic leader of Philadelphia, at least two hundred thousand spectators saw the presidential car move through the streets.

His speech at the hall where the Republicans had held their convention made the most of the "non-political" occasion. Praising Jefferson as the founder of the Democratic party and as the advocate of unlimited suffrage, and attacking Alexander Hamilton as the apostle of wealth and privilege, the President declared his preference for the judgment of all the laborers, managerial personnel and owners of a factory "rather than the judgment of the few who may have financial control at the time." He summarized the New Deal's social legislation. "Even today," he then said, "in certain quarters there are, I regret to say, demands for a return of government to the control of a fewer number of people, people who, because of business ability or economic omniscience, are supposed to be just a touch above the average of our citizens."

The task of answering Willkie's charges in the West was left to Henry Wallace, who left on September 22 to follow the general route of the Republican candidate. The job had to be delegated to Wallace because of Roosevelt's firm decision to remain within twelve hours from Washington. The suggestion that he might fly to distant parts of the country was rejected by the President for reasons of security. In view of his subsequent travels by air under wartime conditions, that he had devised a weak subterfuge seems even more obvious.

8

From the twelfth until the twenty-eighth of September, the Willkie train toured the nation as the candidate started the most vigorous campaign since William Jenning Bryan's in 1896. He waved his arms and called for help from every voter in sight as he spoke from the rear platform of his train and before larger audiences. A gathering of ten or more seemed sufficient to justify a speech.

Willkie's special train was a virtually self-contained mobile campaign headquarters. With him almost constantly, in addition to his wife and Davenport, were such other aides as John Hollister, who was Senator Taft's law partner and an increasingly important Willkie figure, as well as the candidate's younger brother, Edward. Ed was a six-foot-six former athlete who served his older brother in numerous ways. One of his vital functions was to shield Wendell from the flock of self-appointed advisers. Willkie's mail was also full of "advice," which usually conveyed the particular writer's views rather than sound political strategy: but there were those who, at every stop he made, took themselves too seriously to believe that a mere letter would suffice.

Then there was the corps of speech writers under Davenport. They worked together in one astonishingly jammed railroad car filled with typewriters. The place became known to the newsmen as the "squirrel cage." Although the staff had become nearly two dozen in total strength and Willkie frequently turned to various other people for contributions to his speeches, Davenport usually molded the finished product. Of considerable annoyance to the regulars was the absence of any professional politicians from his entourage. Republican leaders had already had enough exposure to Davenport's work to distrust his efforts. Nevertheless, contributions were made to Willkie's speeches by such additional people as Raymond Moley, Henry Cabot Lodge and San Francisco lawyer Bartley Crum. The candidate was also under almost constant pressure to forget about his determination to make no tactical or ideological compromises.

His crowds varied. They were skeptical and even hostile at urban industrial areas, such as the Chicago stockyards, and wildly enthusiastic in downtown shopping sections and financial districts. At Cicero he carelessly blurted out "To hell with Chicago!" after an aide corrected his assertion that he was in the big city by pointing out that he was speaking outside its limits. The comment received wide circulation with the cooperation of Chicago's Democrats and did not endear him to its natives. His strained voice began to give out that night when he addressed fifteen thousand Negroes at the American Giants baseball park. By the time he got to Davenport, Iowa, he could only say, "The spirit is willing, but the voice is weak." A throat specialist was summoned to join the train, and Willkie was able to continue, although with a raucous, ugly voice.

A great mass of local ranchers and farmers welcomed him at Coffeyville, Kansas, where he was introduced by former baseball pitching ace Walter Johnson, another local hero; and the little town got its greatest thrill since the escapades of the Dalton boys. But then a disappointingly small crowd met him at Amarillo, in the Texas panhandle.

Both the excitement and the crowds seemed to grow as his campaign gained momentum, and he invaded Southern California shouting praises for its isolationist senator, Hiram Johnson, as a "true liberal." Willkie was determined to avoid repeating Charles Evans Hughes's snub of Johnson in 1916, when the loss of California helped Wilson win. Johnson hadn't declared for Willkie, but the presidential nominee repeated his name wherever he campaigned, as though the old strong-willed and independent Senator had been his boyhood hero. Eighty-five thousand filled the Los Angeles Coliseum but responded mildly as he read his speech and erupted only when he departed from his typescript. He did much better in San Francisco. At Modesto, in California's lush Central Valley, an egg struck the train and splattered over the top of the speaking platform. When a tomato came his way in Missoula, Montana, Willkie recovered his wits sufficiently to say, "That's the only kind of argument I get from the other side." When he got to Mitchell, South Dakota, he donned an Indian headdress and looked just like every other candidate.

Everywhere he spoke he made FDR and the third term the main issues. In Joliet, Illinois, he denounced the President for having "telephoned to Hitler and Mussolini and urged them to sell Czechoslovakia down the river." Lem Jones explained that the candidate had "misspoken," had only meant to say that the President had supported the convening of the conference, and Willkie was more accurate thereafter; but the candidate was generally believed to have blundered. He warned those at Coffeyville that re-electing Roosevelt would place the nation "under a totalitarian government before the long third term is finished" and declared that the President had "lost his grasp on American principles." He asked the southern Democrats in his Amarillo audience to place the two-term tradition above party loyalty. At San Francisco, after having told Californians that business deserved a fair chance, he accused Roosevelt of having "torn economics from the textbooks. I didn't go to Harvard," he said. "I went to a Midwest school. There I learned in Indiana University that no nation can spend itself prosperous." Iowans were warned that "If the American people have arrived at such a state as to elect 'one indispensable man,' this way of life may pass." After the prepared portion of his Empire City Race Track address at Yonkers, New York, on the night of September 28 had left the crowd unexcited, he spoke without notes and warned that "this way of life will pass" if the Republicans failed to win. In the best tradition of a crusade, he said: "Won't each of you go out and preach the doctrine?"

At least one important Republican committeewoman was enthusiastic about Willkie's Yonkers speech. In a letter to Sam Pryor on September 30 she expressed the hope that Willkie's words had "helped to dispel the wave of pessimism in the East." Then she added: "I have never been more disgusted and disappointed in my life than I have been at the attitude of a great number of the educated voters in the East. They are so pro-British they might as well be colonists, and I hope, when they have succeeded in getting us into this war, that William Allen White and his cohorts will be sent to the battle line in the most unseaworthy destroyer we have! Heaven help a war, if it is going to be run by Winston Churchill and Franklin

Roosevelt, two impulsive amateurs whose disastrous experiments are glorified into feats of valor. . . . Don't call me pro-Nazi. I am just plain pro-American—and I know you are too."

However much Willkie had not wanted to compromise, he was realistic enough to know that views such as the committeewoman's represented a large portion of his party. Yet, curiously, he also learned that he couldn't criticize the President as she had done without making a tactical concession, too. He had discovered that direct accusations against FDR by name antagonized voters, but that they would tolerate the same charges if he substituted such euphemisms as the "Indispensable Man" or, simply, the "Third-Term Candidate." Among his other compromises, in addition to having praised so stubborn an isolationist as Hiram Johnson, had been his endorsement of the marvels of public power during his campaign through California's Central Valley and the Northwest.

Then, within hours after that Yonkers speech, he held important meetings with two men, individuals who represented completely different interests.

The first was with CIO president John L. Lewis. It took place after Willkie left the race track with Joe Martin and went to the Manhattan apartment of Sam Pryor with the national chairman. From about midnight until 2 A.M., while Joe Martin slept, they engaged in a brisk exchange.

The meeting had originated in early September, when Pryor received a phone call from a wealthy oilman named William Rhodes Davis. At Davis' home in Bronxville, New York, Pryor was told that the oilman was out to defeat Roosevelt and was ready to contribute up to a million dollars to that cause. An offer of such dimensions was enough to induce Willkie's friend to use his private airplane to fly Davis to meet with Willkie, who was then in Rushville. Willkie, who had never heard of Davis and asked no questions about his background, pointed to the Hatch Act's provision limiting individual contributions to five thousand dollars and suggested that some money be given in legal amounts to various clubs that could benefit the campaign. Davis said he would be willing to carry the cost of a nationwide radio speech in which his acquaintance, John L. Lewis, would publicly endorse Willkie. The Hatch Act could be circumvented by having the money distributed among Davis' associates so that, through an intricate series of check exchanges, the total amount needed, fifty-five thousand dollars, would be received as individual contributions of five thousand dollars by the Democrats for Willkie, which could then sponsor the broadcast. An arrangement was then made for Willkie and Lewis to meet in New York on the night of the twenty-eighth.

Lewis had been alienated from the President since FDR's neglect in aiding the CIO during the General Motors strike in the early part of 1937, and he had also become bitterly suspicious of FDR's sympathy for organized labor. Their animosity was also a product of a personal clash between two ambitious men. As a vehement isolationist, Lewis had given his public endorsement, in the spring of 1940, to Senator Wheeler for the Democratic nomination; and, as recently as early July, he had told the fifth annual convention of the Townsend National Recovery Plan that Roosevelt's renomination would result in his ignominious defeat by Willkie. Bishop Bernard Sheil of Chicago and Lewis' biographer, Saul Alinsky, then made an effort to reconcile the President and the CIO leader. But the meeting at the White House was fruitless.

Lewis, then, was ready for an opportunity to oppose Roosevelt's race for a third term. Wooing him, Willkie said that, if elected, he would honor the gains labor had won through the New Deal. He did not promise Lewis a post in his Cabinet, nor can it be stated that Lewis made such a request, but Willkie did say that his Secretary of Labor would be chosen from labor's ranks. Lewis volunteered his support if Willkie agreed to repeat that statement publicly in his labor speech scheduled for Pittsburgh on October 3. Willkie agreed, and their midnight session ended.

The Republican candidate's address before a Forbes Field audience of thirty thousand did repeat his assurances to labor, most of which he had stated on previous occasions. He also announced his intention of having a labor man represented in his Cabinet. But when he emphasized that it was a "man's job," which was a direct jibe at Frances Perkins, he incurred the wrath of indignant women throughout the country.

Only hours after his New York meeting with Lewis, as the Republican candidate started West again, he did some further mending. At a railroad siding in Albany that Sunday afternoon, hopefully far enough away from the big city to minimize the possible impact of the story, Willkie met with Joe Pew, who was accompanied by Jay Cooke, the

GOP's senatorial candidate in Pennsylvania. They had responded to Willkie's invitation. For the presidential candidate it was a concession undoubtedly extracted by his aides, as he had vowed to have nothing to do with the reactionary political boss. From Albany until they left the New York Central train at Syracuse, Willkie had enough time to make his peace with the Pennsylvania leadership.

But Willkie had already made a much bigger concession. Having begun the western tour amidst the vituperations of angry isolationists for his approval of the draft and the destroyer deal, he began efforts to suggest that maintaining peace hinged on his election. In the Chicago area he repeatedly said, "And I promise that, when I am President I shall not send one American boy into the shambles of a European war." He told a Portland, Oregon, audience that the President "has left us virtually alone in the world and brought us to the brink of war."

Strange sounds began to come from other unlikely sources. Hamilton Fish stated on the floor of the House of Representatives on October 3 that "I can say without any reservations that the Republican members of the House of Representatives are unanimously for Mr. Willkie in his efforts to keep America out of war and will back him to the limit." Undoubtedly, the Congressman's remarks represented the efforts that Joe Martin had been making to demonstrate to the voters that their candidate and Congressmen were not really at odds. Two days after Fish's statement Willkie's New York headquarters asked Miss Hope Spingarn of Amenia, New York, to discontinue her group's efforts to unseat the isolationist from Dutchess County.

The original Willkie Club organizer in Maine, the man who ran an exporting business in New York, noted that his friends on William Allen White's committee were losing their enthusiasm for the candidate and attributed the let-down to "some of the things Willkie has said and of other things he has left unsaid in connection with the foreign situation." Another correspondent, also from Maine, agreed that Willkie was going downhill and attributed the change to his "somewhat doubtful utterances in his criticism of Roosevelt." Sam Pryor replied: "In this campaign, it seems to be that 'you are damned if you do, and damned if you don't.' One group suggests that the New Deal failures be played up to the limit, and another group wants all the emphasis on policies and aims."

On September 19, while Willkie was still heading west, *The New*

York Times joined the long list of newspapers that had already endorsed the candidate of the GOP. The paper had supported Roosevelt in 1932 and 1936. Citing the two-term tradition, the *Times* said: "When we consider how the powers of the Presidency have grown, what immense patronage, what gigantic expenditures, what enormous power to perpetuate himself in office is now within the grasp of any President of the United States." But, as was indicated by the sparse attendance at Senator Edward Burke's committee hearings on an amendment to limit the Presidency to a single six-year term and confirmed by a Gallup survey, most Americans were still not ready to tamper with the Constitution.

The world situation deteriorated even more when, on September 27, Japan joined in an alliance with Germany and Italy. The pact had followed an American announcement that the export of metal would be barred to all countries but Great Britain and those of the Western Hemisphere. The latest development furthered the belief of many that Roosevelt's defeat would bring despair to the remaining European democracies and would thus encourage Hitler and Mussolini.

CHAPTER ELEVEN

Political Speeches

1

WENDELL WILLKIE, after a day of vigorous campaigning through Indiana and Michigan, addressed the National Federation of Republican Women's Clubs in Detroit on the last day of September. Meeting the argument that FDR should be elected because "you can't change horses in the middle of the stream," he declared that the "closer Mr. Roosevelt gets to war, the more people say that we ought to change horses in the middle of the stream." Then he asked: "Well, for one thing, what are we doing in the middle of the stream?" In Cleveland, a few days later, after a strong statement about the need to continue aid to Britain "even if it means the sacrifice of some speed in building up our own air fleet," he left his prepared text to expand on what he had said in Detroit. "There comes a time," he said, "when it is very wise to get off that horse in midstream because if we don't, both you and the horse will sink."

Having been shaken by the Axis pact, and realizing that the in-

creased fear of war could most likely strengthen his opponent, Willkie
sought to place the Administration on the defensive. Alf Landon
contributed in a similar vein when he asked a Nebraska audience,
"Will the President have Congress declare war after the election? Or
will he so conduct our national affairs that declaring war is a mere
formality?"

Going into the final month, the campaign was becoming less moderate all the time. As the Willkie motorcade was passing in the street
below, a thirty-one-year-old woman hurled a metal wastebasket from
her room at the Book Cadillac Hotel in Detroit, injuring a spectator.
Just outside Grand Rapids, Michigan, a stone crashed through the
window of the rear dining car of the Willkie train. Tomatoes and eggs
as missiles were also becoming more frequent. There was even a
potato in New England. Police along the campaign route began to
search youngsters for hidden apple cores or other potential weapons.
In New York City vandals raided and damaged a local Willkie headquarters.

New York's Governor Lehman told the Democratic state convention that Roosevelt's rejection by the voters would give the dictators
their ultimate satisfaction. He explained that "If Mr. Willkie were
ever to be elected President, he would have to deal with the same
miscellaneous assortment of appeasers and extreme isolationists in
his own party that he has to deal with as a candidate." Still in Michigan, Willkie denounced Lehman's innuendo and asked the Governor
to make clear that he did not intend to imply that the Republican
candidate had "any other attitude than that of a defender of democracy."

Despite some hostility in industrial areas and from teen-agers, the
crowds that greeted Willkie in downtown Detroit and Toledo were
sufficient to convince even skeptics that the campaign was catching
on. At Shibe Park, Philadelphia, the home of both local major-league
baseball teams in 1940, his followers were delirious when he called
for an end to the "drift to war." Again he said that productivity was
the key to more jobs and a stronger America. He charged that the
New Deal had only money and power. With greater wisdom, the
United States would not have been close to war.

2

But however much Willkie tried to discuss the issues with reason, sometimes seeming to lean toward the non-interventionists and at other times, such as at Cleveland, reiterating the need for international responsibility, an "underground campaign" of scurrility was already in progress, to some extent from official sources and more from less responsible individuals. Gradually, the fight for the Presidency became one of the most vicious in American history.

On October 6 the annual convention of the New York State Women's Christian Temperance Union was told by the main speaker, Clinton N. Howard, that Americans should vote for the Prohibition party candidate because Willkie represented a threat to the temperance ideal. A Los Angeles publication called *The National Voice* had already declared in its headlines: "EVERY BOOZE JOINT IN THE U.S. MAY BE HEADQUARTERS FOR WILLKIE." The candidate's brothers, Robert and Fred, were officials of the Seagram Distillers Company, hence the evidence. About the candidate himself that paper said, "He pays little attention to what he eats, is fond of 'rat cheese,' smokes two packages of cigarettes a day and likes a Scotch highball or two when he knocks off work." Correspondence that reached Willkie headquarters revealed many Americans' concern with such information.

But there were charges that Willkie himself was forced to note. At a Brooklyn high school on October 5 Willkie said, "I understand that a whispering campaign is going on about me because one of my parents was born abroad. I say that any man who questions my patriotism is a coward and a cur and I care not what position he occupies, public or private. I only want the votes of intelligent, free-thinking Americans." He was quite likely alluding not only to Lehman's remarks but also to the activities of a New Haven, Connecticut, man named Theodore Heller. Republican headquarters were already aware that Heller had been mailing out copies of a leaflet called "Hands Across the Sea." When asked for an explanation, Heller said he was just doing a favor for a man who had stopped him on the street and asked him to mail the literature. He disclaimed any knowledge of the content or of the organization called "Guardians of America," which was listed as the publisher. The four-page leaflet stated that Hitler was aware of Willkie's German ancestry and, continuing along a "once a German always a German" theme, explained that his victory would enable the Fuehrer to mobilize all German-Americans "to exert his will on our national life." Hopefully, Republicans tried to connect Heller with Charlie Michelson, director of publicity for the Democrats, called by the Republicans "the Goebbels of the Democrats," but they were frustrated when the Senate committee investigating campaign expenditures concluded that it had no jurisdiction to censor campaign literature and so could not pursue the matter.

At the same time, Republicans were able to link smear material to an official Democratic source. The Colored Division of the Democratic National Committee issued a mimeographed handbill titled "Democratic Campaign Facts—1940" from its Madison Avenue headquarters. Its message reminded the voters of Hitler's racial attitudes and Willkie's German background. "Willkie was nominated in Philadelphia by the Hitler formula, otherwise known as the blitzkrieg method," it declared. The handbill also noted that Willkie's floor leader was Stassen, "the Governor of the 'German' State of the Union —Minnesota." Cartoons in the pamphlet illustrated Willkie's alleged anti-Negro attitudes and quoted him as liking to maintain that "I am a white man."

Willkie denounced the pamphlet as the "most scurrilous and indecent" that had ever been used in a political campaign. Ed Flynn also attacked the document, and the chairman of the division, Julian D. Rainey, resigned his post. It did not prevent Willkie from receiving the support of former New Deal Negro newspapers such as the *Afro-American,* the Pittsburgh *Courier,* the New Jersey *Guardian* and the New York *Age.* Most Negro voters, however, had been brought into the Democratic party by FDR and intended to remain there in 1940.

One episode that was too rich for the Republican brass to resist concerned Elliott Roosevelt. FDR's second son, the operator of two radio stations called the Texas Network, applied for a captain's commission in the Army Specialist Reserve. Poor eyesight made him unfit for combat duty or for flying, although he had once held a pilot's license. He was ineligible for the draft because of his sight, a wife and two children and his age. With the Air Corps undergoing a rapid expansion program and undertaking the recruitment of non-flying reserve officers for various administrative functions at the Air Corps material division at Wright Field in Dayton, Ohio, Roosevelt was promptly commissioned as a captain, a standard procedure for those of his age who were accepted under that classification, and assigned there as liaison officer between the Air Corps and the Signal Corps and in the procurement of radio equipment. Wright Field, at that time, had twenty-five other similarly classified non-flying officers and the service was seeking to commission four hundred others. But only Elliott was the President's son.

This was recognized at once as an issue with popular appeal. Hugh Johnson led off by charging that the President's son received preferential treatment. Elliott responded by calling the general "a disgusting old man" who had spent the last war behind a desk. Johnson retorted that if the act were not undone, there would be "a stench to heaven."

Coming so soon after the debate over the Burke–Wadsworth Act, the popular uproar was inevitable. Letters pouring in to Willkie campaign headquarters and newspaper editorials showed the widespread interest. Sam Pryor denounced the commission and was praised for his statement. Willkie himself couldn't resist mention of Elliott in his Cleveland speech. A Greenwich, Connecticut, lady advised that the Republicans also "keep an eye on young Franklin." A New York stockbroker attacked Walter Winchell as "that 'Peeping Tom' kike" for having defended the appointment; and, urging the Eastern Division to exploit the issue, he said it would cost Roosevelt more votes "than the billions of dollars that will be wasted on National Defense." A newspaperman attacked the captaincy in a column that he wrote for the Scripps-Howard papers. He sent a copy to a friend at Republican headquarters. "You will find enclosed a copy of my first article on Captain Rosenfeld," he wrote.

On October 4 a Republican publicity director suggested that Young Republicans in twenty-five of the larger cities form "I want to be a captain" clubs and wear buttons carrying that slogan. "It looks to me like a sure-fire publicity getter and it is one of the things which everybody understands and in which the country generally seems to be interested." He also noted that Willkie's greatest response in his Cleveland speech was to his phrase "overnight captains." Actually clubs of this kind had already appeared, along with buttons bearing the slogan above a picture of Elliott. The American Music Company of Nashville, Tennessee, published the words and music for a song called "Elliott, I Wanna Be a Cap'n Too!"

Fuehrer Hitler made his Captains, from his secret chosen few;
Il Duce followed Hitler—and he made his Captains too.
They've wrecked the whole of Europe—and brought misery and tears;
Now King Franklin makes his Captains and he asks for four more years.

On October 14 young Roosevelt submitted his resignation. It was promptly rejected. "His services are needed," stated his commanding officer, ignoring partisan politics.

Then there was Joseph Weldon Bailey, Jr., son of a former United States Senator from Texas, a graduate of Princeton and the University of Virginia and a member of the House of Representatives from 1933 to 1935. Bailey was a Dallas lawyer and chairman of the Texas-for-Willkie clubs. An additional campaign contribution from him was a series of radio programs, broadcast at eighteen different times in Dallas, San Antonio, Houston, Corpus Christie and Amarillo, that were called "On Guard America."

Introduced by announcer Jimmy Collins as a "native Texan, a real American, and a true-blue Democrat," Bailey devoted his air time to attacking several persons who were closely associated with the New Deal. One program that was devoted to CIO vice president Sidney Hillman contained the following segment:

BAILEY: The cooperation of labor in our national defense rests in the hands of Sidney Hillman, the President's appointee, yet this same Hillman is a *Russian-born, left-wing, pro-Soviet* Socialist leader: This same Sidney Hillman once served on the defense committee of the notorious I.W.W. He was—

COLLINS: *Hold on a minute, Mr. Bailey. Excuse me for interrupting, but those are serious charges. Can they be proved?*

BAILEY: Proof, did you say, Mr. Collins? I hold in my hand Volume One of the official transcript of the Dies Committee. Let me read from the testimony on Pages 649 and 650 of this record. . . . Quote: "Sidney Hillman, born in 1887 in Zagaro, Lithuania." (That's part of Russia, you know.) "Educated in the Jewish seminary in Zagaro; came to the United States in 1907; spent most of his time in promoting Marxism and radical labor unionism; organized the Russian-American Industrial Corporation of which he became the President in 1922. . . . He is well known in most of the revolutionary circles in the United States, having served on many of their organizational boards. He is reported to have served on the I.W.W. defense committee several years ago, according to the Northwest Messenger." Unquote. Again I say that Sidney Hillman, at present a member of our National Defense Council, is a *Russian-born, left-wing pro-Soviet* menace!

Subsequent broadcasts cited vice-presidential candidate Wallace as a constant reader of Robert Frost, the Bible, Tom Paine, Rousseau, St. Augustine, Adam Smith and Karl Marx, which was apparently thought shocking enough for any listener. After reminding his audience that Marx was the author of *Das Kapital,* "the Bible of Communism," Bailey added that "Quite possibly it shaped Henry Wallace's mind, as well; certainly some of his communistic experiments with agriculture seem to bear that out." Bailey also pointed out that Rexford Guy Tugwell was a professor, not a farmer, and that he desired to replace free enterprise with the Russian model. Before signing off, announcer Collins promised revelations "beyond the shadow of a doubt" about Harry Hopkins, "Madame" Perkins, Harold Ickes and Robert Jackson. Impressed listeners suggested that the broadcasts be made available in the East. But the Hatch Act's limitations were offered as an excuse for not doing so.

One final attempt was made to smear Willkie's German ancestry. It came from a Ravenna, Ohio, man who was apparently known to one of President Roosevelt's aides, William Hassett. Willkie's oldest sister, Julia, a chemist, was employed by the Jordan Wine Company of St. Catherines, Ontario, Canada. The Ohio man wrote to her under the pretext that he wanted to assemble information about the Willkie family that "might be useful for publicity purposes," and he tried to find out about relatives who might still be living in Germany. Julia, penciling a reply on the bottom of the letter, discussed the origin of the Trisch and Willkie names and added that "altho [sic] no very near relatives remain in Germany I see no reason for subjecting anyone to persecution."

The man from Ohio had not really lied by stating that he needed the information for "publicity purposes," because he immediately sent Julia's reply to William Hassett at the White House. And he wrote to Hassett on October 29, "I have encountered the most extreme difficulty in getting any information from any of the Willkies as to where their forbears came from in Germany. It looks to me as though they are trying to cover something and the usual excuse . . . is, as you see, the claim that they fear persecution by Hitler. If you see any value in this call me Long Distance and I will write this up, or handle it otherwise." Nothing came of such efforts.

3

By October 6, the Gallup poll was able to show the depth of the Willkie slump. It gave Willkie only six states and thirty-two electoral votes. Moreover, Roosevelt's portion of the popular vote had gone up to 56 percent. The Republican party was able to counter the discouraging figures with a report that predicted Willkie's victory by at least 334 electoral votes, in a sweep that would be reminiscent of Harding's in 1920.

C. Rogers Dunn, who had specialized in statistical research since 1934, operated from a Manhattan apartment. His method, called the Dunn Survey, did not involve the usual poll or straw vote; rather, Dunn made a studious analysis of population groups and tried to chart trends in what he called the "totality of opinion," which would consist of the "pressures and influences which determine opinion." Therefore, favorable newspaper support was considered by Dunn as a factor, among others, that should boost a man's popular support. When questioned about his wide error in forecasting a Landon victory in 1936, Dunn had a simple explanation: He had failed to note that many would cast votes for Roosevelt because they had benefited from WPA projects or relief payments. The employment of each WPA worker, Dunn believed, was good for four votes. Now, even considering so important a factor, Dunn was able to predict that Willkie would win by a comfortable margin. And the Republican National Committee gave the survey fond publicity. Senatorial candidate Bruce Barton used it to predict a minimum plurality of 250,000 votes for Willkie in the key state of New York.

Willkie himself devoted the middle of October to appearances in New York City, in Jersey City—where he delighted crowds by assailing Frank Hague's political machine—and in New England. He hit the Administration hard on both the defense and employment issues as he toured the industrial towns of Connecticut and Massachusetts. While he concentrated on the East, Landon, Dewey, Hoover, Bridges and Taft were cultivating the Midwest. McNary made many appearances in farm areas. A few days later, Willkie got additional support in the Far West when Senator Hiram Johnson reciprocated the attention he had received from the Republican candidate by coming out for him in a radio address.

There were some setbacks, however. Dorothy Thompson, who had been so warm toward Willkie's candidacy earlier, wrote a long column explaining that Roosevelt's grasp of the world situation had convinced her to support him. The St. Louis *Post Dispatch,* which had been a bitter opponent of the destroyer deal, also announced for the President. The paper was published by the namesake and son of the famous publisher of the New York *World,* Joseph Pulitzer. When the New York *Herald Tribune*'s Ogden Reid heard the news, he wired Pulitzer: "Joe, say it isn't so." Rising defense orders that had improved the nation's economy and provided jobs caused many industrialists who had been expected to make large contributions to the Republican campaign to fail to fulfill their promises.

But, on the whole, the campaign was doing very well. The Maryland struggle over control of campaign funds that had been so desperate was rectified. Robert Willkie arrived in Baltimore on October 11 and managed a truce. Both sides even posed together for news photographers with the candidate's brother in the middle. In Kansas, Jay Scovel and Henry Bubb, rather than be relegated by the organization to subservient positions, decided to go along on their own in a friendly competition with the authorized Willkie clubs; the two organizations managed thorough coverage for the state. But the Ohio clubs, which Representative Frances Bolton had noted as having created dismay by tying themselves too closely with the regulars, continued to have a hard time.

4

Franklin D. Roosevelt managed to get to Dayton, Ohio, on Columbus day to deliver another "non-political" speech. He did not mention the campaign but attempted to salve Italian-American feelings that were still irritated by the "stab in the back" speech. He said that Americans "join with our fellow citizens of Italian descent to do honor to the name of Columbus. Many and numerous have been the groups of Italians who have come in welcome waves of immigration to this hemisphere." He conveniently ignored the barriers that had been erected to minimize such "new" immigration. "They have been," he continued, "an essential element in the civilization and makeup of all the twenty-one Republics."

On October 16 he made another radio address. It was the occasion on which sixteen million young men were scheduled to register for the first peacetime draft in American history. To some it seemed a bold way for the President to act so soon before the approaching election. Yet, as he reminded the nation that its youth were "obeying that first duty of free citizenship by which, from the earliest colonial times, every able-bodied citizen was subject to the call for service in the national defense," it was not without the awareness that he was trying to seize the defense issue from the opposition.

The Gallup poll confirmed FDR's political sagacity. Since Japan's pact with Hitler and Mussolini there had been increased sentiment toward aiding Great Britain even at the risk of war. Only 16 percent had been prepared to go so far as recently as May, but now Gallup reported that the number had gone up to 52 percent. Actually, such sentiment had reached its peak immediately after the pact and had begun to slide off by mid-October. Support for the war was strongest in the East, the Far West and the South.

Earlier in the campaign Willkie had vowed to tour the solid South, which had been so unproductive for Republicans, with the exception of Hoover in 1928. But Joe Martin had given different advice. "As a young boy," he said, "I used to go picking berries. I found that I could get my pail filled the fastest if I went where the berries were the thickest." Willkie never did get below the border states.

He was in a border state when he spoke in St. Louis on October 17. It was there, too, that he received the greatest ovation thus far. Confetti and streamers poured over the downtown streets as his motorcade drove through the screaming throngs. Speaking to an audience of twenty thousand that night, he charged the Administration with an ignorance of the function of production that had contributed to the forces of war instead of the cause of peace. He cited Winston Churchill, who had written in 1937 and 1938 that the President's actions had retarded American economic recovery and had, therefore, made this nation incapable of rendering effective aid to Britain. His great theme was clearly that the Administration's policies were leading to war.

All along his latest invasion route in the Midwest, crowds indicated the rise of the Willkie fervor. In Chicago, only the day before the St. Louis triumph, Emil Hurja predicted to a meeting of businessmen that the Republican ticket would win and possibly even by a landslide. Hurja, who now conducted a poll for *Pathfinder* magazine, had been Jim Farley's political analyst when the latter was the Democratic national chairman. The latest Gallup poll, published on the eighteenth, agreed with the indicated trend. It showed shifts placing the states of Michigan, Indiana, Wisconsin and Illinois in the Republican column. Willkie's electoral-vote projection had gone up to 117 from the previously reported 32. In Washington, Franklin D. Roosevelt, Jr., had begun to ask his father to abandon his passive campaign.

5

Everyone from the local politicians to the President's political family urged him to give up the subterfuge of "inspection trips" and meet the opposition head on. Ed Flynn sent FDR, Jr., to the White House to persuade his father to change his mind; but the President was much too cautious to allow himself to be trapped into any promises. At their solitary dinner in the Oval study, Roosevelt allowed his namesake to tell him that everybody at the Biltmore headquarters worried that their candidate would do nothing. "Are the party workers out ringing doorbells?" asked the President. When reassured that they were, FDR answered, "Good . . . then they're not relying upon me." Beyond that, the President refused to go. "I'll let them know," he concluded.

The progress of the Republican campaign convinced almost everyone connected with the Democrats that the President's determination not to campaign was justifiable cause for worry. The press was cheering Willkie and burying Roosevelt news in the back pages. The Democratic machine was suffering badly from Farley's absence, and Ed Flynn seemed to have arrived too late to be built up as a truly national figure. Farley told the Vice President in September that he would vote for the ticket because that was owed to the party, but he would not make speeches for the candidates. And the regular party members were not fully recovered from the convention blues. Real enthusiasm seemed to emanate mostly from the Norris–La Guardia "Independents for Roosevelt," which annoyed the regulars further, as did the President's Jovian attitude. He might be able to stay on Mt. Olympus and manage all right, but the Democrats needed him to mingle with their constituents so that his prestige might rub off on their local candidates. The White House mailbags were filled with letters urging action.

It may have been this urging that prodded the President. It may have been, as Farley suggested, that Wilkie "smoked him out." Or it may have been that the old campaigner couldn't stay away from the noise of battle any longer. Newsmen said that from early October they detected that Roosevelt's restlessness was increasing. When visitors to the White House begged for action, they no longer received a cool rejection. Rather, FDR would nod his refusal sadly. He was resigned but regretful. In reality, he was gathering his strength and his cunning. After being held in abeyance so long, it was possible that the Roosevelt magic might be even more powerful when released.

On October 17, the press was informed that the prerogative retained in the acceptance speech "to call the attention of the nation to deliberate or unwitting falsification of fact" would be exercised. At the same time, the President announced that he would make five speeches in the time left before election day. Inspection trips would be made along the way but "will be paid for, of course, obviously by the Democratic National Committee because they contain political speeches," Roosevelt said. Secretary Ickes, who had been agitating for this change of plan, called the President after the announcement. "I am fighting mad," said FDR. "I love you when you are fighting mad, Mr. President," answered his Secretary of the Interior. Lowell Mellett spread the word that FDR had just about consented that everyone could go for Willkie now with, as Ickes put it, "our bare hands."

Roosevelt's entrance into combat was judged tardy by many, perfectly timed by others. The third-term issue was insufficient to deprive the President of the bulk of his party. The country, from coast to coast, was well supplied with "No Third Term" equipment, from buttons to billboards, but it was almost all nothing but Republican propaganda. The war overshadowed a sentimental tradition.

Even in the West, the cradle of isolationism, a new look was being taken at the creed. Several factors were at work. Aid to Great Britain was being endorsed from Iowa to the Pacific Coast states. Friends of Senator Wheeler cautioned him to modify his isolationist views lest he endanger his chances for re-election. National defense was a cause with which no one dared to quarrel. And the government spending program began to look better to Westerners when part of the money was being spent on defense plants that provided them with jobs. The Elliott Roosevelt episode had aroused some controversy but not enough to cause really meaningful damage.

Basic farm problems such as low farm prices and low farmer income had not been truly solved by the Administration. However, the farmers were somewhat assuaged at the moment because their benefit payments were arriving on time, as was inevitable in an election year.

Willkie had tried many issues, including abuse of presidential power, but he had not succeeded in developing a few major questions or trends that would pinpoint the campaign. Roosevelt had two overwhelming advantages: the world situation and himself. The former was beyond his control, but the latter was about to be exploited to the fullest. The President had the prestige of his office and his record. He had also a powerful psychological weapon—the attitude of a winner.

But the professional politician does not deal in intangibles or metaphysics. He prefers a close political look at the campaign map and a close study of the campaign figures. Some critical states remained on the doubtful list. Pennsylvania looked safe for the Democrats because of the probability that FDR would carry Philadelphia. The industrial sections of Ohio supported Roosevelt, but Willkie had made gains in rural areas and sections that had large blocs of German voters. The critical state of Illinois seemed to lean to Willkie despite the efforts of the Kelly–Nash machine. The Gallup poll and the straw votes were giving the state to the Republicans probably because of isolationist sentiment. The Democratic cause was being threatened in California by old-time liberal Hiram Johnson's defection to Willkie. Though the Senator claimed it was because of the third-term issue, his past record would dispute his position. Johnson had been the vice-presidential candidate on Theodore Roosevelt's third-term ticket in 1912 and in 1916 had voted his delegates for TR's third-term candidacy. The cause for his defection was, therefore, personal pique because the President had failed to pay enough attention to his demands. Nevertheless, to fail in California the Democrats would have to lose a huge percentage of their 1936 lead of 900,000. This seemed unlikely because Democratic registration in San Francisco, for example, was promising a record turnout.

A study of the key areas would seem to clinch the election for the President were it not for the independent vote, which might go in a bloc to either party. Some promising Republican indications were: group votes such as the Germans in Ohio, Hiram Johnson's radio speech scheduled in California, persistent fear in the Midwest that Roosevelt would send their sons to overseas battlefields and, on the West Coast, fear of a war in the Far East.

The Democrats worried about the votes of all the ethnic groups. Campaign literature went out from their headquarters in thirteen different languages ranging from Finnish to Yiddish. Letters to the White House that pointed up any difficulties were immediately referred to the proper department for expert handling. A letter from Walter White, president of the National Association for the Advancement of Colored People, warning that there was considerable pro-Willkie sentiment among the Negroes was regarded as highly significant.

6

After his St. Louis success, Willkie delivered an eloquent extemporaneous address at Jefferson City, Missouri. He condemned the smooth "professional" maneuvers of the President. He also urged that he be regarded as a political amateur ignorant of how to manipulate Congressmen to control their votes. One could then wonder how, if elected, he planned to get his domestic and foreign policies approved by Republicans, particularly as their Congressional majority, if that should be obtained, would install Hamilton Fish as chairman of the House Committee on Foreign Affairs. When a reporter questioned him on this point, Willkie replied that he could cope with that problem once he had the power of the Presidency.

Upon hearing that his scheduled speech in Baltimore might coincide with the date of the President's appearance in that city, Willkie again challenged FDR to a debate on the issues. Everywhere he went Willkie challenged his Democratic rival. At Milwaukee he warned him not to take credit for business revival, which was really the result of defense expenditures, for that kind of solution would be reminiscent of the "ultimate boast of the all-powerful state" and was the solution of dictators. He also asked why, if FDR believed the gravity of the international situation was sufficient to violate the two-term tradition, he had not permitted Secretary Hull to be nominated. His constant reference to the "third-term candidate" pleased the crowds. Republican leaders began to feel that he had placed the President on the defensive.

At Chicago he hit even harder. Speaking in the same city where, on September 13, he had promised that he would "not send one American boy into the shambles of a European war," Willkie recited the discrepancies between the Democratic platform of 1932 and the actual record of the Administration. The President had not even tried to balance the budget; he had experimented with "commodity dollars"; he had ignored the interests of international economic cooperation by wrecking the London Conference in 1933; there were still nine million men and women unemployed. "Mr. Third Term Candidate," he demanded, "when you begin your belated discussion of the issues tomorrow night, tell the American people whether Wendell Willkie falsified that part of the record." He kept repeating his challenge with each citation of the record, and the crowd was delighted.

Then he recalled that, on September 11, FDR had said: "I have one supreme determination—to do all I can to keep war away from these shores for all time." Accordingly, Wilkie now observed: "My fellow citizens: In the light of the record I challenge [this promise]. The third-term candidate has not kept faith with the American people. How are we to know that he will begin to keep it now?" And, departing from his prepared text, he added: "If his promise to keep our boys out of foreign wars is not better than his promise to balance the budget, they're almost on the transports!" Two days later, at a stopover just northeast of Erie, Pennsylvania, he made the same point.

Before he left from Chicago's LaSalle Street station, two eggs hit the Willkies, one striking Wendell's left cheek, raising a welt and spattering his clothes, and the other landing on Edith's back. Only a restraining policeman kept the candidate from pursuing the thrower. But it was a minor incident, hardly marring the spectacle of admiring crowds. Confidence rose.

Nevertheless, those officials at Willkie's Eastern Division head-quarters who read the "personal and confidential" report that was submitted by a private research organization at the end of the third week in October were less ecstatic. It analyzed the meaning of Gallup's figures and the sources of each candidate's strength. "The prime concern of the people in the United States," it read, "now is national security." Among those leaning toward Roosevelt, "it is evident that the war crisis is weighing heavily in their calculations," in addition to the feeling that he "has helped the poor man." "The 'enemy at the gates' psychology," said the report, "has given the Administration a new lease on its political life, and may result in a third term." The Willkie people, on the other hand, were mostly concerned with the "third term, dictatorship, need for a change, need for a business point of view in government, alarm over federal debt and fear of war." Roosevelt's principal appeals, based on his experience and help for the poor, were more effective than Willkie's, which were mostly anti-Roosevelt rather than pro-Willkie. "Willkie has declared the crusade," it said, "but he does not appear to have dramatized himself sufficiently as its Moses." In order to win, Willkie would have to take all the states north and east of the Ohio and Mississippi rivers but, at that moment, the candidate was losing some strength in Pennsylvania, New Jersey and New England. His best gains were in the Midwest. An international incident, bringing a clear threat of war, could guarantee the President's victory; but any crisis that could be interpreted as indicating that FDR wanted to lead the country into battle could carry Willkie to the Presidency.

7

Without having done a thing but publicly avoid formal campaigning, Roosevelt had developed a situation that made his first formal campaign speech seem like the climax of his campaign instead of its beginning. Exuding confidence, the President planned his Philadelphia speech. Although, including a night on the train, he would be away from Washington only a scant twenty hours, FDR would travel through parts of Delaware, New Jersey and Pennsylvania, giving two platform speeches along the way.

The President's wife and son Franklin had persuaded him to time his speech with National Youth Day, October 23, whose theme was "America Looks to the Future." Roosevelt's progress to the Philadelphia Convention Hall on that day was like a triumphal march. A circuitous route from Frankford Arsenal to the hall was lined with cheering spectators. The size of the crowd compared favorably with the Willkie reception of two weeks before. It was noisier and, particularly in the industrial areas, considerably larger. When the cavalcade arrived at its destination at 9:07 P.M., sixteen thousand citizens welcomed FDR inside and an overflow crowd outside, twice as great, milled around to try to get a glimpse of the President. On the arm of Captain Daniel Callaghan, to the rhythm of cheers and the chant "We Want Roosevelt," the smiling, waving President walked to the platform. He was in top form. The crowd loved him.

"My friends of Philadelphia," rang out the clear, familiar voice. Robert Sherwood, one of the author's of the speech, wrote that, reread after seven years, "it does not qualify as one of his best efforts." But heard and even reheard, it was a sensation. Sherwood himself admitted at the time that "That man would be one of the best actors on our stage with his fine sense of timing and the way he can modulate his voice and change his expression." He used every trick of inflection that he knew and never mentioned Willkie by name. The audience thought the delivery glorious.

The purpose of the speech was to answer the "more fantastic" misstatements of the Republicans. FDR started with a denial of the charge that he had made a secret treaty, a secret commitment or a secret understanding with another nation that might lead the United States into war. Another falsification, said the President, was the accusation that this country was still in a depression, had not recovered and was heading for bankruptcy. Roosevelt supplied his listeners with the "plain facts" as an answer. National living standards, improved labor conditions and industrial production, he asserted, had exceeded the levels of 1929.

In recognition of the occasion, National Youth Day, Roosevelt concluded with a promise to young people. He offered them an additional right—the right to work. Finally, the nation was reassured by a recital of the Democratic party platform on foreign relations. Roosevelt stated: "It is for peace that I have labored; and it is for peace that I shall labor all the days of my life."

The crowd moved along to a high pitch of enthusiasm during the

President's address. They laughed at his irony, booed at references to Republican ineptitude and "me-tooism" and cheered the accomplishments of the Roosevelt Administration. Everyone was pleased with the results, even FDR.

8

The day chosen by FDR for his Philadelphia speech was designated by the opposition as "Anti-Third Term Day." Willkie's appearance, at the same time, was at the tenth annual Forum on Current Problems sponsored by the New York *Herald Tribune* at the Waldorf-Astoria. The GOP candidate, despite a hectic schedule that day, had listened to the President's speech. With his Forum address carried by two national networks, Willkie observed that since Roosevelt had been so optimistic about the state of the union there was hardly need for an indispensable man to serve a third term. Again, he repeated his challenge for a debate. That same day Al Smith told an Academy of Music audience in Brooklyn that he shared "a general belief among people that the New Deal is trying to get us into war." The date also marked the start of a final series of almost daily broadcasts featuring prominent Republican speakers. Three were planned for McNary, two each for Hoover, Taft, Al Smith and author Kathleen Norris. Dewey, meanwhile, winning acclaim as one of the party's best speakers during the campaign, Vandenberg, Irvin S. Cobb and Frank Lowden were also scheduled to participate in the final radio barrage. Willkie himself was scheduled for at least six different spots.

When he spoke at Akron on October 24 he declared that Roosevelt's defense of the Administration had been like the national defense system, "either obsolete or on order." Campaigning through the southern-tier counties of New York State, Willkie kept hammering away at "the third-term opposition." At Jamestown he said, "I would like to hear what his views are about a fourth term. And also I wish he would discuss with us the fifth term." Those close to the candidate feared that both his voice and his stamina might not last through the few remaining days.

Though Roosevelt consistently turned down a direct confrontation between himself and Willkie, the President, nevertheless, followed Willkie and also participated in the annual *Herald Tribune* Forum.

Roosevelt made the final address in the series from the White House. He took as his text the final words of Lincoln's Cooper Institute speech of February 1860, in which he said, "Neither let us be slandered from our duty by false accusations against us, nor frightened from it by menaces of destruction to the Government, nor of dungeons to ourselves." The modern parallel, Roosevelt said, was the sane answer to "the foreign propagandists who seek to divide us with their strategy of terror." The speech was an attack on dictatorship and defense of democratic principles. And in conclusion, though he did not mention Great Britain by name, Roosevelt took the opportunity to speak of the men and women who "displayed such courage, such unity, such strength of purpose under appalling attack."

The next day, October 25, John L. Lewis made his radio broadcast from Washington. As William Rhodes Davis had arranged, it was sponsored by the Democrats for Willkie. His words in support of Willkie were vigorous in denouncing the President. He accused the New Deal of not solving unemployment and of neglecting labor's other problems; but his most emphatic warning was that FDR was leading the nation into war. Although he told his listeners that he was speaking as a private citizen and not as the president of the CIO, his speech was climaxed by the astonishing announcement that he would quit his office if Roosevelt won the election. Astutely, Albert K. Lasker, who had been working hard for Willkie, reacted to this statement by observing that it proved the extent of the Republican's difficulties. If the election was a contest between Lewis and Roosevelt, as the labor leader implied, anti-Lewis union men could accomplish their purpose by voting against Willkie.

The President was not really surprised at Lewis' endorsement of Willkie, which, he felt, was just a return to his former political faith. Also FDR was aware that Willkie's agents had been cultivating Lewis. But the threat to resign, which in effect ordered every member of the CIO to vote against him, did trouble the President. Sidney Hillman, who visited the White House the next day, said that both Roosevelt and Hopkins were depressed by Lewis' action.

Almost immediately it became obvious that labor's rank and file was not going to follow the leader. Reaffirmation of Democratic support came in from locals all over the country. Even CIO officials split over the issue. Vice President Philip Murray and Secretary-Treasurer Thomas Kermody both came out for Roosevelt. Reassuring telegrams and messages of support bombarded the White House. A western Senator wired that his survey of the reaction of the leaders in the coal mines and metal mines of his state was very reassuring. "They uniformly condemn the action of Lewis and regard him as a deserter of the workers of the country," he told the President. Vice-presidential candidate Wallace, in Albany, New York, dubbed Lewis a "Goebbels" and then diagnosed his problem as hostility to the President because he had not been allowed to dictate the government's labor policies.

There was much more going on behind the scenes of the Lewis–Roosevelt rift than was public at that time. As early as 1939 Davis had been in discussion with Goering and others about plans to utilize John L. Lewis. Both Goering and Ribbentrop admitted this later. Joachim Hertslet, a Nazi posted in Mexico City, was in charge of keeping in touch with Davis and Lewis. When the German Embassy was informed early in 1940 that Lewis was opposed to FDR's third term, Hans Thomsen saw the possibilities. He did not fool himself with the notion that Lewis favored the Nazis, but he realized that Lewis believed that American involvement in the war would result in a loss of labor's objectives. Therefore, Thomsen said, there was no need to pour a lot of money into this venture. It would take care of itself. But Goering preferred to make contact with Lewis in the hope that, should the United States go to war, a general strike might be effected. There is no evidence that the Germans influenced the labor leader. There is sufficient evidence that the attempt was made.

Knowledge of this Nazi activity clarifies a story that Saul Alinsky told in his 1949 biography of Lewis. He revealed that on October 17, Lewis was summoned to the White House, where he was ushered into the President's bedroom. FDR, he declared, looked nervous and ill and spoke longingly of retirement. Roosevelt asked Lewis directly for his support. "What assurances can you give the CIO?" asked Lewis. Roosevelt answered that he had always been a friend to labor. Lewis then accused Roosevelt of ordering the FBI to tap his phones and to follow him. The two men disputed heatedly for a time. Lewis asserted that Frank Murphy had admitted to him that he had seen an order to the FBI for these activities. Roosevelt continued to deny it. It would seem that this episode was linked up with the Nazi interest in Lewis. There is a strong likelihood that the government was aware of all or part of the German efforts to contact the labor leader.

Willkie, when asked by Marquis Childs about his having accepted Davis' money to sponsor the Lewis broadcast, replied that he had never heard of the oil speculator before; but he added that, had he known about his background, he would have refused his money. Not only was Willkie naïve in this respect, but he was also careless, for the avoidance of any opportunity for the opposition to link him with Nazis had to be a major consideration.

CHAPTER TWELVE

The Third Term

1

WILLKIE'S FINAL CAMPAIGN APPEARANCES were extremely hectic. He appeared at the New York World's Fair on Saturday, October 26, and delivered four speeches in Brooklyn and Queens, including a major one at Jamaica High School, where he branded as false the kind of prosperity achieved through defense spending. He received a mixture of boos and cheers when he attended the Fordham–St. Mary's football game at the Polo Grounds that afternoon. By Monday he was in the Midwest again and received one of his greatest ovations in Indianapolis. At Louisville he said the Democratic party had been suffocated by the "fungus-like" growth of the New Deal and warned of the end of the two-party system.

On Monday, October 28, the Democrats held their traditional pre-election rally at Madison Square Garden in New York. The major speech, of course, was to be made by the President, who, earlier that day, completed a fifty-eight-mile tour of the city's streets. Over two million shouting New Yorkers saw him. Along his route he stopped at the ground-breaking ceremonies for the Brooklyn-Battery Tunnel and the dedication of the new Queens Midtown Tunnel and delivered six speeches in all. After his strenuous day he arrived at the packed Garden. Every one of its 22,000 seats were occupied and so was all the standing room. The President's face was gray and lined with fatigue. But the sight of his admirers and the sound of their cheers revived him. His voice became alive and there was no trace of weariness.

Roosevelt answered the Republican charge that America's rearmament was too slow to meet the threats from abroad. He pointed out that Republican Congressmen had continually spoken and voted against spending for defense. Yet "today," said FDR, "they proclaim that this Administration has starved our armed forces, that our Navy is anemic, our Army puny, our air forces piteously weak. Yes, it is a remarkable somersault. I wonder if the election could have something to do with it."

The President added, "I say that the Republican leaders played politics with defense in 1938 and 1939. I say they are playing politics with our national security today." Now, he said, they were yelling "me too" about helping Britain but, the previous fall, when they had the opportunity to vote on the repeal of the Embargo Act, they turned it down.

"The act," continued Roosevelt, "was passed by Democratic votes, but it was over the opposition of the Republican leaders. And just to name a few, the following Republican leaders, among many others, voted against the act. Senators McNary, Vandenberg, Nye and Johnson; now wait, a perfectly beautiful rhythm—Congressmen Martin, Barton and Fish."

The crowd howled with delight. The lilting phrase tickled the imagination of the listeners. It was reminiscent of Eugene Field's children's poem "Wynken, Blynken and Nod," which, it was said, inspired it.

When, a minute or so later, the President worked in the happy rhyme again—"Great Britain and a lot of other nations would never have received one ounce of help from us if the decision had been left to Martin, Barton and Fish"—the audience repeated the three names with him in chorus with uproarious pleasure. Somehow the essence of the Willkie opposition was caught in the phrase, probably because it linked the Republican candidate in the public mind with Old Guard Republicanism.

Willkie recognized the damage done to him by that felicitous jingle; other Republicans hearing the audience reacting to the master's dramatics privately wondered whether there was any point in continuing. In Charleston, West Virginia, Willkie reacted to the President's Madison Square Garden speech of the previous night and noted that FDR was supersensitive to the suggestion that he was "about to load the boys on the transports." He also ridiculed the Chief Executive's expressions of sorrow that the Italian and Greek people had been brought to war and challenged him to repeat his "stab in the back" reference to Italy with the election just a few days away. Elsewhere that day Willkie defended the Republican record in Congress on the defense program, pointing to those Republicans, particularly Warren Austin, who had helped to achieve the gains.

The Italian invasion of Greece caused Roosevelt to reassess his campaign plans and to consider the possibility of canceling them. Though he was in touch with Cordell Hull on the telephone, he felt that he should be in Washington so that, if nothing else, he could preside over the details. Particularly since his future excursions, including Boston and Cleveland, were farther from the capital than he had ventured recently, and because there were rumors of a forthcoming explosion in the Far East, the President believed that a curtailment of political activities might be proper. Some of his advisers felt that such a move might be even more effective and dramatic than the proposed trips. But campaign commitments overcame FDR's hesitation.

Roosevelt was often a trial to his associates. He refused the expert political counsel which urged that he postpone the drawing of the numbers under the Selective Service Act until after the election. Instead, on October 29, a day that saw war hysteria at a peak and the Gallup poll reporting a Willkie gain, Roosevelt, back in Washington, attended the ceremonies and delivered a radio address. By presidential fiat, the day was not to be marked by military fanfare. On the contrary, the President wanted a homely flavor with historical overtones that would evoke the American past. For this effect he used the word "muster," redolent of the battles of Lexington and Concord in the American Revolution. Three letters from clergymen of the three major faiths in the United States were introduced, in part, into the speech. The words "draft" and "conscription" were carefully avoided. But, to the Democratic politicians, Roosevelt had failed to lock with the problem that might lose him many votes. He was not giving adequate assurance to the mothers of America who demanded an absolute guarantee that their sons would not be sent overseas to fight. Strong pressure was placed on him to make up this deficiency in his next campaign speech, which would be made in Boston on October 30.

The announcement of the proposed Boston speech also served the purpose of putting another persistent rumor to rest or at least to bring it out in the open to air it. It was firmly stated that the President would serve out his four-year term if elected, thus answering talk that he would resign after the present emergency was resolved. A reporter queried, "Does this mean, Mr. President, that if re-elected, God willing, you will serve out a full four-year term?" Roosevelt affirmed that it did and thanked the newsman for including the "God willing."

En route to Boston, despite the rain and cloudy weather, the presidential train was stopped for brief speeches in Connecticut and Worcester, Massachusetts, which made Roosevelt unavailable to his speech writers, who were still preparing some of the more difficult parts of the Boston speech. When he could, FDR sat with the speech in his lap in his private car, with Grace Tully, Missy LeHand, Hopkins, Rosenman and Sherwood working on carbon copies. Telegrams poured in along the route urging, once more, that parents be reassured that their sons would not be sent to war. Ed Flynn added his pleas to the others. For some reason this seemed to irritate the President, who kept insisting that he had repeated assurances a hundred times and it was part of the Democratic platform. Robert Sherwood answered, "I know it, Mr. President, but they don't seem to have heard you the first time. Evidently you've got to say it again and again and again." And that phrase was put into the speech. Roosevelt said, "And while I am talking to you mothers and fathers, I give you one more assurance. I have said this before, but I shall say it again and again and again: Your boys are not going to be sent into any foreign wars."

The President's stubbornness made him refuse to heed Judge Rosenman's reminder that the Democratic party plank had included the additional phrase "except in case of attack." He replied rather snappishly that "Of course we'll fight if we're attacked. If somebody attacks us, then it isn't a foreign war, is it? Or do they want me to guarantee that our troops will be sent into battle only in the event of another Civil War?"

That Boston speech had another troublesome repercussion. As a friendly gesture to the Boston Irish, Roosevelt made complimentary reference to "my" Ambassador to the Court of St. James's, Joseph Kennedy. The sound of the personal pronoun struck both Hopkins and Rosenman at once. They suggested a change to "our" Ambassador. Roosevelt insisted that he was technically correct and refused to make the change. There was later Republican reference to this as an example of the President's arrogance and dictatorial tendencies.

The crowds in Boston were not too friendly through the Back Bay area. When FDR visited his son John at his apartment on the Charles River, some MIT students welcomed him with a large banner that read "We Want Willkie" and the chant "Poppa—I wanna be a captain." But in other parts of the city there was a tumultuous welcome. About 500,000 lined the streets cheering and tossing shredded paper at the cavalcade.

The Boston speech had a combination of several variations on the theme "We are going full speed ahead," in defense building, in production and in farm recovery. The incompletely stated promise to keep the boys out of war was there, at the insistence of Ed Flynn, the political wisemen and countless others. Sherwood and Rosenman telegraphed Flynn after the President's capitulation, "Listen in tonight. 'Mother' is finally in. Congratulations!" But Roosevelt was not happy about the inclusion. He still believed that it encouraged fears instead of relieving them.

Devices to appeal to the voter abounded in this speech. In describing the defense buildup, tribute was paid individually to some of the areas of the country—Seattle, Buffalo, St. Louis, Southern California, Hartford, among others—and the citizens who worked in those defense plants. But the cleverest bit of showmanship was the introduction of a brief and sarcastic diatribe against Joe Martin, which set the stage for audience participation in the chant "Martin, Barton and Fish." One overenthusiastic participant chimed in too soon and Roosevelt asked him to wait.

The speech also contained a news bulletin to add some further excitement to the rally. "The British within the past few days have asked for permission to negotiate again with American manufacturers for 12,000 additional planes . . . they will bring Britain's present orders for military planes from the United States to more than 26,000," revealed FDR. This report to the people had been prepared with the help of a memorandum from Prime Minister Churchill. The purpose of the draft, on which Arthur Purvis, the brilliant and charming head of the Anglo-French Purchasing Mission in Washington, and Frank Knox both worked, was to get Britain what she needed and also to help re-elect Roosevelt. It would answer Willkie's accusation that the Roosevelt Administration had not given Britain all possible aid short of war. The President was pleased with the nation's response and believed that he had effectively answered his opponent. In retrospect, there is little doubt that this was the most significant part of the speech.

2

At the very beginning of the campaign it had been decided that not only the President but also his family would stay out of the campaign. Ed Flynn changed his mind, however, and sent Franklin D. Roosevelt, Jr., all over the country. FDR, Jr., organized the Young Democrats drive, helping to set up about 3,000 clubs, most of them on college campuses or in college towns.

Once the clubs were organized, young Roosevelt's cross-country tour was mapped out. He went to forty states and made about 475 speeches. On the tour he did not limit his speaking engagements to youth groups but spoke to everyone. Endowed with good looks, vigor and a generous dose of Roosevelt charisma, Franklin Roosevelt, Jr., also had the advantage of resembling his father closely and displaying many of his mannerisms. And he had a style of his own. He commanded the audience with ease and livened his presentation with colloquialisms, the most popular being "my old man." He would say, "My old man is going to keep us out of war," or "Mr. Willkie is probably a pretty fine man, but I'm sure that you'll agree with me when I say I know my old man is an awful lot finer." The audience was delighted with him and so was his "old man." Just before election day when he omitted the phrase from a speech that the President heard over the radio, FDR wrote to his son, "You did a grand job only I wanted to hear you say 'my old man'!"

Young Roosevelt was received with great enthusiasm everywhere. Crowds turned out even in small towns. Most of the interest seemed to be in Selective Service and national preparedness. He was seldom questioned about the third term. Reference was made to Elliott's captaincy, particularly by young people. The issue probably hurt his father, FDR, Jr., said.

Recognition that the Midwest was the most troublesome area of the country as far as Democratic vote-getting was concerned caused a concentration of attention in that area. Roosevelt was due in Cleveland on November 2, but before that the Democrats were rushing their best speakers into Ohio in the hope of halting the Republican trend. Ohio was one of the cluster of states that Willkie had to win in order to take the election.

Gallup polls continued to offer some hope to the Republicans. On October 30 a neck-and-neck finish was predicted. In the next couple of days Connecticut and Missouri were moved into the Republican column. But fifty Washington reporters in a straw vote conducted by *Newsweek* believed that the President would win, also asserting that it would be a close race.

As was traditional, on the Friday night before election day Roosevelt addressed an election rally of the Brooklyn Democratic organization at the Brooklyn Academy of Music. Because it was a strongly Democratic area, the size of the Democratic majority that could be piled up in Brooklyn could determine which way the state of New York would go. Roosevelt's speech was flanked on either side by radio addresses delivered by two of his Cabinet members—Harold Ickes in Wilkes Barre, Pennsylvania, and Cordell Hull in Washington.

Farley, who had not missed a Brooklyn rally since 1928, sat on the platform with Roosevelt. This fourth major address in the President's campaign started humorously with a recital of Republican contradictions on many issues. There was good-humoured audience laughter accompanying the remarks. One of the most important elements of the speech was the emphasis that was made on the varied support that Willkie was acquiring from the right and the left. The Communists were supporting him because, during this interval of the Nazi-Soviet pact, the Communist party line was to defeat FDR because of his pro-British, anti-Hitler position. Roosevelt referred to this support as an "unholy alliance" and the "very strange assortment of bedfellows who have been brought together in the Republican political dormitory."

Arthur Krock unwittingly played into the hands of the Democrats for the benefit of this speech. In his column in *The New York Times* he admonished a Republican lawyer from Philadelphia for statements he had made in a campaign speech that Roosevelt's only supporters were paupers who earn less than $1,200 a year and the Roosevelt family. When this was reported to Roosevelt, Rosenman and Sherwood, they received the news with unrestrained glee. Not only was it ready-made copy for the speech, but it enabled the President, who thoroughly disliked Krock, to enjoy the thought of his discomfort when he heard the speech.

In answer to this statement, which was quoted in Brooklyn, the President said that we should forget the Roosevelt family, "but these Americans whom this man calls 'paupers' . . . are only millions and millions of American families, constituting a very large part of the nation! . . . 'Paupers' who are not worth their salt—there speaks the true sentiment of the Republican leadership. . . ." Roosevelt lost not a moment to champion the common man in ringing tones and to conclude with "And I will not stop fighting."

The day before, Willkie had made an appearance at Baltimore's Fifth Regiment Armory. Nearing the end of his arduous campaign itinerary and facing a large crowd in the huge building, the Republican candidate again warned that re-election of FDR could result in war. Unlike his previous assertions about the consequences of the President's foreign policy, he told his audience that such a war would probably come by April 1941. Secretary Hull, who had insisted all through the campaign that he would stay out of it, angrily replied to Willkie's statement. He said that the Administration was making the public aware of danger and supplying countries under assault with necessary materiel so that war might be avoided. In answer to the charge that United States activities had placed us in a position of "loneliness in world affairs," Hull declared that all the nations of the Western hemisphere were our friends, as well as the nations who were fighting for survival. He made a mild statement of support for FDR's election, citing the disadvantages of a change in leadership at a time when the President's familiarity with and experience in international affairs were a valuable asset. Ardent Roosevelt supporters complained that the speech was anemic.

The President's campaign train waited at Grand Central Station to carry him to Cleveland for his final pre-election address. The speech was to be a summation of all that had been said before on domestic and foreign issues, hopefully without sounding repetitive. At midnight, however, there was not yet a speech. The President went to bed while the faithful team of Hopkins, Sherwood and Rosenman started to review the speech material that had been relayed to them from the White House, including some valuable material from Archibald Mac-Leish, Dean Acheson, Dorothy Thompson and, of course, FDR's notes. Hopkins retired at about 2 A.M., but the other two continued through the night. End-of-the-campaign fatigue was plaguing everyone, but there was complete agreement that this speech was critical.

Short stops along the way at Rochester, Buffalo, Batavia, New York, and Erie, Pennsylvania, included platform talks or brief visits to aircraft plants. At lunch the President looked gray and tired, but after a long, dull monologue on sailing days along the New Brunswick coast, he revived remarkably. For six hours, except for the interruptions of his appearances, he worked energetically on the speech.

Samuel Rosenman said that, except for Roosevelt's 1944 speech to the Teamsters Union regarding his "little dog Fala," the November 2 address delivered at Cleveland was his best. Not only was the speech superb but the delivery was his finest.

Roosevelt's final campaign address was presented in a mood removed from partisan politics. The Republican opposition was ignored and its challenges forgotten. No ridicule, no clever phrases, no repartee was included. In serious, sometimes almost poetic prose, the President described the New Deal's role in the American democracy and his own vision of his country's future. Ever present in the speech was an awareness of the European war.

"This generation of Americans is living in a tremendous moment of history," said the President. "The surge of events abroad has made some few doubters among us ask: Is this the end of a story that has been told? Is the book of democracy now to be closed and placed away upon the dusty shelves of time?" FDR's answer was, "It falls upon us now to say whether the chapters that are to come will tell a story of retreat or a story of continued advance. I believe the American people will say: Forward."

The continuance of "dynamic reform in our social and economic life" was assured by FDR. "For this is the road to democracy that is strong," he explained. And this refrain was repeated after each promise of further reform.

A similar device was effectively employed in the passages that described the America to come. "I see an America of great cultural and educational opportunity for all its people," Roosevelt said. "I see an America whose rivers and valleys and lakes—hills and streams and plains—the mountains over our land and nature's wealth deep under the earth—are protected as the rightful heritage of all the people" was another vision. The result of the repetition of "I see an America" was most successful, partially because of the President's flare for the dramatic style.

Roosevelt captured his motive for seeking a third term in a strong paragraph. He said: "There is a great storm raging now, a storm that makes things harder for the world. And that storm, which did not start in this land of ours, is the true reason that I would like to stick by these people of ours until we reach the clear, sure footing ahead." His audience was enchanted. But when Roosevelt added that at the end of the next term there would be another President, shouts of "No! No!" rang from the galleries. With great presence of mind, FDR put his mouth close to the microphone and continued with his speech so that the radio audience would not hear the shouts. Later, on the presidential train, George Allen referred to the statement that after this term there would be another President. "Well, that's going to cost us a million votes in 1944," he joked. Everyone laughed.

On November 2, Willkie's train arrived in New York, having completed its 18,759 miles of campaigning by rail. He had also traveled 8,884 miles by air. That night Willkie held his Madison Square Garden rally.

Twenty-two thousand packed the arena. Many more jammed the streets outside. Eighth Avenue was virtually impassable. Willkie told the rally that the victory that was certain to come would not be a personal one but, instead, a victory for the people. The "We want Willkie" cries filled the building. Those present in that confident and hysterically admiring crowd could, understandably, find it impossible to believe that all of America was not with them.

The candidate was exhausted and fell into bed in his two-room suite at the Commodore Hotel. Joe Martin was also there. "Joe, how are we coming out?" asked the weary candidate.

There was no point in being blunt. "We've got a chance to win, Wendell," Martin said. He added that some fourteen important states, which could go one way or the other, would decide the issue.

Willkie listened in silence.

"The difficulty that we're really under," the national chairman finally added, "is that we've got to take all of them."

Nevertheless, on November 3, Martin told the press that Willkie would win with 324 electoral votes out of the total 531. And Willkie, on that same day, issued a statement that promised a call for a Constitutional amendment limiting the President to two terms in office. It would be part of his very first message to Congress.

Monday, November 4, was the final day of the campaign. The President was at Hyde Park and made his usual tour through the surrounding counties. In Salem, Oregon, Senator McNary said that the New Deal was taking "deeper and deeper refuge in paternalism and statism." The Republican vice-presidential candidate had gone through the West wooing farmers and reminding cattlemen that the New Deal had purchased Argentine beef and, in particular, lowered tariffs, which had sacrificed them to a "flabby good neighbor policy." Willkie worked in his fourteenth-floor Commodore room while his brother sealed him off from visitors.

That afternoon Willkie delivered a radio talk to the women of America. "I promise, as I have promised many times before," he said, "not to send your husbands, sons and brothers to death on a European or Asiatic battlefield. I will avoid bringing about a condition of affairs that will make a war necessary." Any war that cannot be avoided would come only when "your representatives in Congress declare it." Two other broadcasts followed, both with brief Willkie talks.

Roosevelt's ten-minute election-eve address was broadcast from his country home. It was an intimate, non-political speech spoken in a particularly engaging manner. He emphasized the difference between life in the United States and across the seas, where "life has gone underground." He said, "We thank God that we live in the sunlight and the starlight of peace" and that "In our polling places are no storm troopers or secret police to look over our shoulders as we mark our ballots." The President concluded his address with an admonition to all to vote and an old prayer that he was fond of, "for the dignity, the integrity and the peace of our beloved country."

The final Republican broadcast, from midnight until 1 A.M. was a kind of all-star program sponsored by the Associated Willkie Clubs. It was broadcast from the Ritz Theatre, on Manhattan's West 48th

Street, where an overflow crowd was delighted to see the candidate himself make a surprise appearance. His brief message was almost lost amidst the voices of Ray Baldwin, Lew Douglas, Clare Boothe, Charlie Halleck, Hugh Johnson, Hiram Johnson and movie stars Bing Crosby and Mary Pickford.

To Oren Root, Willkie said he hoped the "silent vote" would materialize for him. The man who had initiated the petitions and the Willkie clubs back in April listened and knew that a candidate who talks about a "silent vote" knows he is through. And it was all over. They had done all that anyone could do. Willkie told Lem Jones that his victory would require a miracle.

The final predictions were in. Emil Hurja said that Willkie would win with a 353–178 electoral vote. Joe Martin had already said his man would get 324 electors. George Gallup noted that a Willkie trend was continuing, but his final figure showed the President about to get 52 percent of the popular vote. Elmer Roper, in *Fortune* magazine, saw 55.2 percent for Roosevelt.

On election day the three members of the Willkie family voted shortly after 9:30 A.M. at Public School 6, which was then located at Madison Avenue at 85th Street. They then went for a forty-five minute drive through Central Park and along Riverside Drive as far north as 140th Street. After a brief stop at their Fifth Avenue apartment they went to the Commodore, where they were joined for lunch by Mr. and Mrs. John Hollister.

On the afternoon of election day Roosevelt, Hopkins, Watson and Dr. McIntire played poker. Franklin D. Roosevelt, Jr., and his wife and the John Roosevelts arrived later in the day. The President then retreated to occupy himself quietly with his stamps. Eleanor Roosevelt served creamed chicken, ice cream and coffee at a buffet supper at her cottage near the main house. FDR dined alone with his mother.

About nine o'clock the First Lady's guests returned with her to the big house. The dining room, where the President would be stationed to listen to the returns, was set up for the occasion. Roosevelt was seated at the table with tally sheets, sharpened pencils and a telephone connected with Ed Flynn at the Biltmore Hotel headquarters in New York. His jacket off, his tie removed, the President was comfortable and waiting. In a small adjacent room the teletype machines were ticking. The guests moved in and out of the dining room except for Missy LeHand and the President's sons. Others sat in a little study off the main hall or wandered into the large library. There was tension, of course, but everyone was optimistic. At 9:40 Ed Flynn telephoned the first report of victory. Cleveland's *Plain Dealer* had conceded the election to the Democrats.

At Willkie's New York headquarters a crowd of more than five thousand campaign workers packed the downstairs ballroom and watched the returns being posted on a bulletin board. The Willkies remained in their own suite. With them were Edward Willkie and his wife. The candidate sat in a large chair in the bedroom with his feet propped up. He smoked cigarettes and nervously ran a hand through his heavy black hair, while his eyes concentrated on a television set, which Ed occasionally had to adjust. At his side, also, was a portable radio. After ten o'clock there were some visitors—Tom Dewey, Roy Howard and Russell Davenport. Groups of newsmen also came in, arriving in shifts of two or three. Occasionally Willkie got up and walked aimlessly around the room, then returned to his chair.

The first returns, from rural parts of Ohio, showed that Willkie had taken the lead. But it did not look good; his margin was far smaller than the vote he needed from such areas. Roosevelt was doing well among the farmers. Soon it appeared that Willkie was trailing in those vital midwestern states. When the first Indiana districts reported a lead for the President, Willkie said to the reporters, "They're probably from Gary." At eleven o'clock he heard radio announcer Elmer Davis state that FDR appeared to have been re-elected. Willkie, obviously discouraged, said nothing. There was still the possibility that late returns from rural areas might yet overtake the Democratic tide in the cities.

The President, who seemed to have no nerves, was surprisingly conservative about claiming the prize. He protested that Flynn's victory announcement at eleven o'clock was premature. But success was obvious to the others. The traditional repast of scrambled eggs was served to the guests, and the traditional parade from the village arrived. Red flares and a band playing "The Old Gray Mare" gave the scene an old-fashioned, rustic flavor. One young lad proudly carried a sign reading "Safe on Third." The President, leaning on Franklin, with his wife, elegant in a flame-colored chiffon gown, came out with the others to greet the cheering villagers. He said, "We are facing difficult days in this country, but I think you will find me in the future just the same Franklin Roosevelt you have known a great many years." He was particularly happy that he had carried his home district.

The mood at the Commodore had grown progressively gloomier. After midnight Willkie went downstairs to the ballroom, where the loyal crowd, now much smaller, applauded and chanted, "We want Willkie!" At 12:20 the Hoosier made a brief statement that was not a concession speech. "I congratulate you in being part of the greatest crusade of this century," he told them. When some people shouted, "Don't give up!" he replied, "I guess those people don't know me."

He returned to his suite. A loudspeaker in the room told him that, on the West Coast, McNary had conceded. But when Willkie announced at 1:30 that he was retiring for the night, he said there would be no statement until the morning.

Roosevelt sat in his high-backed Governor's chair, in his library, and received the congratulations of his friends. But he was too restless to sleep. He returned to the dining room and the telephone. He and his wife talked to their other children over the long-distance wires. Ed Flynn called to tell him that Willkie had gone to bed without conceding. At 2:30 Roosevelt was finally satisfied that the results would not be upset and went to bed.

Willkie's telegram of concession, when it was finally sent to the President at 10:51 on November 6, was proper: "Congratulations on your election as President of the United States. I know that we are both gratified that so many American citizens participated in the election. I wish you all personal health and happiness. Cordially— Wendell L. Willkie."

On Wednesday morning Sam Pryor walked into Willkie's room at the Commodore. The big hotel was a far quieter place than it had been just a few hours earlier, when optimistic party workers were still hoping for the appearance of that big pro-Willkie "silent vote" that, for some reason, had refused to reveal itself to the pollsters. Nothing that Pryor and Willkie could say to each other about the campaign mattered much any more; but Pryor, as generous and kind as he was, could not resist twitting his friend about why things had gone awry.

"I want to say something and I'll never say it again, and I hope we'll be friends for a long time," said Pryor. "You could have won this election if you had kept John Hamilton as national chairman and Ray Baldwin as your running mate; and, third, if you would have met some of these men on common ground to see some good in their philosophy. You refused to see John Bricker. Look how he won Ohio and how you lost it. You could have been President and there's only one person to blame for it, and that's you."

Willkie listened and nodded. It was easier to agree. Finally, when Pryor said he was going to his vacation cottage on Jupiter Island in Hobe Sound, Florida, Willkie arranged for his own family to join the Pryors. So they all went to Florida planning to spend two weeks and remained for six.

On Armistice Day, before he left, Willkie delivered a radio address to the nation. He spoke mostly about the importance of a "Loyal Opposition" for the continued viability of the American Constitution in a two-party system; he asked Americans to avoid falling into the "partisan error of opposing things just for the sake of opposition" and reiterated his belief that Britain must be helped. It was his greatest speech. From Democrats came new expressions of respect, as well as from such Republicans as Henry L. Stimson, Frank Knox and Kenneth Simpson. But to many others in the GOP it was merely ample proof that Willkie was still telling "you Republicans" what to do.

4

Almost fifty million Americans had voted, a figure that remained the all-time high for a presidential election until the Eisenhower–Stevenson election of 1952. FDR's third term was approved by 27,308,-000 voters, or almost five million more than Willkie's 22,321,000. Of some satisfaction for the Hoosier was the fact that his losing total was, nevertheless, a larger number than had ever been given to any previous Republican candidate, and he had brought "the Champ" down to the narrowest of his three victories. While 4,200,000 more persons had voted than in 1936, Willkie received 5,646,000 more than had Landon.

As is usually the case, the electoral vote was more decisive. Roosevelt finished with 449 in the Electoral College, while Willkie won ony ten states that gave him eighty-two votes. The Republican candidate had failed to accomplish what would have been his second upset victory of the year; and his party had been unable to terminate the Democratic hold of the Presidency and the Congress, although it had already become obvious that the war had, in effect, halted the New Deal.

Losers invariably find that someone else was at fault. James G. Blaine had Reverend Burchard's "Rum, Romanism and Rebellion" comment as a handy reason. Those behind Al Smith in 1928 blamed the bigots for having been responsible for denying the nation's highest office to a Roman Catholic. In a vituperative outburst following his defeat for California's governorship in 1962, Richard Nixon blamed the press. Barry Goldwater castigated those Republicans who had refused him support. So, in 1940, it was perhaps natural that the interloper who had stormed Convention Hall with his legions and had walked off with the party's top honor would become the victim rather than the myth-maker.

Everything about Willkie's background and personality made him a natural target for those who preferred to blame the candidate and not the party. If only he had cooperated more with conservatives like John Bricker and had paid more attention to the advice of the professionals; if only he had not relied so much on intellectual theorists like Russell Davenport, whom one Willkie biographer, Mary Dillon, virtually views as the Rasputin of the campaign; if only he had been less outspoken about wanting to aid England and thus make it difficult to draw a fine distinction between himself as a "peace" candidate—the badge of American Legion patriotism in 1940 when the enemy was only Hitler—and Roosevelt as a man sure to bring war; if only he had sounded like a real Republican and had tried to demolish the New Deal rather than having pursued Democratic and independent votes by endorsing so many of FDR's reforms; if only he had not allowed the Willkie clubs to live after the convention and frighten regulars into feeling that they were competing with a mistress who would get all the favors of his devotion. Others liked to cite his intemperate comments such as "To hell with Chicago!" and his unfortunate charge about FDR and Munich. Some complained that he wisecracked too often, others that he lacked humor. A few claim his endurance, and particularly his throat, could have been preserved longer if he had not exhausted himself prematurely at Colorado Springs. As usual, however, most of these reasons overlook what really happened. And to find out, one must start with an analysis of the voting pattern.

Of the ten states won by Willkie, five—North and South Dakota,

Nebraska, Kansas and Colorado—were in the Great Plains. Three others—Indiana, Michigan and Iowa—were in the Midwest. Maine and Vermont, the only others he won, were Landon's only consolations in 1936. But for a more incisive view it would be helpful to relate Willkie's performance to Landon's by comparing the percentages of the popular vote they were able to get in various states.

The national view makes it quite obvious that Willkie's greatest gains were in the upper Midwest, the Rocky Mountain states and the Far West. In almost every one of those states his share of the vote was ten or more percentage points higher than Landon's. In North Dakota he made the greatest improvement, 25 percent, and the difference was 15 or more percent in Minnesota, Wisconsin and Nebraska, while in South Dakota it was 13 percent. It was at least 10 percent all along the Pacific Coast, 19 in Arizona and 13 in Nevada. Along the Rockies he was preferred by 13 percent more than Landon in Colorado, 12 percent in Montana and Idaho and 9 percent in Wyoming. Utah's relatively mild 5 percent was in sharp contrast with the surrounding area.

A secondary level of gain, but a consistent pattern, was registered along the prairie belt of the Midwest and extending into the two most important states of the Northeast. In Iowa, Missouri, Illinois, Indiana, Ohio, Michigan, Pennsylvania and New York his gains were between 8 and 10 percent. He was also within that range in New Jersey, Arkansas and Oklahoma.

In general, then, Willkie did best beyond the Appalachians. When the eastern seaboard is examined, and New England in particular—which had been the nucleus of his drive at the convention—a contrast appears. The South was the only region that was not filled with "We want Willkie!" enthusiasm before the convention and also remained cool toward his candidacy in November. Outside of Dixie, then, Willkie received much better support on election day from those areas that had sent the most loyal Taft, Dewey and Vandenberg delegates in June than he got from the states that had been most instrumental in making him the candidate.

His showing in New England was most disappointing. The "sure" Republican state of Maine, which had given Landon 57 percent of its votes, gave the Hoosier a most unenthusiastic 51 percent. Moreover, he was also off 2 percent in both Vermont and New Hampshire. In Rhode Island he slipped by less than 1 percent. In Massachusetts, Joe

Martin's state, he went up just 2 percent; and Connecticut, where the Willkie regulars were Sam Pryor and Ray Baldwin, gave him just 4 percent more than it had given Landon, which was 46 percent of its total two-party vote. One can easily surmise that many New Englanders who had clamored for his nomination in June voted for FDR in November.

The only real effort in his behalf through the South was made by local businessmen and bankers and trade associations. He lost 5 percent in Georgia and 1 percent in North Carolina and did only a fraction better than Landon had in South Carolina. Elsewhere, with the exception of a 7 percent gain in Alabama, his improvement was in the neighborhood of 2 or 3 percent from Texas through Virginia and including Florida.

All of the above must be considered along with the fact that Willkie's over-all two-party percentage of the popular vote was 8 percent higher than Landon's. And, as had been the pattern since 1928, all of the largest cities, with the exception of Cincinnati, went Democratic. Often they did so with majorities that were sufficient to overwhelm the Willkie vote in the rural areas. Willkie, for example, carried upstate New York by half a million but lost New York City by seven hundred thousand. Successes such as the two-to-one Republican majority in Nassau County were thus obliterated.

As both candidates had expected in the closing days of the campaign, what finally budged voters from their normal economic interests or from following their usual geographic and ethnic customs could only have been their attitude toward interventionism in the war. Both men had pledged to keep the peace; both had even favored helping England; but there is no doubt, as the Axis powers realized, that the Willkie effort was, to a large degree, generated by a party and by individuals whose chief cry had been that Roosevelt was leading the country toward war. The internationalists who had prevailed at Philadelphia could not have prevented the isolationist majority from contaminating the campaign. The war, then, was the greatest single reason why voters deviated from their 1936 pattern, why states like the Dakotas and Wisconsin and Minnesota, with their large German populations, why neighborhoods populated largely by Italians still fuming over FDR's "stab in the back" speech went over to Willkie en masse. And it was also why the Northeast and the South, both much more ready to go to war if necessary to save England, remained most loyal to the President. Analysts such as Samuel Lubell have pointed to the tendency of voters to support the parties according to economic lines, with the more affluent going Republican. Yet a study made by William F. Ogburn and Lolagene C. Coombs in 1940 showed that the economic division had already been established, and, despite charges that Roosevelt had incited a "class war," there was no evidence of any widening gap. In 1940 an isolationist in Wisconsin with a $2,000 annual income would have been more likely to have voted for Willkie than a Bostonian who earned twice that amount.

For the Republican party itself, personal letters of both the prominent and the so-called "grass roots" voters confirmed that the real issue was getting rid of the New Deal and FDR. They could disagree among themselves about how much the United States should risk by helping England, but there was complete harmony in believing that the Administration was an enemy of private enterprise, which they were still fond of calling "free" enterprise. Even the issue of the third term was subordinate to this factor. As a Gallup poll showed, those who wanted to get rid of Roosevelt for other reasons liked to offer the third term as an excuse, while New Deal supporters minimized its importance. As a real issue, it never became basic.

A few days after the election, Willkie himself offered his own reasons, not in the form of a public condemnation of a scapegoat but in private and confidential letters to newspaper columnist Mark Sullivan. "In my judgment," he wrote, "the reason we did not prevail was due to two reasons—one, defense money and the inevitable consequent prosperity. This was most evident in Connecticut, although it was well localized in key states. Second, Republican Congressional record on conscription, international affairs and defense. This was most evident in New England and New York." Almost two years later, Willkie wrote to Westbrook Pegler that "during the course of the campaign I advocated the giving of the fifty destroyers to England, the passage of the Selective Service Act, opposed the Fish Amendment, and advocated other preparatory measures. I advocated these despite the fact that most people in my party opposed them."

Undoubtedly, even while Willkie was stressing that more than nine million were out of work, new jobs were being found as defense expenditures rose. The war emergency was belying his own statement that the nation could not spend itself into prosperity; if anything, that the war finally ended the depression proved that Roosevelt had not spent enough all along. However, even attempts to isolate this economic factor are not entirely successful. For example, Willkie's biggest gain in the entire South was in Alabama, which in 1940 had the single largest concentration of heavy industry in all of Dixie. Yet, in agricultural Georgia, where defense contracts did not play a significant role, Roosevelt gained 5 percent over his 1936 landslide. This consideration must place the economic upturn second to the international issue. And Willkie's references to his own party's obstructionism toward preparedness, even as they were charging the New Deal with neglecting defenses, only points to the Republican party as having been the better bet for noninterventionists.

Finally, if Willkie lost because he had not been subservient enough to the professionals, there is no reason to believe their advice would have been helpful. Bruce Barton, who had had a typically Republican voting record as a member of the House and who was certainly a bona fide member of his party, lost his attempt to become a Senator from New York by getting 543,000 fewer votes than James Mead, while Willkie lost the state by only 225,000. Willkie also got one hundred thousand more than Barton in New York City, although Barton had represented a Manhattan Congressional district. All in all, Willkie's vote was better than his party's Senatorial candidates in nine of the thirty-one states where such elections were held, and he did better than his party in seven of the thirty states where the governorship was being contested. His vote was also greater than the combined total of all Republican Congressional candidates in nine states. Willkie's showing is more impressive when it is realized that no other Republican candidate was matched against Roosevelt himself. To Mark Sullivan, on November 25, 1940, Willkie observed: "I think it would be almost tragic if the Republican Party falls back into old-guard reactionaries [sic] in the belief that it could have won if that had been its program in 1940. I am writing this to you entirely personal [sic] and off the record."

Probably the most important single reason for the outcome was Franklin D. Roosevelt. As tarnished as his name may have become among many voters, he was the President whose fireside speeches comforted Americans with the feeling that there was a man in the White House who cared about them and about the world. That he was running for a third term proved to be but a minor impediment, a break with tradition that seemed irrelevant in a world being overwhelmed by barbarism. His party, too, had become identified with a willingness to help the many rather than the few. The depression was hardly a dim memory in 1940, and if it hadn't been Hoover's fault, few could argue that his party had not helped to create its causes.

Judging by the prediction that Roosevelt himself had made on August 1, he and the Democratic party had done better than they had expected. Those on relief voted for him, but so did employed labor, despite John L. Lewis. FDR's loss of the Germans and Italians was balanced, to a certain extent, by his acquisition of the Polish vote. Although Willkie had attracted many of the Irish Catholics in the major cities, the President retained the Negroes and was overwhelmingly supported by the Jews and all others who had reasons for being vehement about Hitler.

An examination of campaign financing that was made by Louise Overacker showed that Willkie's vow to limit total expenditures to three million dollars was no more realistic than his confidence in being able to defeat Roosevelt. Rather than adhering to the Hatch Act's three-million-dollar ceiling on contributions and expenditures, various committees organized under a wide array of names spent at least fifteen million dollars. The combined expenditures of the Republican party's national committee, the Willkie clubs and the Democrats for Willkie came to over four million. Additional sums were spent by more than eighty other groups working independently, such as the Willkie War Veterans, the People's Committee to Defend Life Insurance and Savings, the Citizens Information Committee and the Jefferson Democrats of California. Furthermore, there were other independent groups that were too fragmentary for their expenditures to be included within that fifteen-million-dollar total. Contributions received from individuals also showed the futility of trying to limit such sources to five thousand dollars each. It was simple enough for every member of several wealthy families to be listed for that amount to many different groups. For example, the roster of family contributions to the Willkie campaign shows that $199,780 came from the DuPonts, $108,500 from the Pews, $56,000 from the Rockefellers and $42,375 from Edgar Monsanto Queeny and his family. That "Wall Street interests" did invest heavily in Willkie's campaign cannot be denied; but Delaware was nicely represented by the DuPonts, Pennsylvania by the Pews and Missouri by the Queenys, and, furthermore, any close examination of contributors and committees as

well as of the activities of individuals shows that Wall Street did not
have a complete position of control. And such contributions that did
come from the financial district were not so different from those in
most political campaigns.

The Roosevelt people, while spending considerably less, were also
unable to adhere to the spirit of the Hatch Act. They too had their
important families. The Morganthaus, the Biddles, the Edwin W.
Pauleys, the J. Paul Gettys and the Nathan Strauses were all generous
but fell far short of what was given by their leading counterparts in
the other party. And while the Democratic National Committee remained under the Hatch Act's limitation, additional amounts attributed to local and independent committees brought their total to at
least $5,855,082. The aggregate campaign outlay for the two camps
can be estimated as having been around twenty-one million dollars.

Nevertheless, despite what was spent, for Wendell Willkie and the
Republican party, it was a lost effort. But for the nation, which had
two men who, on the whole, fought the campaign with a recognition
of the major needs, it was a fortunate choice of candidates. Willkie's
support had enabled the Administration to go ahead with such major
preparations as Selective Servive and the destroyer deal. A rank isolationist may very well have forced the master politician to withhold
even those preparations, which, on December 7 of the following year,
were to prove less than adequate.

Never Again

ROOSEVELT HAD WON the election but had not established a new precedent, even though, in 1944, he went on to a fourth victory. Running against Governor Dewey of New York, he was the leader of a nation at war; and most Americans felt more secure in keeping the President in his post than in making substitutions when the major military tasks were still incomplete. Furthermore, the great post-second-term barrier had already been broken. However much Dewey referred to government by "tired old men," no "fourth term" issue ever developed. Willkie, the man who had challenged Roosevelt's right to a third term, had already been destroyed as a contender by increasing opposition from conservative Republicans and then, decisively, by his poor showing in that spring's primary election in Wisconsin. His subsequent withdrawal was inevitable, and he died less than one month before election day without having made any public statement of support for either party's candidate. Some disenchanted Willkieites, many of whom had spoken so vigorously in 1940 against a third term, favored Roosevelt for a fourth. Among them was Russell

Davenport. Nevertheless, most Republicans were determined to pursue at least one part of their 1940 platform, a prohibition against some future FDR occupying the White House for more than eight years.

The project was begun by the Eightieth Congress, in 1947. It was the first Republican-controlled federal legislature since 1930; but, more important, it represented the postwar conservative reaction. (The same Congress mustered enough votes to override President Truman's veto of the Taft–Hartley Act and thus give organized labor its first major legislative setback on Capitol Hill since the 1920s.) There was little doubt that a majority of the Congressmen were eager to revenge the "calumnies" of FDR. It was, in a way, their postWorld War II version of a "return to normalcy."

And "normalcy" meant, as in Warren Harding's day, a less aggressive Chief Executive. Such a reaction against vigorous presidential leadership had not only followed Woodrow Wilson but also had already become an American characteristic. Resentment against Lincoln's exploitation of his prerogatives had undoubtedly contributed to the difficulties of his successor, Andrew Johnson. Nobody can contend that William McKinley's concept of the Presidency was anywhere as bold as had been the frustrated efforts of Grover Cleveland; and William Howard Taft was no Theodore Roosevelt. Truman, however, blocked the revival of the figurehead type of Presidency, as his anti-Taft–Hartley fight certainly dramatized. Historian Marcus Cunliffe recently noted that having Truman as FDR's successor probably increased the normal Congressional impulse to reassert its authority over the White House.

Of significant assistance to the conservative cause, which had become better represented by Congress than by the Presidency, was the popular realization that the shooting war against the Axis had been replaced by a different kind of war against the Soviet Union. Almost one year before the Eightieth Congress convened its first session, Winston Churchill told an audience at Fulton, Missouri, that an "iron curtain" had descended across Eastern Europe. And Bernard Baruch soon followed with the term "cold war." Soviet intransigence at the United Nations and Russia's rejection of an American plan to internationalize atomic energy made the communization of a large portion of Eastern Europe seem even more ominous. In the fall of 1949 there was additional consternation when the Russians exploded their first atomic bomb and the Red Chinese completed their conquest of what was left of Chiang Kai-shek's holdings on the mainland. At home there were countless spy stories, with such names as Alger Hiss, Judith Coplon, the Rosenbergs and, ultimately, Senator Joe McCarthy becoming part of every man's Cold War dictionary. A third world war seemed particularly near when Truman and the United Nations committed troops to stop the invasion of South Korea and, within a few months, found themselves having to contend with "volunteers" from Communist China. Few Americans—whether they endorsed whatever George F. Kennan meant when he wrote about the need to "contain" Soviet expansion or whether, with Senator McCarthy, they thought that the problem of subversion was as serious at home as abroad—doubted the accuracy of the somber words that had been used by Churchill and Baruch.

The situation could not have been better planned to aid the Roosevelt-haters. By 1950, they had dismissed FDR's efforts to plan the successful conclusion of the war and to promote his idealistic desire to create a United Nations that would finally fulfill Wilson's elusive dream. Instead, they concentrated on his attempts to establish a postwar working relationship with the Soviets. Roosevelt's role in the Yalta Conference was condemned as a "sell-out" to Russian expansionism. Few Republican campaign speeches in the early 1950s failed to mention that sunny Crimean resort on the Black Sea. And, in the fervor of self-righteousness, few Americans bothered to try to find out what had really occurred when Roosevelt conferred with Churchill and Stalin. Ironically, then, FDR's reputation fell to its lowest level in the years immediately following his greatest triumph. Therefore, it was the most propitious time for an anti-Roosevelt move that had a largely symbolic intent. Barring future American Presidents from a third term seemed like a good idea to Roosevelt-haters and also to more dispassionate critics of the growth of presidential power.

The Eightieth Congress started the process on January 3, 1947, the very day it convened for the first time. A proposed Twenty-second Amendment was presented by Representative Earl C. Michener, a Republican from Michigan and the chairman of the House Judiciary Committee. In its original form the document fixed an eight-year limit for both the President and the Vice President. However, a change was introduced by Senator Robert A. Taft. It permitted a Vice President who had succeeded to office after half of the President's term had been served to be elected twice more. The Taft version was accepted, and the House of Representatives endorsed the amendment on February 6 by a vote of 258–121. Every one of the 238 Republican members of the lower house voted for it; and when the Senate concurred little more than one month later, the forty-six Republican Senators maintained their party's unity on the issue.

Congress allowed a generous seven years for ratification by the required minimum of thirty-six states. But it was soon apparent that the uncertainty of public approval had induced the cautious lawmakers to submit the document for ratification to the state legislatures rather than through popularly elected ratifying conventions. That would have risked extensive public debates during state campaigns to elect delegates. There could be no doubt that the Eightieth Congress had delivered a posthumous attack on Roosevelt for having shattered the two-term tradition.

While most Americans were distracted by the Cold War and the issue of communism during the next four years, the amendment progressed from one state capitol to another. Although, for the most part, Democratic lawmakers usually opposed the change and voting followed party lines, the most remarkable thing was the lack of strong organized opposition. A liberal political group, Americans for Democratic Action, which had been organized in 1947 to express the views of the anti-Communist left-wing of American politics, went on record against the amendment. But that was in February of 1948; the organization was still young and its influence was confined largely to labor leaders and intellectuals whose popular influence was insufficient to frighten a single politician. There was, in addition, a group called the "National Committee Against Limiting the Presidency." That obscure organization was apparently so feeble that its name did not reach *The New York Times* until after the Twenty-second Amendment had been ratified. Although the ratification process did seem to stall for a while, by the end of January 1951 approval had been granted by twenty-four state legislatures.

That progress was insufficient for Republican strategists who were really concerned about the 1952 presidential election. Although the amendment clearly spared the incumbent, and Truman was free to run again, his candidacy for an additional term could, they hoped, give the GOP an election issue. Since the President had served virtually all of what would have been FDR's fourth term and had won his own election in 1948, a possible argument in 1952 could have revolved around Truman's moral right to run for a virtual third term. To get the amendment adopted before the 1952 campaign, a meeting of the Republican National Committee considered the problem early in 1951 and stressed the importance of stimulating its adoption by more states. In the subsequent few weeks GOP activity was so intense that the necessary twelve additional states were obtained by February 26, which was well ahead of both the time limit and the coming presidential campaign.

The reactions were predictable. Representative Joe Martin called it a "victory for the people and their Republican form of government . . . defeat for totalitarianism and the enemies of freedom." *The New York Times* agreed. Its editorial pointed out that any President in office in a period of great emergency "will surely find it possible to do what Mr. Roosevelt failed to do in 1940 and 1944—namely, develop within his own administration, or elsewhere within his party, an alternative leadership to his own, fully capable of presenting his policies adequately to the electorate." Democratic Representative John McCormack of Massachusetts, however, warned that during some emergency the voters will lose "the best man under the circumstances." President Truman gave an uncharacteristic response to inquiring reporters: "I have no comment. It doesn't affect me."

Despite the swift action by the representatives of the people, many Americans thought the move unwise. The amendment, they felt, had introduced a rigidity to presidential tenure that had been rejected in Philadelphia in 1787. Had the limitation been in effect in 1940, Roosevelt would have been forced to retire despite the feeling of a substantial majority that the critical situation should not be turned over to a novice. They would have been ignored in a democracy that was supposedly responsive to the desires of the people. An inevitable development from such a situation would have been strong demands for abolition of the restriction.

Historical evidence was also cited to oppose the amendment. Critics pointed out that Presidents usually lose some of their power even in their second term. Jefferson's post-Louisiana Purchase consensus was marred by his second-term attempt to impose an embargo as a way of avoiding involvement in the Napoleonic Wars. Andrew Jackson inspired a conglomeration of opposition before he yielded to Martin Van Buren. As brief as was Lincoln's second term, his own party's rebellion against benevolent Reconstruction terms challenged the possibility of effective leadership. By 1937 and 1938 Franklin D. Roosevelt was no longer the leader of a solid Democratic coalition because of the schisms provoked by the plan to "reform" the Supreme Court and the attempted purges of Congressional opponents. Harry S Truman's second term, although it followed a highly prestigious personal victory in 1948, was wracked by partisan abuse against limiting the war in Korea and the issue of Communists in government.

The critics who cited such realities questioned the assumption that continuing the same man in office would enable him to acquire powers in defiance of both the American tradition and the built-in strictures against the possibility of a dictatorship. The greater likelihood was that a third term would be rare, anyway, perhaps as unusual as second terms had been in the era of Hayes, Arthur, Cleveland, Harrison and McKinley. Movements to continue the same man in office would probably be in response to a national consensus that such a step would be in the best interests of the country. Meanwhile, Congress would provide the necessary checks to assure the limitation of presidential power. Certainly there was little question that the legislature could thwart an ambitious Chief Executive, particularly in the field of domestic legislation. The Senate could even scrutinize appointments more carefully to protect against his possible aggrandizements. The real need, they pointed out, was to maintain an independent legislature and an independent judiciary. When even so popular a figure as FDR himself, only months after his overwhelmingly one-sided second-term election, tried to manipulate the size of the Supreme Court he was stopped by an indignant majority that included those who believed he had sought the change for all the right reasons. All an anti-third-term amendment would achieve, they argued, would be the automatic creation of a lame-duck President after he had been re-elected. The writers of the Constitution had undoubtedly been wise to avoid such limitations, and American history provided no evidence, except to the Roosevelt-haters, to show that such tampering was warranted.

Their arguments held much validity. It was, nevertheless, not entirely certain that the Supreme Court would inevitably check presidential ambitions. The Court-packing scheme of 1937 was, after all, soon followed by the creation of a "Roosevelt Court" even though

FDR had supposedly lost his legislative battle. The longer a President held power the greater would be his opportunity to place his men on the bench of the top court as well as in regional Federal courts. The "advise and consent" powers of the Senate could become a perfunctory matter in an era of virtual one-party domination of the upper chamber. All of these dangers had always existed. Yet, as is frequently pointed out, the authors of the Constitution did not anticipate a two-party system or the possible perversion of government by purely partisan political considerations. George Washington recognized that threat in his Farewell Address when he warned against "the baneful effects of the spirit of party generally." Yet, one would have to admit that the Republic had survived such challenges.

In retrospect, however, one of the best examples of foresight in writing the Constitution was the provision for amendments to cope with future exigencies. The modern American Presidency, with its multiplicity of Executive offices, affords the possibility of tremendous expansion of personal power not only via the judiciary but through appointments to the military, the diplomatic service, regulatory agencies and other domestic bureaus. Those who railed against Roosevelt's potential accumulation of dictatorial powers in 1940 did not even anticipate that within three more decades the head of government would preside over a nation with an annual budget in the neighborhood of $200 billion. Even more important is the Constitutional latitude given to the President in the field of foreign affairs. As much as the need for rapid responses to emergencies in the nuclear and space age may require a strong President with the ability to provide instantaneous leadership without even the nominal acquiescence of Congress, the modern world can view with more alarm his ability to develop his own brand of foreign policy with only a minimum of restraints on his authority. Truman's dispatch of troops to Korea in 1950 was without Congressional approval; Eisenhower did not have first to secure acceptance of the so-called Eisenhower Doctrine as a prerequisite to his being able to commit Marines to Lebanon in 1958; and the gradual build-up of American forces in Southeast Asia had little to with Congressional approbation, except for financing. Nor was Congress even aware of preparations for the Bay of Pigs. And appropriating money for such purposes is more like having to pay for the family's medical needs. Clearly, as with Lyndon B. Johnson and the famous Gulf of Tonkin Resolution of 1964, the President is quite free to utilize a real or pretended emergency so that, in the name of patriotism and national security, Congress must go along. It may well be, then, that only a Constitutional limitation of presidential tenure will maintain the desired balance of power among the three branches of our government. And the members of the Constitutional Convention provided the tool.

To point to 1940 and question what would have happened had the Twenty-second Amendment been in force then is a specious argument. For the Democratic party to remain in office, or for the New Deal to perpetuate itself, provisions would have been made for responsible future leadership. Never again would a man become President with as little preparation as Harry Truman in 1945.

Since the adoption of the Twenty-second Amendment the satirical character Alexander Throttlebottom has been permanently relegated to the musical-comedy stage. The three Vice Presidents since the amendment has been in operation—Richard Nixon, Johnson and Hubert H. Humphrey—were given far more authority than their predecessors, as demonstrated by their inclusion in the National Security Council and by numerous diplomatic and domestic political assignments. Hence, Nixon could campaign legitimately in 1960 as a man of experience, and nobody questioned Johnson's ability to take over in 1963. Would any Vice President who had been in office before the adoption of the Twenty-second Amendment have been prepared to make such an efficient and smooth transition after the Kennedy assassination? Could anything have been more abrupt?

With the adoption of the amendment in 1951, fears were voiced about the creation of a lame-duck second term that would hinder a President by reducing his political power. In the only experience we have had with such a situation thus far, the second Administration of Eisenhower, there is no evidence at all to suggest that the amendment created more difficulties for him than the normal second-term reactions had troubled his predecessors. In fact, when considering foreign affairs, in particular, the death of John Foster Dulles in 1959 left President Eisenhower in much more control of the diplomatic situation than he had had earlier. Even his greatest party weaknesses had been at the start of his first Administration in 1953 and not at the end. When one recalls how Republican presidential hopefuls jockeyed for ex-President Eisenhower's endorsement prior to the party's 1964 convention, there can be no doubt that politicians will want to maintain their credentials with the former occupant of the White House.

There is little question about the contribution that Roosevelt made to his country during his third term. He, along with Churchill, provided the leadership that led to a great victory. By the time he died on April 12, 1945, the war in Europe was virtually over and the end of the Pacific conflict was less than six months away.

The public felt and many historians still concur that FDR was a major force in saving the world from Hitler. Other than Wendell Willkie on the Republican side, it is now hard to imagine anyone else taking over the responsibilities at that time. Undoubtedly, the wartime emergency had enabled Roosevelt to win his third term and to glide into a fourth. But, in the Atomic Age, emergencies have become constant. There is never a convenient time to "change horses in the middle of the stream." It is at least some comfort to know that under the Twenty-second Amendment we have learned to prepare for the inevitable transitions. Furthermore, no democracy can be dependent on a single leader.

Shortly after the amendment was ratified, James A. Farley wrote a letter to *The New York Times* that recalled earlier days. "Am I immodest if I point out that I raised the issue at considerable political risk to myself in 1940?" he wrote. "I am still glad that I took my stand in 1940 even against the advice of some of my closest friends and sturdy supporters." He went on to note that the Presidency's "great powers seem to have become a burden almost insupportable in weight and complexity. We saw tragically in the case of President Roosevelt an utter breakdown of his great strength in his third term. We saw his nomination in 1944 when it was widely known among political leaders that he was a dying man."

It is even possible that future Presidents will be thankful that they can point to the Twenty-second Amendment and say no to self-interested party leaders. If anything, the burden of the office has increased since FDR's days. Before the passage of the Twenty-fifth Amendment, which provided for filling the office of the Vice Presidency and for coping with presidential disability, there were serious suggestions that a second Vice President should be chosen to relieve the additional difficulties of the Chief Executive. When Dwight Eisenhower began his eight years in the White House he had serious doubts about the wisdom of the two-term limitation; before he retired, he had changed his mind.

Notes on Sources

The New York Times and the New York *Herald Tribune* were examined for each day of the period studied. Supplementary material and additional insights were drawn from other major dailies and a multitude of local papers representing all parts of the country. At the British Museum the files of the *Times* of London and the *Daily Express* were helpful for an appraisal of English sentiment. Further information was obtained by scrutinizing such magazines as *Time* and *Newsweek*, as well as *The Nation, The New Republic* and other journals of opinion. Such partisan publications as *The Republican* contained helpful material.

A publication of the United States Department of State, *Documents on German Foreign Policy*, Series D, Volume X (Washington, D.C., 1949), exposes the correspondence between Hans Thomsen and the German Foreign Office. Closely related to this topic, two recent books have also clarified the extent of German activity in the United States during 1940. They are: Alton Frye, *Nazi Germany and the American Hemisphere, 1933-1941* (New Haven, Connecticut: Yale University Press, 1967), and James V. Compton, *The Swastika and the Eagle* (Boston: Houghton Mifflin Company, 1967).

A helpful contemporary investigation of Nazi sympathizers in America is John Roy Carlson's *Undercover* (Philadelphia: The Blakiston Company, 1943). For an intelligent reconsideration of an intriguing subject see Manfred Jonas, *Isolationism in America, 1935-1941* (Ithaca, New York: Cornell University Press, 1966). Also helpful in this area are Wayne Cole, *America First* (Madison, Wisconsin: University of Wisconsin Press, 1953), Charles J. Tull, *Father Coughlin and the New Deal* (Syracuse, New York: Syracuse University Press, 1965), and Walter Johnson, *The Battle Against Isolationism* (Chicago: University of Chicago Press, 1944), a study of the formation and activities of the Committee to Defend America by Aiding the Allies. A recent popular account of American foreign policy during that period is T. R. Fehrenbach's *FDR's Undeclared War: 1939-1941* (New York: David McKay Company, Inc., 1967), but the most authoritative work is still William S. Langer and Everett S. Gleason's *The Challenge to Isolation, 1937-1940* (New York: Harper & Brothers, 1952).

The following books provide useful insights into American politics during 1940. The most pertinent synthesis is William Leuchtenberg's *Franklin D. Roosevelt and the New Deal, 1932-1940* (New York: Harper & Row, 1963). In Samuel Lubell, *The Future of American Politics* (rev. ed., Garden City, New York: Doubleday & Company, 1956), Paul Lazarsfeld, *et. al., The People's Choice: How the Voter Makes Up His Mind in a Presidential Campaign* (New York: Columbia University Press, 1948), and V. O. Key, Jr., *The Responsible Electorate* (Cambridge, Massachusetts: Harvard University Press, 1966), the reader will find useful interpretations of American voting habits. Although Arthur Schlesinger, Jr., has not reached 1940 in his three-volume *Age of Roosevelt* (Boston: Houghton Mifflin Company, 1957-1960), he has provided brilliant portraits of some of the personalities who appear in this book. A revealing contemporary report by a journalist who was active in 1940 is Marquis Childs's *I Write from Washington* (New York: Harper & Brothers, 1942).

Columbia University's Oral History Collection provided recorded depositions by Walter S. Mack, Jr., Clarence Budington Kelland, Edward Flynn and Arthur Krock. Others that would have been useful will not be available for some time. For a list of personal interviews and correspondents, see the introduction to this book.

Happily, the Roosevelt papers are conveniently housed in the Franklin D. Roosevelt Library at Hyde Park, New York. The excellent cataloguing and scrupulous attention from the staff provided easy access to the files of the presidential campaign papers of 1940 and other related subjects, including letters from Harry Hopkins, Wendell Willkie, William Allen White, Morris L. Ernst and others.

The Public Papers and Addresses of Franklin D. Roosevelt (13 vols.; New York: Random House and The Macmillan Company, 1938-1950) are indispensable, but unfortunately the editing by Samuel Rosenman and FDR occasionally altered the original text and reduced its authenticity. A collection of Roosevelt letters compiled by Elliott Roosevelt and called *FDR: His Personal Letters* (4 vols.; New York: Duell, Sloan and Pearce, 1947-1950) offers glimpses of Roosevelt's mind.

The best analysis of the President's personality is John Gunther's *Roosevelt in Retrospect* (New York: Harper & Brothers, 1950). Of the many biographies, the two most valuable are Rexford Guy Tugwell, *The Democratic Roosevelt* (Garden City, New York: Doubleday and Company, 1957) and James MacGregor Burns's *Roosevelt: The Lion and the Fox* (New York: Harcourt, Brace & World, Inc., 1956). A fascinating and thorough account of Roosevelt appears in Robert E. Sherwood's *Roosevelt and Hopkins* (New York: Harper & Brothers, 1948).

Memoirs of the prominent associates of FDR are in abundance. They all contribute something of value to an understanding of the President and his Administration. The following are the most useful: Eleanor Roosevelt, *This I Remember* (New York: Harper & Brothers, 1949), *The Memoirs of Cordell Hull* (2 vols.; New York: The Macmillan Company, 1948), James A. Farley, *Jim Farley's Story: The Roosevelt Years* (New York: McGraw-Hill Book Company, Inc., 1948), Edward J. Flynn, *You're the Boss* (New York: The Viking Press, 1947), Frances Perkins, *The Roosevelt I Knew* (New York: The Viking Press, 1946), and Samuel Rosenman, *Working with Roosevelt* (New York: Harper & Brothers, 1948). Very intimate and helpful are: Grace G. Tully, *FDR, My Boss* (New York: Charles Scribner's Sons, 1949), and James Roosevelt and Sidney Shalett, *Affectionately, FDR* (New York: Harcourt, Brace & Company, 1959). Harold L. Ickes' *Secret Diary,* particularly the third volume called *The Lowering Clouds, 1939-1941* (New York: Simon and Schuster, 1954), added an astringent commentary to the entire scene.

Roosevelt as a campaigner was examined in two useful books: Harold Gosnell, *Champion Campaigner: Franklin D. Roosevelt* (New York: The Macmillan Company, 1952), and Bernard Donahoe's recent *Private Plans and Public Dangers: The Story of FDR's*

Third Nomination (South Bend, Indiana: University of Notre Dame Press, 1965). And the problem of the third term in American history is most carefully handled in Charles W. Stein, *The Third Term Tradition* (New York: Columbia University Press, 1943).

Much of the Republican campaign story came from three major collections that were made available to the authors. The massive files owned by Edith and Philip H. Willkie were scrutinized mainly for the records of 1940; and, in addition to offering some useful insights into the thought and character of Wendell L. Willkie, the search turned up valuable information about the activities of the candidate's closest strategists. Also, the numerous pieces of correspondence sent to his headquarters by ordinary citizens are of particular interest to the political scientist. The papers of the Associated Willkie Clubs of America, housed in the Lilly Library of Indiana University, consist of a large accumulation still in their original file drawers. Amidst the inevitable minutiae is information about the methods, activities and problems of the local clubs and their leaders throughout the country. Most striking, perhaps, are those pieces that pertain to the difficulties of conducting a grass-roots campaign in harmony with the efforts of the party's professionals. The third major collection contains the files of the Eastern Division headquarters of the Willkie campaign committee. The exhaustive coverage of people and topics that appears within these papers render them of particular value for acquainting the researcher with the many personalities who are sure to reappear throughout the remaining work.

There are several biographies of Willkie. The most copious, by far, is Ellsworth Barnard's *Wendell Willkie: Fighter for Freedom* (Marquette, Michigan: Northern Michigan University Press, 1966), while the most readable but controversial is Joseph F. Barnes's *Willkie* (New York: Simon and Schuster, 1952). Mary Dillon's *Wendell Willkie, 1892-1944* (Philadelphia: J. B. Lippincott Company, 1952) frequently sounds strident and must be used with care because it gives undue weight to questionable sources. A campaign biography by Herman Makey, *Wendell Willkie of Elwood* (Elwood, Indiana: National Book Company, Inc., 1940), is amateurish and superficial but, nevertheless, is useful for information about the family background. Alden Hatch's *Young Willkie* (New York: Harcourt, Brace & World, 1944) is unsophisticated and takes too many liberties. Although not a biography in the usual sense, Donald Bruce Johnson's *The Repub-*

lican Party and Wendell Willkie (Urbana, Illinois: University of Illinois Press, 1960) is a good work of scholarship concerning Willkie's brief political career. Of interest, too, is Roscoe Drummond's essay in Isabel Leighton's collection called *The Aspirin Age* (New York: Simon and Schuster, 1949). A recent book by Marcia Davenport, *Too Strong for Fantasy* (New York: Charles Scribner's Sons, 1967), adds disappointingly little to the Willkie story but offers a personal view by the wife of Russell Davenport.

Willkie's own writings should not be ignored by anyone attempting to understand this remarkable man. His "We, the People" article that appeared in the April 1940 issue of *Fortune* is perhaps the clearest and most complete statement about his economic and political ideas. One should not overlook the March 18, 1940, issue of *The New Republic,* which has Willkie's "Fair Trial" essay. Numerous other articles by and about Willkie appeared in various magazines, especially after 1937, but most are repetitive after one has read "We, the People." To understand the quality of the man's basic liberalism, the reader should examine the text of his "loyal opposition" speech of November 11, 1940, the remarkable little book that resulted from his five-week around-the-world trip in 1942, *One World* (New York: Simon and Schuster, 1943), and his final statement, *An American Program* (New York: Simon and Schuster, 1944).

Many other books helped to fill in background information that is vital for an understanding of the Republican party, the issues and other leading figures. Helpful general histories of the GOP may be found in George H. Mayer, *The Republican Party, 1854-1966* (2nd ed., New York: Oxford University Press, 1967), and in Malcolm Moos's *The Republicans* (New York: Random House, 1956). Donald McCoy's *Landon of Kansas* (Lincoln, Nebraska: University of Nebraska Press, 1966) was particularly helpful for Landon's pre-convention position, while Joe Martin's memoir, *My First Fifty Years in Politics* (New York: McGraw-Hill Book Company, Inc., 1960), gives some interesting details.

As with any work of this sort, many other sources were used, but two articles should be cited for their usefulness in helping to tell about the Willkie story. They are: Henry O. Evjen, "The Willkie Campaign, 1940: An Unfortunate Chapter in Republican Leadership," *Journal of Politics* (May 1952), pages 241-256, and Hugh Ross, "Was the Nomination of Wendell Willkie a Political Miracle?"

in *Indiana Magazine of History* (June 1962), pages 80-99. A more personal and appealing view of Willkie appears in Janet Flanner's "Rushville's Renowned Son-in-Law," *The New Yorker* (October 12, 1940).

Several articles were useful for information about American political attitudes and the methods used by the pollsters who, at that time, were really pioneers in the field. See in particular William F. Ogburn and Lolagene C. Coobs, "Economic Factor in the Roosevelt Election," *American Political Science Review* (August 1940), pages 719-729; Daniel Katz, "The Public Opinion Polls and the 1940 Election," *Public Opinion Quarterly* (March 1941), pages 52-78; and Archibald M. Crossley, "Methods Tested During the 1940 Campaign," *Public Opinion Quarterly* (March 1941), pages 83-86.

Finally, there is a thorough analysis of how both sides financed their campaigns in Louise Overacker's article "Campaign Finance in the Presidential Election of 1940," in the *American Political Science Review* (August 1941), pages 701-727.

Index